CHRIST AND CONTEXT

CHRIST AND CONTEXT

The Confrontation between Gospel and Culture

edited by

Hilary D. Regan
and
Alan J. Torrance
with
Antony Wood

T&T CLARK
EDINBURGH

T&T CLARK LTD
59 GEORGE STREET
EDINBURGH EH2 2LQ
SCOTLAND

First Published 1993

ISBN 0 567 29235 5

British Library Cataloguing-in-Publication Data
A catalogue record for this book
is available from the British Library

Printed and bound in Great Britain by Redwood Books, Wiltshire

Preface

This collection of essays and interactive responses emerged from an international theological symposium which was given the title "Christ and Context: The Confrontation between Gospel and Culture" and which took place in Dunedin, New Zealand. As such it was the first conference of its kind to have taken place in New Zealand. Its ecumenical nature reflected the remarkable inter-denominational co-operation which has developed in the University of Otago — New Zealand's oldest university. It served, moreover, to bring together two of the University's activities of which it is particularly proud: its leading role in New Zealand theological studies and its extension work through its department of University Extension.

The Presbyterian Knox Theological Hall, the Roman Catholic Holy Cross College and the Anglican Selwyn College — the University's oldest student hall of residence — provided the basis for the University's Faculty of Theology, which was formally established in 1971. Prior to that, in 1967, the University had also developed teaching in Religious Studies. Dunedin has also been fortunate in having the sisters and friars of the Order of Preachers — the Dominicans. Together these served to make Dunedin a natural venue for an ecumenical theological symposium and one in which a planning committee could draw on the expertise of people from a wide range of perspectives and traditions.

The role of the University's Extension department was to bring together and service, over two and half years, an inter-denominational and interfaculty group which undertook the planning and organisation of the symposium, drawn from the Faculty of Theology, the Dominican Friars and the Political Studies Department. The members of the planning committee were: Helen Bergin, Terry Hearn, Gregory McCormick, Alan Torrance and Antony Wood under the chairmanship of Hilary Regan, and with Neil Howard as treasurer and Bill Webb as secretary.

But an event on this scale and of this quality would never have been possible without the very substantial financial assistance given by a wide range of religious and secular organisations and individuals, including gifts from Australia. It was thanks to these benefactors that it was possible to bring to the symposium, as its keynote speakers, scholars of international renown from Germany, England, the United States, South America and South Africa.

Regrettably, both Dr. Metz and Elisabeth Moltmann-Wendel advised us at the very last minute, that, due to ill health, they were unable to attend the symposium in person. (Hence there are no replies by them in chapters 4 and 8.) Fortunately, however, and at very short notice, Professor Daniel W. Hardy was able to come in their stead.

The event itself was a profoundly stimulating one and was attended by over 300 participants not only from the Australia-New Zealand region but from much further afield as well. The purpose of the symposium was to generate critical discussion in an area of central importance for contemporary theological and ecclesiastical debates. It is our hope that the dynamic engagement that emerged at the symposium itself will be inspired similarly in those who read this collection.

Finally, the editors would like to express their thanks to the following for their help in the proof reading of this volume: Brent Baldwin, Bruce Hamill, Hamish Kirk, Murray Rae, Robert Thompson, and Neil Vainey. The task of producing the indexes fell to Hilary Regan.

Table of Contents

1

Introduction

Alan J. Torrance

The contemporary world is one in which cultural diversity is becoming ever more pronounced. A sense of cultural identity — not least as it is witnessed in independence and separatist movements and the struggles so often associated with these — features increasingly as one of the most significant factors in socio-political life and consequently in international politics. What is also clear is how integral religious conviction can be to a people's sense of cultural identity. The combination of a romantic sense of cultural identity with a religious interpretation of history (where a people's "story" takes on a hermeneutical or interpretative function) continually gives rise to a sense of divine ratification of an exclusive, cultural self-understanding — a recipe which all too often leads to armed struggle, conflict and oppression, be it in the Middle East, South Africa, Northern Ireland or Fiji. We see it in "first-world" contexts where "civil religion" can so often define foreign, as well as internal, policy. The issues here were graphically illustrated in a cartoon which appeared in the Otago Daily Times during the period of the Gulf War. It showed God in the form of a rather fatherly figure holding President Bush in one hand and Saddam Hussein in the other and saying, "I'm going to have to have a word with the two of you about name-dropping!" Two very different self-understandings and historical accounts were being combined with a great deal of culturally conditioned God-talk in order to ratify the use of arms and to ascribe easy or compliant moral warrant to mutually opposing and incompatible agendas.

Indeed, it is arguable that the theological affirmation of "culture Protestantism" which so shaped German self-understanding in the first half of this century contributed in no small measure to this century's two world wars. Germany was a deeply religious nation where the needs and demands of German culture too readily defined the church's agenda.

We need to avoid, therefore, two popular and widespread tendencies if we are to be theologically responsible. There is a need, first, to avoid what one might call a "fundamentalism of culture". This is where the demands of a culture, defined in terms of its own prior self-understanding, are accepted uncritically as defining theological conclusions — an approach which unfortunately still continues to be adopted by those who would regard themselves as theologically informed. Second, we need to beware of a more sophisticated form of this, which one might call "cultural foundationalism", where it is believed (explicitly or implicitly) that culture defines the necessary form of theological questioning, even though those who advocate this may wish to deny (problematically) that they are conditioning in advance the actual content of their conclusions.

At the same time, however, we must avoid here any over-stressing of the problems of cultural religion to the extent that the door may be opened to a naïve and destructive concept of a "culture-less" or culturally neutral Christianity where the inevitable and, indeed, necessary cultural and contextual "interwovenness" of the church is overlooked. The result of developments of this latter kind can be the overwhelming endorsement of the prevailing culture or, rather, a subliminal fundamentalism of one's own culture. Such an endorsement results from the transparency to its members of their own culture and their consequent deeming of their own world-view to be culturally "neutral" or post-culturally modern. This approach in its ecclesial form can reflect what Professor J. B. Metz describes as the "fiction" of a "pure and naked Christianity". It is to state the obvious to suggest that this kind of approach easily gives rise to a *de facto* oppression of all those resources seen to be "foreign" and regarded, accordingly, as being "culturally" non-neutral. This has been one of the more traditional failings of European Christianity which has in various ways — not least through its theological forms of expression and interpretations of the church — engaged in (culturally rooted) oppression of other cultures precisely in the name of the liberation of the Christian faith from "culture".

[Similar concerns are reflected in Professor Dan Hardy's emphasis that Christian witness must guard against two common contemporary traps, namely, the tendency to use "Christian faith to bless —

prematurely and uncritically — situations which have a purely secular provenance and prospect, or to use the authoritativeness of Christian faith as a substitute for careful consideration of situations and developing a fully Christian response."]

One of the tragedies of the latter approach is the extent to which it is destructive of an adequate appreciation not only of other cultures but also of one's own. It fails theologically to appreciate the manner in which God may be seen both to be active and, as Hardy suggests, to *have being* in this activity within the dynamics of one's own culture. This, of course, requires careful, theological interpretation. In other words, the fiction to which Metz refers, can simply serve to induce an eclipsing and enclosing of one's own self-understanding not simply vis-a-vis other cultures but also vis-a-vis the active presence of God in our world. To say this, of course, is in no way to detract from the radical obligation placed upon us to supply an adequately theological hermeneutic of culture if we are to avoid the dangers of cultural foundationalism!

When we use the term "culture" it is easy to assume that "culture" refers simply to those more obvious expressions or forms of life characteristic of national or ethnic identity. But this would be to overlook some of the most important contemporary challenges which a discussion of Christ and context must also address and which are also covered by the term. First, as several of the authors of essays in this book help to bring into focus, perhaps the single most widespread form of oppression, exploitation and suffering that is witnessed in the contemporary world derives from an orientation toward male self-interest characteristic of the majority of cultures world-wide. The forms of suffering to which this gives rise range from the widespread and personally destructive "non-coincidence of self with self" at one level, to which Sr Veronica Brady alludes, to the massive loss of life at another level (due to the male-biasing of medical and other health-related resources) to which Dr Janet Martin Soskice refers. Social, political and economic structures conditioned by a male self-understanding and apperception (often functioning subliminally) are shown to lead to a large-scale abuse of power informed by self-interest. What will concern us specifically in this volume is the extent to which this has received sanction and endorsement from dogmatic theological formulations and the language of the church — an issue to which several contributions refer and which, as we shall see, is addressed specifically in Dr Elizabeth Moltmann-Wendel's essay.

A second, and arguably related, topic with which it is obligatory for a contemporary discussion of Christ and context to engage, concerns the ecological consequences of the consumerism which is so integrally part of the culture of the first-world and which has been so detrimental to the environment. Yet again, the underlying attitude can be seen to have received endorsement within Christian thought from false notions of stewardship and what is regarded as humankind's divinely decreed dominion over the earth and its resources.

A whole range of different questions emerge in the course of a discussion of Christ and context. However, it would seem that we can define four general questions or categories of question which, although inter-related, are essentially distinct and which it is profoundly important not to confuse.

First, in relation to what one might refer to as the *context-Christ* direction, there is the question how far and in what ways our interpretations of Christ *are and have been conditioned*, as a matter of fact, by our various and diverse contexts. How far has the one who is God's Word to humankind been translated into a "christ" who is a product of prior, unconditioned human agendas and who thus functions as a "ventriloquist's mask" (to apply an expression from one contributor) to afford divine endorsement to prior human interests?

Second, there is the very different question as to how far our theological and christological interpretations *ought to be conditioned* by our context. If it is suggested that they should, the question immediately arises: In what way should this take place and what kind of critical controls operate here? Does our context provide prior conditions which we define in advance and then apply in our interpretations of God's Word to humanity? If so, how do we take due cognisance of the freedom of God whereby God is acknowledged as the one who may re-define and re-order not only the content of our questions but their very form?

In that this second question concerns prescriptive rather than descriptive issues, it clearly raises a whole variety of further questions as to how one determines what precisely is of value (theologically and otherwise) in a particular context, what criteria operate, what value systems one adopts and, most importantly, where the theological warrant for such value systems lies — a consideration that seems continually to be overlooked in easy forms of prescriptive cultural religion.

In other words, how far is it possible to affirm that the context defines the theological agenda without opening the door to the dangers testified to by feminists as well as by South African blacks and so many others, whose suffering has been compounded by a concept of Christ which is the product of a cultural agenda imposed on theology and determined by perspectives conditioned both by ignorance and by vested interests.

In parallel to these two questions there are two obverse questions relating to what might be referred to as the *Christ-context* direction. First, we may ask: How far are our understandings of our context conditioned in fact by our interpretations of Christ, that is, by theological apperceptions be they good or bad? How much does Western democracy, for example, and its notions of human dignity and human rights owe to Christian interpretations of value? Or, perhaps less comfortably, how far has its interpretation of the natural environment been shaped by an anthropic principle as this may be traced to the influence of Christian thought — a question which emerges from Professor Jürgen Moltmann's paper?

Finally, there is the very different question as to how far our interpretations of our contexts ought to be conditioned or moulded by a critical theology and perception of God's purposes for humanity expressed in Christ. To what extent does the Word of God to humanity demand a theological restructuring of our world-views and (cultural/contextual) agendas as God actively questions, re-defines and reinterprets these agendas together with the questions they pose? In what ways may this take place?

Few people this century wrestled with the problems of Christ and context to the degree that Dietrich Bonhoeffer did. This is witnessed not only in his life and, indeed, his death at the hands of the Gestapo, but also in his writings — a feature reflected by the extensive discussions of his work in contexts of cultural oppression and culture Protestantism, for example by Professor John de Gruchy.

In the opening paragraphs of what are now published as Bonhoeffer's lectures on Christology he argues that, from our perspective, God's Word to humanity in Christ is better denoted by the term 'Counterlogos' than by the term 'Logos'. The reason he gives is that the latter title too easily opens the door for us to subsume, categorise and interpret the Logos under prior categories of thought and with a predetermined agenda. When this occurs, the Logos becomes the ratification, the divine stamp on our world-view — the Logos becomes our own human logos given a capital "L". However, if the Logos is to be taken seriously as the Word of God to humankind, then this Word stands over and against our systems of thought and prior, (often subliminally self-oriented and self-interested) cultural agendas and context-conditioned directions of thought. The Word serves, rather, to liberate and to reorientate our world-view, to bring us to new, more inclusive and often more radical ways of interpreting and reinterpreting the world around us. To the extent that this Word stands to transform our agendas and to re-define our questions and interests, this Logos is more accurately described from our perspective as the Counter-Logos. This is not to interpret Christ as a Word spoken in negation of humanity, quite the opposite! The Word of God is spoken to and for humanity in order to liberate it from all those prior human agendas and controlling interests which dehumanise and interrupt God's reconciling and integrative purposes for humanity whereby communion may be established both amongst human beings of all sexes and races and also within the created order as a whole.

There are many more questions raised by the theme which this volume has set out to address but it was a conviction of those responsible for initiating the Symposium on "Christ and Context" that clarity in the areas of the four questions raised above is of fundamental importance if the Christian church is to avoid the further legitimation (in the name of theology) of oppressive attitudes, regimes and approaches toward those of other cultures and contexts.

As is already clear, there was a concern to obviate the all too common pseudo-theological move of translating uncritically *descriptions* of cultural-religious contexts, informed from within a particular perspective, into evaluative *prescriptions* characterising the agenda of the Church and the expressions of its faith. For this reason the symposium was given the slightly provocative sub-title: *The Confrontation between Gospel and Culture*— so that it might be seen that we wished to redress the uncritical assumption of divine ratification for agendas immanent in our various cultures and contexts.

Clearly, such an attempt to avoid dangers of one kind inevitably opens the door to risks of another kind. And the weakness of the apparent negativity of such a subtitle is that it can fail to communicate adequately the fact that God in Christ does not exist in isolation from this world and the machinery of human interaction but rather that the Triune God is both active within the whole sphere of human contextuality and, furthermore, *has being* in and through this dynamic engagement. As Hardy shows, this suggests that there is an even more fundamental and more specifically theological question that requires to be addressed. This concerns how God *is* in this, that is, how the being and activity of God are to be understood in the interwovenness of human beings with their contextuality. It is therefore to the enormous benefit of the entire dynamic of this volume that it opens and concludes with two discussions of these issues as theologically profound as those offered by Professor Hardy. Indeed, not only does his opening essay really make redundant any additional theological introduction to the subject but his closing essay serves as an extraordinarily constructive recapitulation of the theological challenges which emerge throughout the course of this book and goes on to define an integrative, theological perspective which serves to elevate and, in many ways, to re-define the entire debate.

It would be quite inaccurate to imply that there is a uniform approach adopted by all the contributors to this volume. Indeed, some of the perspectives represented are quite diverse — although it is of interest to note that this diversity seems to cut across the denominational affiliations of the contributors. Whereas it was never the intention of the organisers of the Symposium, from which this publication has arisen, to produce a volume in definition of any one particular line in the debate on theology and context, it was, however, the concern of the planning committee to seek to encourage constructive dialogue and interaction between some of the most respected and influential theologians of our time. For this reason each of the authors of the main papers was also requested to respond to one other paper to which the author of that paper would then be given the right to reply. This final reply, by the person responsible for writing each essay, is largely reproduced in the off-the-cuff form in which it was presented at the Symposium. This serves, we believe, to communicate something of the dynamic of the debate and to reflect the "gut reaction" of the key speakers to the issues raised and criticisms made. One hopes that this will serve to stimulate further the involvement of the reader in the debate.

In that most of the papers have two respondents, the additional respondents are academics and theologians from New Zealand and Australia where these issues are of particular significance not merely for the academic, theological debate but much more importantly for the whole life and well-being of the church.

It now remains to provide the reader with a brief overview of the kinds of approaches represented by the main essays in this volume.

Dan Hardy opens the discussion by drawing attention to the intertwining or interwovenness of ourselves and our culture and sets out to ask about the manner in which God in Christ is present in and through this braidedness. In this way he seeks to oppose the atomistic forms of interpretation and the tendency to hypostatize culture which lead to a fragmented understanding not only of the relationship between human beings and their contextuality but also of the being of the Triune

God. His concern here is not to conflate God and culture but rather to think in terms of the active presence of the Triune God in human life in its various forms and relations thereby avoiding deistic notions which reflect false dichotomies between the being of God and the activity of God in the created order.

In this way he seeks to establish a dynamic and inclusive understanding of human contextuality and God's active and compassionate participation in this. To do this involves asking about "our proper interwovenness with nature" and about "the interwovenness of people and cultures in which God is present". Herein, he believes, is to be found the agenda of theology for the future and the grounds of rediscovering the deep unity between peoples which has been lost in a fragmented and individualistic world torn by the conflicting claims of self-interested groups.

Reflections of insight into this intertwining of people and the natural world are to be found, he suggests, in the songlines of the Aboriginals as also in Celtic Christianity. However, such insights have been lost in the formalistic structures and practices of Christianity grounded in Roman law and aided by the convoluted and esoteric mental strategies of academics who are overconcerned with being seen to be scientific and whose thought is divorced from the life of the church. Consequently, theologies have emerged from an obsession with appearances reflecting the "plastic life" of contemporary Western culture and which have undermined the possibility of richer, more dynamic and integrative forms of theological interpretation. A consequence of the bad habits that have resulted from such theological vanity are confrontational styles of theology and a disengagement of faith from intelligent understanding.

The way ahead involves finding and affirming that *cantus firmus* that "all things share one breath" by way of a "creative poiesis" in and through which the multi-stranded reality in which we live is, in a manner reminiscent of the Aboriginal song-lines, "sung as a hymn of praise to God the Creator". Theology may thereby provide wisdom (the creative use of our knowledge and practice) and a reorientation of that sense of direction which has been lost. The creative poiesis which reveals the full congruence of people both with each other and with nature, and how this derives from the presence and activity of God amongst them, is found, Hardy suggests, in the inmost structure of the Christian faith.

Indeed, this divine creativity can be seen to characterise the lives of Jesus' followers after the resurrection where there is witnessed, as in the activity of God amongst people today, a binding and a freeing liberation of women and men for a love that "shifts the boundaries of our being"

(O'Siadhail). This love is not a cost-free compassion but testifies to what he calls a "generativity" whereby new life is found in that compassionate sacrifice for others which participates in the Triune life of God — and where God's own Triune life is also characterised in these terms. God's love shifts the boundaries of God's own being in a way which leaves us no grounds from which to think of God as anything other than present in the extremities of our life.

It is the dynamic of this gratuitous love (on which, Dr Gutiérrez also focuses in his essay) which, Hardy argues, "transforms the way in which we are with each other as peoples, cultures and contexts"and in which is provided "the fundamental pattern by which, in the interweaving of human beings and cultures, the presence of God is found."

In this way, Hardy provides the theological ground and direction of an integrative approach which may point to possibilities of a new congruence and harmony where there is cultural and contextual alienation. Likewise, Janet Martin Soskice sets out in her contribution to address the epistemological challenges of conceiving of an integrated or shared perception of the truth given the immense variety of formulations of the truth witnessed not only in the conflicts and divergences of opinion of our contemporary world but in the major debates of the church's history. This concern is summarised in her alternative title: *On seeking the unity of truth from a diversity of perspectives.*

How can we claim to subscribe to a universally valid Christian message when we must also recognise that theology is always done "in context" and where it is so often the case, therefore, that "the truth looks different from here." Reviewing the notorious debate between Cardinal Sadolet and John Calvin, she defines the essential problem which we have to confront as being "a certain view of truth and human knowing... one which presents us with stark alternatives: either we know things clearly or we know them not at all. Either claims are objectively true or they are completely false; either they are from God or from men and women. In its extreme form it poses the alternative to absolute certainty as total relativism." This a position which sees truth as direct correspondence and the ideal form of knowledge as that accruing to a solitary and free knower absolutely detached from and unaffected by the constraints of language, culture, custom and other human "limitations".

Repudiating this kind of approach, Soskice shows how integral a role models have in scientific knowledge and where, although not directly descriptive of reality they are "reality representing". Even the hardest forms of science are interpretative ventures and they do not pretend "to give us 'the world' or 'the truth' neat". Here the "epistemological modesty of modern science", Soskice argues, "is thus not only a useful complement to the propositions of theology, which has always at its best moments admitted the limitation in any of our efforts to talk about God, but also provides a foundation for theological perspectivalism — the thesis that "the truth looks different from here."

Soskice goes on to illustrate the relevance of theological perspectivalism as a means not only of encouraging openness to, but further of discovering the validity of, and indeed mutual compatibility of, the causes of different groups whose central theses and agendas may seem at first sight to be irreconcilably different from our own.

It is clear to Soskice that post-modernism, with its radically relativistic interpretations of contextual formulations and their consequent denial of the validity of universal truth-claims, is not an adequate alternative to the kind of approach described above. Both liberation theology and feminist approaches, each of which takes contextuality utterly seriously, will continue to want to make universal claims in the area of morals. It would be equally inappropriate for Christian theology to give up the universality of its claims. However, it will always be the case that the Christian ultimately cleaves to the conviction that "the truth" inheres in God and that our formulations of that truth are approximations to it and open to bias and human error. We must avoid the temptation of believing that the theology of the church is done by angels free from human limitation and we must accept, therefore, that although "the truth may be one... our apprehension of it is limited and perspectival."

At least two theological reasons at the heart of the Christian faith suggest that epistemic certitude is not part of the Christian promise: first, the unutterable goodness and holiness of God before which all human speaking is as straw, and second, "the pledge of the Spirit and the hope of the kingdom" which reflect that "the Christian story, like the Jewish one, is a story that awaits completion."

The chapters which follow, with the theological questions which they raise and challenges which they pose, share in common the fact that they are the result of concrete reflection upon a variety of specific, perspective-defining domains. The contexts and perspectives portrayed are those of the poor in South America, of women struggling against the confines of male self-interest with its attendant, hierarchical social structures, of those oppressed on racial grounds in South Africa and finally that of environmental destruction and the abuse of the natural world.

Poverty is not simply a lack of money or of food or clothing. It is, as Gutiérrez argues, "a way of feeling, knowing, reasoning, making friends, believing, suffering, praying, celebrating and loving." Ultimately, poverty means death and the one who is poor is the one who is anonymous in death as in life. Furthermore, poverty is not to be romanticised since it involves the destruction of individuals, of peoples and of cultures. The consequence of all this is that to be committed to the poor is not simply a matter of helping the poor or of being politically committed to them but rather of staying and living with them, of being friends with them. It is to enter, or to stay, in the world of the poor.

It is out of this that theology and theological method must derive in that they emerge from this "Way" of *being* Christian. They derive from reflection on the Christian faith as this is irreducibly bound up with being in the Christian Church and, therefore, with belonging to, and therefore sharing in, the life of the world-wide Christian community.

Gutiérrez's discussion leads to the conclusion that any theology which does not emerge from participation in the whole Christian community, as this involves identification with the poor, must necessarily be an inadequate theology, that is, a diminished or incomplete reflection upon the Christian Church as it concerns the "way" of being in the world which is the way of the community of Christ.

This brings us to the question of the motivation or intentionality of our participation in this as Christians. It does not and cannot derive from any moral idealism on the one hand or idealisation of the poor on the other. Rather, Gutiérrez argues that this identification with the poor derives from a perception of "the gratuitous love of God" (what Hardy refers to as the divine *compassion*) which is the very reason for creation itself. It is God's love which initiates that dynamic by which we are brought to share and participate in the life of the community of Christ as this includes and involves identification with the poor and with whom we become 'friends'. Consequently, Gutiérrez argues that justice is "very important", "we cannot avoid speaking from, and about, the suffering of the innocent". However, he continues, "But grace, gratuitous love, is the last word, not because the former is eliminated, but the full meaning of justice is in the context of this gratuitous love."

It is at this point one begins to perceive the rationale for the title of the paper "Joy in the Midst of Suffering" for the form of life which he spells out is characterised by a "paschal joy", a passing from death to life, from sin to grace, from suffering to joy as this stems from its source in this gratuitous love of God. It is from this that we live but further it is this which liberates us from being closed in upon ourselves. It is this which in the words of the opening essay "shifts the boundaries of our being".

What does this suggest about the nature of the theological enterprise? It means that theology has its place "between orthodoxy and practice" in that it attempts to understand the relation between the two. It seeks, therefore, to do theology as Job sought to do it in the face of suffering rather than as his friends sought to do it who neither knew, nor could identify with, the suffering of the innocent.

Representing the perspective of those who suffer and are marginalised because of their sex, we have Elizabeth Moltmann-Wendel's article "Christ in Feminist Context" which, together with the two responses to it, serve to add substantial support to the case for an extensive theological rethink in relation to so many different areas of the church's thought and activity.

Moltmann-Wendel focuses on the problems that have emerged for women over the last twenty years with regard to the maleness of Jesus. The question she poses is whether "this figure can still serve as a point of identification for women who today want to rediscover themselves and their history" bearing in mind the subordinationist and hierarchical social orders and structures (not only within the church but also within Western culture more widely as it has been shaped through the influence of Christian thought) which have been associated with the male Christ-image.

The fact that the focus of the dogmatic expression of the Church's understanding of Christ relates to Jesus' sonship of God and to the event of the salvation of the world defined with reference to this relationship gives rise to attitudes which, she suggests, have led to the legitimation of "the selflessness of women and their subjection".

The question she asks therefore is: "How can Christ in the context of women become alive again? Is it possible at all to relinquish the male context of the Christ event and the interpretation of Christ?" Can a male saviour save women?

By appealing to feminist Biblical scholarship and theology she seeks to show how we might begin to rediscover both the feminine in theology and also the concept of humanity which has been lost in patriarchal theology and which includes what she terms "non-deformed maleness". In this way she believes we may be re-introduced to the notion of our essential mutuality which stands at the heart of the Christian faith and which, in mutual taking and giving, maintains and affirms human dignity conceiving it anew in relational terms.

Consequently, she directs the reader to Martha's confession "You are the Christ, the Son of God who has come into the world" with its specific emphasis on God's humble identification with the concerns of this world as reflecting something of the way forward for theology and the church. The emphasis in this confession is different from that of Peter's in that it centres on God's involvement within this world and identification with its problems. That is, it reflects an inclusive cosmocentricity where the orientation is not simply to the individual human but to the cosmos as a whole. Such an approach, Moltmann-Wendel argues, typifies the concern of women for the cosmos and the healing of its disunity. It is this reconciling and healing approach as it receives expression in the confessions of the women in the Gospel of John that theology needs to recover. "Here salvation occurs. Here with the Christ who has come, the separating power of death, (John 11) which tore apart sister and brother and the law of the religious divisions which divided Jews and Samaritans, is lifted."

If it is only fairly recently that the full extent and character of sexual discrimination has begun to be exposed, discrimination on the basis of race and colour in South Africa has been the explicit grounds of government for decades and as such has been a topic of international concern for most of that period. Under the spotlight of world publicity, sustained attempts have been made by sectors within the church to proffer theological justification for separate development, and therefore for the legitimation of apartheid and racial hierarchy. The manner in which this has been attempted, particularly by scholastic neo-Calvinists appealing to the concept of "orders of creation", "pluriformity" and divinely ordained "cultural mandates", is well-documented. The consequence of this is that there are few contexts where reformed theologians have in recent years been so required to think again through the very grounds of their understanding of the responsibilities of the Church vis-à-vis its cultural context.

Professor John de Gruchy's essay is written from the context of the failure of much of the church vis-a-vis its responsibilities here but also at a time of enormous (and unexpected) socio-political change and transition. Consequently, he sets to explore the role of Christian witness in transforming culture at the point of the "striving for birth of a new nation". This chapter reflects that all too rare combination of sensitive and informed historical and socio-political analysis with "in depth", critical, theological discernment.

One particularly telling insight (and almost universal oversight) relates to the dynamic nature of culture. "Culture, truly understood, is not something which we simply inherit and pass on to the generation which follows us, rather it is a dynamic process in which its various elements, including such fundamental components as language and values, change and develop in response to new historical developments." This understanding means that culture is not to be seen as inherently exclusive and as a static ground of division but rather can be seen as offering profoundly creative resources for the transformation and shaping of the future. This leads de Gruchy to ask the question: "In what way then, does this understanding of culture as dynamic process relate to our understanding of the gospel of God's reign in Jesus Christ?" This he addresses in terms of the "fundamental presupposition" of Christian witness as "the conviction that in and through the death and resurrection of Jesus Christ and the gift of the Spirit, God's liberating and reconciling power has become operative in the world as a whole in a new and decisive way which leads to human and social wholeness". This form of witness is in word and deed, critical reflection and action, and as such commits the Christian to a transforming praxis shaped by the anticipation of God's liberating reign in Jesus Christ. De Gruchy's argument here inspires engaged theological discussion and response on the part of Dr Campbell and Hardy, but we can only leave the reader to interact with this for herself.

The conclusion which de Gruchy goes on to draw from this is that the constructive transformation of culture in the light of the Gospel involves two central facets of Christian witness, namely, identification with its victims (involving *metanoia* on the part of the guilty) and representation of the guilty. These must take place in such a way that the hurts and angers of the past and the fears and anxieties of the present are dealt with. This is of critical importance if there is to take place the creation of a new culture by way of the radical transformation of society as a whole which is needed. As such what is involved is considerably more than merely changing laws. There is needed a changing of the "habits of the heart" as well as of socio-economic realities. The challenge here is clearly enormous.

If there seem to be almost insurmountable grounds for pessimism in the face of the potential problems presented by such a context, de Gruchy reminds us that faithfulness to the gospel means being captive to the promise of a "new heaven and a new earth" and it is this "hope against hope" that keeps alive the commitment to the struggle for the just transformation of society.

Where de Gruchy is concerned with the question of motivation in the struggle against injustice and grounds this in the hope which springs from the promises of the Gospel, Hardy sets out in his response to explore the theological dynamic of cultural transformation, the presence of "the dynamic economy of the Trinitarian life of God in the cultural dynamics per se" rather than simply referring to the work of the Spirit through the life of the church. He argues that a radically theological approach aims not simply for equality and justice but for a much deeper and radical ex-centricity, what he refers to as "the ex-centricity of love, which 'shifts the boundaries of our being'" and which stems from the divine "compassion".

Addressing the related issues of reconciliation in cultural division and reflecting insight into the situation of Aotearoa-New Zealand Campbell examines Ephesians to explore the extent to which "Reconciliation rests on a christological re-working of being." In this way he further seeks to ground the debate in theological and ontological affirmations without which the ethical imperatives and exhortations so popular today are groundless and ineffective.

In several of the essays in this volume reference is made to the disturbingly detrimental relationship of humankind to our shared environment. Moltmann-Wendel represents much feminist thought in suggesting that women are perhaps more holistic and cosmocentric than the Western male has tended to be in this regard. Gutiérrez points out how much closer to nature the poor are than the rich of the 'first world'. What we are forced to recognise is that Western attitudes have reflected tragically exploitative and 'decontextualised' attitudes with respect to the natural world. It is now clear that the world-wide legacy of this could be extremely costly if not ultimately catastrophic.

Professor Moltmann sets out to inspire a Christological rethinking of our understanding of nature. His "text" is "the biblical tradition of the creation wisdom, the wisdom-messiah and the cosmic Christ" and his "context" is "the ecological crisis of the Earth-system, in which we live and move and have our being". There is no context without a text and no text without a context. The two have to be conceived and interpreted in their mutuality and inter-relationship and this leads Moltmann to explore a christology of nature where redemption is seen to relate to the whole of nature and where christology is thereby "expanded to its cosmic dimension".

This introduces us to a re-examination of three themes: creation through the Spirit and the Word; the securing of creation interpreted within the kingdom of grace (where nature and grace 'are so closely interwoven that it is impossible to talk about the one without talking about the other') and finally, the renewal of creation, where creation is viewed prospectively in the light of the anticipated final new creation of all things.

This leads into a profound and original analysis of a christological approach to evolution and to critical engagement with the thought of Teilhard de Chardin. In this, Moltmann discusses the temporal dynamic of eschatology and its relation to that of evolution. What emerges is a contrast of enormous relevance between the *Christus evolutor* and the *Christus redemptor*: "The *Christus evolutor* is the *Christ in his becoming*. But the *Christus redemptor* is the *Christ in his coming*."

This argument leads us to a thoroughly holistic interpretation of the reconciliation, redemption and recreation of creation with clear consequences for our understanding of our stewardship of creation.

It is easy, however, for those of us who live in the wealthy "first world" to become engrossed in environmental issues by virtue of the fact that they stand to threaten our life-style. Consequently, the motivation can stem not so much from the gospel as from little more than unenlightened self-interest. Moltmann's conclusions radically redress any such risk. He reminds us of Indira Gandhi's statement that "poverty is the worst pollution" and shows how inseparable the issues of poverty and pollution are. Pollutant attitudes in the first-world are integrally bound up with the poverty of two-thirds of the world's population. A perspective informed by a perception of the cosmic Christ inspires and commits us to a radical engagement with both.

Professor Metz is also concerned in his essay with a global challenge to Christianity. Despite the fact that this is a challenge of a slightly different kind, it further serves to question and contest the Western values and ambitions discussed above. His particular aim is to focus our attention on the issues which stem from large-scale cultural polycentricity — a feature which the West has been slow to recognise adequately, let alone engage with seriously, at the theological level. Non-Western countries have been under siege, he argues, from a "second colonisation" by way of "the invasion of Western culture, industry and mass media — especially television, which holds people "prisoner in an artificial world, a world of make believe." Taking the form of a "sugar-coated poison" the whole industry of Western culture functions like a narcotic drug which leads to an alienation of people from their own cultural images, language and history.

Metz argues therefore that in opposition to this, Western Christianity is challenged to "transcend itself" toward a polycentric World Christianity by way of a process of enculturation which seeks oneness in the world not by way of a monolithic universalisation of Western culture but rather by a process of recognising the world's ethnic and cultural diversity and dignity.

A process which reflects a concern for peace and justice will involve a break, first, with the traditional perception of knowledge as domination (as grasping, appropriating and taking possession) and second, with a praxis which has been characterised by the exertion of power over nature. It is this duo which has served to engender destructive forms of subjugation, exploitation and reification vis-a-vis the whole realm of nature and socio-cultural life.

For the necessary liberation to take place from a "dominating anthropology", and all that is associated with it, there is required in the West a "hermeneutic of acknowledgement". It is this alternative form of knowing which allows human beings to see "the trace of God" in the otherness of the other.

The development of a hermeneutic of acknowledgement has been effectively prevented in the society and church of the West by two factors: first, he argues, by the epistemological influence of Greek idealism which advocated that "like can only be known from like"; and second, from the confusion within the church between the universality of the church's mission and the universality of the Kingdom of God — with the resultant failure to recognise the eschatological difference between the church and the Kingdom of God. This parallels Soskice's emphasis on the eschatological tension (and consequent non-identity) between our formulations of the truth in the present and the Truth that resides in God. What Metz and Soskice seem to share is a critical attitude to what has been termed the "drive towards a form of monism" which has so characterised Western culture and its theological expressions and which has so often led to what Metz has termed "a hermeneutic of assimilation, even of subjugation."

What is being advocated is not "a romantic elevation" of the other or that which is alien but an acknowledgement of others in their otherness whereby we may become "bearers and witnesses of a vision without which there will be no peace, no justice, and no saving of the earth."

In her response, Moltmann-Wendel suggests that there can be no acknowledgement of the other without a "new self-experience". It is what one might regard as the "new self-experience" of the contemporary male pakeha (European) New Zealander which forms the basis of the other response by Neil Darragh who describes his response as an attempt "to articulate a theology which contributes to a polycentric Christianity from within the limits and hopes of that group of Christians whom I know best."

The dilemma which emerges here reflects some of the difficulties confronting the debate. How do we recognise the "poly-ness" of the contemporary world without endorsing an individualistic fragmentation within the church where every self-defining element establishes its cultural identity in the form of an "over against"? Is this the alternative to cultural monism? May we not rather think in terms of God's "gratuitous love" for those who are radically *unlike* where God strives for that deep congruence of minds and persons whose differences are not static individuations but are fulfilled and transcended in the form of an *ec-stasis* whereby humanity is brought to share in that divine communion and compassion which, as Gutiérrez suggests, is the ground and condition of all existence? Is it bland idealism to think not simply of a mutual recognition of the other but of an epistemic communion amongst those who are unlike in a shared and ecclesial perception (through a variety of "per-spectives") of the communion that stems from the Triune life of God? Might it be that, in this way, there can be a fundamental unity or integration which neither submerges nor swamps human persons and communities but which may lead into new, dynamic and vital forms of life and cultural expression which are continually both transformed and transforming?

The question whether and how we may think in terms of such a dynamic interwovenness and braiding, by way of that "congruence of God with the world by which God is himself", is the concern of the concluding essay by Hardy. In this he argues that there is a transcendent unity of all that is. However, he argues that this unity is not to be interpreted as merely *preceding* the diversity of things. Rather it is to be conceived as an *immanent* unity and, furthermore, as a dynamic or active one which arises precisely in and through the diversity of people and things. This active contextuality or interweaving can only properly be understood in terms of that "Trinitarian activity of God by which God is one." This is to be understood, moreover, as a reconciling unity which changes the character of universality and avoids the monistic tendencies (whether logocentrist or phallogocentrist) against which the postmodernists, he argues, so rightly protest.

It would be quite inappropriate to try to summarise his concluding essay or even to attempt to anticipate what he accomplishes with such theological depth and precision. Readers must simply be encouraged to engage for themselves with his profound and integrative theological analysis.

Suffice to say that his concern is to articulate the manner in which the very being of God is present in the conferral on human beings, in and through their world, of what he calls "that fuller dynamic order from which the ecosystem operates and which is the dynamic order belonging to the being of God". Hardy operates here with the affirmation of an identity between the being of God and God's act of reconciliation as this denotes God's active renewal of his presence in the diverse contextualities of existence in a manner that restores the full contextuality of human beings not only with each other but also with the natural order as a whole. This dynamic, reconciling act of God is one whereby God is interwoven in the lives of those most 'decontextualised', that is, those who are most diminished in their contextuality, in such a way that their contextuality is restored in an event of love that includes them and those who meet them in such a way that new life is provided for them in their abandonment.

The promise of the fullness of this and the hope or anticipation that this promise will be realised was a central element common to the conclusions of several of the papers. Soskice's expression avoids utopianism by holding together the prospective and the retrospective by referring not simply to present injustice and decontextualisation but also to past, anonymous and forgotten suffering which is as integral to a theology of God's all-embracing communion as the suffering and oppression which is taking place in the present or, indeed, which is still to take place in the future.

"Christian hope looks to a time, God's time, when all will be well; when every tear will be dried, when all the suffering of the world through all its ragged and jagged history will somehow be made whole. And this must mean, for me anyway, this *Christian* hope must mean that Hagar will find her home and that wholeness will return to Tamar and the unnamed concubine in the Book of Judges, to the child prostitute killed by one of her customers, to the rape victim (as well as) to the mother who sees her children starve to death. Unless I can believe in a risen Christ who, somehow — and I don't know how — will redeem these sufferings, as well as promise a better future, I can have no hope."

Many theologians are seduced by that ultimate form of exclusive, contextual privilege, namely, that of existing in the temporal present. However, Soskice does not overlook, theologically, the contextuality of those in the past by reducing Christian eschatology to a fashionable form of realised eschatology — and which so often serves simply to baptise a particular agenda with a pious hope for its successful outcome! Rather than defining hope as a kind of looking forward from *our* present contextuality and thereby 'dating' it with reference to the perspective of our temporal contextuality she reflects what is "temporally" a rather more catholic approach by arguing, "Even if things changed now, overnight, to be wondrously egalitarian and good for women all over the world, how can we forget, what kind of amnesia would let us forget, two thousand, four thousand, six thousand years of pain and death? This *anamnesia*, this painful memory, is only redeemed by Christian hope because it is only God who can promise healing of the past as well as to our future." Such a vision is reflected in Gutiérrez's complaint that so much theological reflection on the resurrection of Christ is empty because it does not appreciate the fundamental implications of Christ's resurrection for those who die young and for those who die unjustly. This is also integral to the whole thrust of Moltmann's paper where he writes, "What is eschatological is the new creation of all things which were and are and will be. What is eschatological is the bringing back of all things out of their past, and the gathering of them into the kingdom of glory. What is eschatological is the raising of the body and the whole of nature. What is eschatological is that eternity of the new creation which all things in time will experience simultaneously when time ends in eternity."

In the final analysis, a radically holistic approach to our contextuality must take full account, not only of our theological geography (Darragh), but also of our historicality in such a way that the activity of God is seen as ultimately bringing reconciliation and integration also to *this* dimension of our interwovenness in the created spatio-temporal order. The perception of Christian hope is that divine love and justice ultimately triumph over the whole spatio-temporal span of human contextuality. It is in this way that we not only hope but discern that all will be well, or rather is well, within God's time, within the time of God's completed, all-inclusive and integrative embrace of the created order, where all may know in its fullness that compassionate re-ordering of existence which stems from and, indeed, participates within that communion constitutive of the Triune God.

2

The Future of Theology in a Complex World:
An Opening to Discussion

Daniel W Hardy

On Being Theologically Responsible

The title I have given for this lecture is presumptuous, of course. How can I, even after many years of involvement with theology across several continents, presume myself fit to address such a topic? I promise you that I do not. Nonetheless, it is most important for the issue of the future of theology to be placed on the agenda for discussion. Each thing which will be said in such a conference as this not only implies but effects some sort of view about the future of theology. My first aim is simply to help you to recognize this.

At the same time, unless theology is simply a curious study of religious thoughts and practices, you and I and we need to be reminded that in what we say we are morally responsible for the future of theology. Not only in what we say, but in the manner in which we deal with the questions and disagreements with which we will be concerned, we are exemplifying theology and fashioning it for the future. It used to be said that theological statements are self-involving, and that is true enough. But theological statements are also God — community — and world-involving; each statement enhances or destroys relationship to God, others and the world. It is facile — if not irresponsible — to suppose otherwise. I have always been amazed that those who engage in discussions and disputes about theological matters do not seem to recognize that the very process by which they do so is theological. It is; we here are morally and theologically responsible for the future of theology in what we do. That is one side of the issue with which we will be concerned in this Symposium.

The Problem of Complexity and Culture

The other side is what I have called the 'complex world' in which we exist as we meet to discuss. It is a complexity which reaches far into the heart of the issues which we will discuss, probably farther than any of us cares to admit. We are too fond of simplicities and the comfort they bring to face how deeply complexity reaches into the issues which we discuss.

Perhaps I can explain this by talking for a moment of the idea of 'context' which appears in the title of the Symposium. Through long habits instilled into western patterns of thought by figures of the past, we are inclined to think in terms of dualities. Whenever, therefore, we need to identify something, we do so by differentiating it from what it is not. We tend therefore to see everything as sharply atomized, this from that, you from me, God from the world, and so on. These differentiations quickly turn into sharp distinctions, and the distinctions into oppositions or confrontations; and it soon seems paradoxical to suppose that there is some fundamental unity between those which/who have been disjoined. And if you see this Symposium in these terms, the title 'Christ and Context' will be taken to mean that Christ and context are naturally distinct and opposed, a notion that the subtitle of the Symposium ('The Confrontation Between Gospel and Culture') reinforces. By the same token, you will see contexts primarily as distinct and disjoined, rather than related in some more fundamental unity.

Context, Culture and God's Presence

But the notion of context needs to be looked at more closely. Etymologically, its meaning is quite different, not at all a designation for something which is divided, stands outside and confronts. The Latin verb contexere means to 'braid', 'weave' or 'connect'. If you understand the Symposium title in this way, 'Christ and Context' speaks of an interweaving, a braiding, of what otherwise — with our usual habits — we see as divided. And the question before us is how that interweaving occurs.

For what it is worth, I would add that there is a similar problem with the word 'culture'. We are accustomed to hypostatizing 'it' as something fixed and outside the Gospel, like a self-same, alien world 'into which' the Christian mission goes — like a divine intervention — in order to 'confront' and convert it by the proclamation of the Gospel. But this is fair neither to the culture nor to the place of Christ in it. Cultures are not fixed and self-enclosed; they are dynamic and intertwined with others. And yet within this intertwining, there is a braiding in which God himself may be present. And the question before us is how, in that intertwining, God in Christ is present, and how, by recognizing the presence of God in Christ, we may further effect the consequences of this presence. To ask such questions is not to evacuate the distinctive character of the Gospel of Christ, or to engage in some new conflation of Christ with culture, but to seek for the fundamentals of God's work in Christ in the human world. For God's identity does not rest on 'being out-side' but on who he is in what he does, on his being in his acts.

Cultures and the Agenda for Theology

What makes this especially difficult is the very dynamism of particular cultures today. Across the world, the old — and by today's standards monolithic — unities, neatly demarcated as lands and nations by ancient geographical boundaries often themselves sacralized, are being called into question. And what often seems to be replacing them is chaos, not simply the chaos of groups and individuals seeking self-realization but a chaos of fundamental divisions which loses the vision of any unity at all.

In view of this, in order to continue to exist, nation after nation is driven to a desperate attempt to preserve a rather low and pragmatic form of unity.

> 'Inclusivity', which... is interpreted as amalgamation of people with vastly different beliefs and ways of life, thus becomes not only the method but also the end of authority's exercise... [A] political version of art for art's sake, inclusion for the sake of inclusion becomes the going wisdom of the day and from this wisdom the notion of sharing and serving a common good is steadily

> evacuated...[All this happens] within a society of strangers who define themselves in opposition one to another rights, possessions, and differing 'life styles.' Within the amalgam, people increasingly define themselves by what they demand. Voluntarism defines religious as well as political communities. Within all social institutions interest groups multiply like amoebas.[1]

Such circumstances produce two very difficult questions. The first question is this: In a world where the possibility of deep unity between peoples, one based on their service of a common good, has been lost in the welter of the conflicting claims of self-interested groups, how are we to recover the intertwining of cultures and peoples? How are cultures dynamic not only in their distinction from each other but also in their intertwining? In itself, that question has nothing necessarily to do with theology. The second question, therefore, is this: how, in the braiding together of cultures and peoples in a dynamic unity, is God himself present? How, indeed, does God's life appear in their service of a common good? And what, then, is the identity of the God who so appears? Those are the questions which are before us in this Symposium. These questions are demanding, to say the least, and require a delicacy of working together, and a willingness to go to the depths of the Christian tradition which we are not at all accustomed to.

Along with these issues comes another which can hardly be separated from them today. With the division of cultures and contexts, both from each other and from the common good or the presence of God, the territories where these cultures are found are seen to be divided also, both from each other and from the presence of God.[2] Given the human preoccupation with such divisions, it is unlikely that there can be any serious attention to ecology, in the sense of a recognition of the interrelatedness of all the natural world. Furthermore, there can be no theological ecology, in which the common good and the presence of God are found in the interrelatedness of all the natural order. In other words, seeking for the dynamic contextuality — the interwovenness — of cultures also presses us for a better understanding of 'the land', the environment with (and in) which all cultures coexist. How is God

---

1. Philip Turner, "Authority in the Church: Excavations Among the Ruins," in *First Things,* December 1990, p.30.
2. It is no accident that disputes over the rights to land feature so prominently in controversies between cultures, and particularly where two groups claim rights to the same territory, for example in Palestine.

present in our contextuality with the natural world? Even if it can easily be forgotten in a beautiful place like Dunedin where we are comfortably provided-for, the situation which we have just indicated is one of unparalleled gravity. As a Nobel prizewinner wrote recently,

> Whatever our professional preoccupations may be, we cannot escape the feeling that we live in an age of transition, an age that demands constructive modification of our environment. We must find and explore new resources, must understand our environment better, and must achieve a less destructive coexistence with nature. The time scale of the qualitative modifications that are required to achieve these major goals is not comparable to the immense time spans involved in biological or geological evolution. Rather, it is of the order of the decade... the modifications that must be made interfere with our own lives and the lives of the next generation.[3]

Can we also find God's presence in our proper interwovenness with nature? Unless we can, finding the answer to our other questions about the interwovenness of people and cultures in which God is present will resemble Nero fiddling while Rome burned.

If we put all these together, we have the *agenda of theology for the future.(1) The first question is this: We live in a world where the possibility of deep unity between peoples, that which is based on their service of a common good, has been lost in the welter of the conflicting claims of self-interested groups. We live in a world where the proper unity or interwovenness of humanity with nature has also been lost. How then are we to recover the proper intertwining of cultures and peoples, and our proper interwovenness with nature?(2) And the second question is: How, in the braiding together of cultures and peoples and nature in a dynamic unity, is God himself present? How, indeed, does God's presence and life appear in the achievement of the common good of cultures, peoples and nature? Who is the God who so appears?* Regrettably, in what follows, we must largely confine ourselves to the question of the braiding together of cultures and peoples, and leave the question of their interwovenness with nature to another time.

3. G. Nicolis & I. Prigogine, *Exploring Complexity*, (London: W. H. Freeman, 1989), p. 1.

Precedents for Such Concerns

It is not that these are altogether new problems. The fact is that people in the past, when faced with these issues simultaneously, have found ways of recovering God's presence in the recovery of the intertwining of peoples and the natural world. Let me give two examples.

One is the 'dream-time' practices of the Aboriginals in Australia which is described in Bruce Chatwin's book *The Songlines*. As he says there,

> The Aboriginals had an earthbound philosophy. The earth gave life to a man; gave him his food, language and intelligence; and the earth took him back when he died...
> [They] were a people who trod lightly over the earth; and the less they took from, the earth, the less they had they give in return ...
> My reason for coming to Australia [Chatwin says] was to learn for myself... what a Songline was — and how it worked...
> [As I found] Every Wallaby Man believed he was descended from a universal Wallaby Father, who was the ancestor of all other Wallaby Men and all living wallabies... Each totemic ancestor, while travelling through the country, was thought to have scattered a trail of words and musical notes along the line of his footprints... these Dreaming-tracks lay over the land as 'ways' of communication between the most far-flung tribes. A song ... was both map and direction-finder. Providing you knew the song, you could always find your way across country... as long as [a man] stuck to the track, he'd always find people who shared his Dreaming, who were, in fact, his brothers... from whom he could expect hospitality. So song is a kind of passport and meal-ticket... In theory, at least, the whole of Australia could be read as a musical score... And [the Aboriginals] could sing [all the white man's gear, even] the railway back into the created world of God.[4]

4. Bruce Chatwin, *The Songlines,* (London: Pan Books, 1988), pp.14-17.

Though not based on a Christian understanding of God, this shows deep similarities to Biblical faith of the sort found throughout the Old and New Testaments, where the presence of God is found in the movements of people through the lands. A particularly interesting example is found in the Wisdom Literature, which finds the presence of the divine in the right practice of human relationships. As the Book of Proverbs suggests, 'The fear of the Lord' is in 'turning your ear to wisdom and applying your heart to understanding... For the Lord gives wisdom, and from his mouth come knowledge and understanding... Then you will understand what is right and just and fair — every good path.'[5]

Incidentally, the understanding that God's presence is to be found in the interweaving of human beings with each other, may be far more widely appreciated by ordinary Christians than the theologians are prepared to recognize. While they, the theologians, are busy re-inventing the wheel, ordinary Christians may simply be getting on with the job. On the way here, on the airplane from Los Angeles to Auckland, I sat next to a Bible salesman — a 'Bible Broker' he called himself — who told me an interesting statistic: if copies of the New Testament are bound with the Psalms, sales go up 10%; but if they are bound with the Psalms and Proverbs, sales go up by 50%. Perhaps ordinary people do see that God's presence is to be seen in the interweaving of human lives.

The other example of God's presence found in the interweaving of human beings is explicitly Christian, drawn from the north of England which I learned to love so much, a place in many ways very like Dunedin. There the tradition of Celtic Christianity is very much alive, not least in Durham Cathedral of which I was Residentiary Canon while I was Professor in the University. It is a form of Christianity quite unlike the pattern which dominates the West. The Celtic view of God in the world was far more dynamic than the form of Christianity which came from Rome and eventually triumphed. The Celts saw God's life and purposes intertwined with those of human beings as they are intertwined with each other and with the natural world. The well-known Irish blessing which goes 'May the road rise up to meet you' hints at the way God cooperates with the order of nature to bring goodness to human beings. In the North of England, wandering missionaries gathered communities around them who lived close to the natural world, and within their natural life together found a God who walked with them and brought them blessing. The best images of this intertwining are the

5. Proverbs 1:7; 2:2,9.

interweaving tracery of Celtic art and stone-carving which mark the great Christian buildings of the North of England. Sadly, the form of Celtic Christianity was nearly lost under the weight of law-based Christianity, and the formalistic theology and practice which goes with it. It was much more dynamic than that which could be captured in the patterns of Roman law, but it was the law-based patterns which predominated in the West as a whole.

The Failings of Theology

Such examples offer some precedents for recovering God's presence in the recovery of the intertwining of peoples. They show people whose very wandering and finding themselves one with other people and with the natural world is a creative realization of the presence of God. But the fact remains that such practices, not only the primacy given to the intertwining of peoples but also to the creative realization of God's presence there, have almost always been displaced by more formalistic practices in theology.

Perhaps, therefore, a note of caution is in order before we proceed with our task. It amounts to this: beware of habits. In my present role as Director of a new institution, the Center of Theological Inquiry, dedicated specifically to the redevelopment of theology for its future role in public life, I have learned well the habits which undermine theology in its prospects for the future. Perhaps you know Hans Christian Andersen's story, 'The Emperor's New Clothes'. Let me tell you that all human beings and institutions, including those engaged in the enterprise of theology, are always a little like the emperor (in the story) who, in his love of finery, allows himself to be deceived by his advisers into parading in an imaginary set of new clothes; and the emperor's loyal subjects are quite prepared to join in the deception.

Like the emperor in the story, theologians wish to be accepted and admired by those around them, and are easily deceived into false agendas, into — quite unintentionally — being what they are not. These days, I think it is very difficult for them not to be led astray, given that there are so many 'experts' who will see to it that theology is woven an imaginary set of new clothes (if not a new set every year!) in which to parade before the whole world. What is more, not a few of them have the influence to coax theology into the 'new clothes' which they invent, and then to parade it through the town, while at the same time convincing bystanders that these imaginary new clothes are better, and that they should applaud such wonderful new garb. During this same symposium, Professor Moltmann and I were commiserating over the increasing separation of academic theology from Church life, as theologians — so anxious to be accepted as 'scientific' by their university colleagues — adopt esoteric and convoluted mental strategies. Such tactics subvert theology.

Let me be more exact. What are these bad habits? In the language of 'The Emperor's New Clothes', they are an interesting combination of 'vanity' and 'new fashions'. The vanity comes where theologians are preoccupied — like the Emperor in the story — with their position. And the means by which they do retain their position is to outdo others in their grasp of the formalisms which have dominated Christian Theology in East and West. By this they perpetuate intellectual habits learned over the past centuries, as if those were the only ways suitable. The unfortunate by-product of this is the disengagement of intelligent Christian faith from the means by which truth and understanding are sought in the modern world, whether by the experts or by ordinary people. Intellectually and institutionally, therefore, faith has come to be promoted in ways that are strictly marginal to modern life.

And this, in turn, leads to a confrontational stance: having confined theology to such formalisms, they go on to say that the truth of theology can only be shown through the confrontation of all else. What they mean, however, is that theology can only be true to itself if it is seen in the formalisms of the past, with the intellectual procedures of the past; and that causes it to be marginal to, confrontational with, the methods of today. So theology itself comes to be seen as an esoteric, abstract and sectarian activity. It's a caricature of theology.

The second bad habit can be likened to the 'new fashions' in which the king's advisers outfitted him. Perhaps the most damaging of these new fashions is that faith can be — even ought to be — disengaged from its engagement with intelligent understanding. This supposition pervades places where religion and theology are taught. Where religion/theology is studied in public institutions, it is supposed that the question of the truth of faith should not be addressed; it is sufficient to catalogue the phenomena of religions, and it is supposed that these must all be equally valuable. That is supposed to be the strategy for preserving the place of religious study in public institutions, or in places where there is disagreement about the value of different traditions. Such an approach mirrors the blandness and vacuousness of much life in the West, where there is nothing but appearance and all appearances must by definition be equal. 'Plastic life' is what it's called in California.

And the study of theology by Christians has usually followed this lead, at least in the Western world. If that is what is deemed academically credible for theological study, it is thought that it should be followed in theological institutions also. For this reason, 'theological' study in private institutions consists usually of ever more detailed study of the religious or theological material which is thought normative for a particular tradition, by means of the historical, phenomenological, sociological or political techniques which are found in the academic market-place. These 'new clothes' are titillating, but their freshness seems often to rely on the discovery of new data or methods. Again, questions of truth are avoided where they emerge in (or about) the material studied. Such study is sometimes accompanied by a rather un-self-critical re-description of the 'substance' of the material, frequently in terms currently popular, or by a philosophical testing of the continued viability of the tradition. But the issue of its truthfulness for today is not addressed.

Such forms of study do, in a sense, preserve the faith of previous generations, but in doing so they repeat the mistakes which led to the disengagement of faith from public life and of faith from the intelligent appropriation of faith. Assumptions about the continuing authority of the tradition replace the engagement with modern understanding and life by which the tradition must be revalidated. Acquaintance with the phenomena of faith, religion and theology replaces intensive engagement with the depth and truth of tradition. The exaltation of private or group opinion undermines the possibility of a common truth by which society may be maintained. The results are profound and many-sided: the intelligent understanding of faith (theology), and the institutions which support it, grow weaker, while the prospects for social unity grow more dim.

Moving Beyond Our Bad Habits

So we must be cautious both about the vanity by which theologians perpetuate habits learned over the past centuries, as if those were the only ways suitable, and about the new fashions which operate in most theological study today. It is the proper task of theology today to respond to the need to find the presence of God in the intertwinings of people in and with the natural world. And that will require reaching beyond the vanity which confines theology in its past, and beyond the fashions which restrict theology from the task of intelligently discerning the truth of faith. I know that is very difficult in today's world; but it always has been. That 'reaching' is the basic vitality of theological work. In religious language, it is the art of transcendence. And, as one woman put it: 'I believe that learning to admit transcendence may be one of the major undertakings of a man's life, perhaps the major undertaking, so that if it is ignored his personality may be stunted or destroyed.'[6] Nowhere is that more true than in the study of theology itself. It is part of the very purpose of theology to reach to the higher goals which it serves, and to hold fast to them even in difficult times.

This task, which we need freely to undertake, is strangely similar to those which are forced upon us by the others which we have discussed: in all the turmoil of conflicting voices and national layers of voices, can we find the presence of God in the interweavingof people and cultures? And can we do so while also finding the presence of God in a true braiding of humanity with nature which will ameliorate the frightful damage being done to the natural world? These are all 'transcending questions', which call us out of our captivity to the vanities and new fashions of theological study.

Approaching the Task of Theology

So far, I have only identified the agenda for theology in the future, and asked you to be bound neither by the habits of the past nor by the new fashions of the present in which theology is so often confined. I want now to turn more directly to the task of theology itself in the complex world in which we live. The most apt way of turning to this is to read a poem by a fine Irish poet whom I know, Micheal O'Siadhail.

> O my white-burdened Europe, across
> so many maps greed zigzags. One voice
> and the nightmare of a dominant chord:
> defences, self-mirroring, echoings, myriad
> overtones of shame. Never again one voice.
> Out of malaise, out of need our vision cries.
>
> Turmoil of change, our slow renaissance.
> All things share one breath. We listen:

6. Monica Furlong, *Contemplating Now,* (Cambridge, Mass.: Cowley Publications, 1983), p.50.

clash and resolve, webs and layers of voices.
And which voice dominates or is it chaos?
My doubting earthling, tiny among the planets
does a lover of one voice hear more or less?

Infinities of space and time. Melody fragments;
a music of compassion, noise of enchantment.
Among the inner parts something open,
something wild, a long rumour of wisdom
keeps winding into each tune: cantus firmus,
fierce vigil of contingency, love's congruence.[7]

What O'Siadhail says about the 'white-burdened Europe', its greed, defensive self-interest, divisiveness in shame (shame always divides), and loss of a common identity, could be found the world over in greater or lesser degree. In all the turmoil of conflicting voices and national layers of voices, can we find the cantus firmus — like the ground bass in a Bach piece — of unity? Can we find and affirm that cantus firmus, that 'All things share one breath'? And what kind of spirit do they share? Those are the questions we must face — as theological questions.

Theology as Poesis

Before we do, we should look for a moment at how to approach these questions as theological questions. Implicit in O'Siadhail's poem is the purpose of poetry itself. Poetry, in its creative perception, provides a concentrated opportunity by which to 'sing reality'. As Chatwin says of the Aboriginal Creation myths,

> [They] tell of the legendary totemic beings who had wandered over the continent in the Dreamtime, singing out the name of everything that crossed their path — birds, animals, plants, rocks, water-holes — and so singing the world into existence... By singing the world into existence,

7. Michael O'Siadhail, "Motet," in *The Chosen Garden,* (Dublin: The Dedalus Press, 1990), p.82.

> the ancestors had been poets in the original sense of poesis, meaning 'creation'.[8]

So the multi-stranded reality in which we live needs to be 'sung into existence'. For a Christian, this means that it needs to be sung as a hymn of praise to God the Creator. It is the task of theology to fashion the creative poesis by which it is sung as a hymn of praise to God.

In more technical terms, poetry — or theology — provides a wisdom, heuristic or direction for exploration, which serves to orientate a search, much as the Aboriginals' songlines provide a 'map and direction-finder' for travel. This is often where we are at our weakest. Our lack of orientation is what allows us to be subverted by our vanity and the new fashions of the world. The crucial question is how we achieve the proper sense of direction.

In a much simpler time, though one not without its own complexities, Plato quotes Socrates as saying,

> This, then, every soul looks for, and for this every soul does all that it does, feeling in some way what it is, but troubled and uncertain and unable to see it clearly enough. The soul forms no fixed belief about the good as it does about the other things... And are the best men in our state, in whose hands everything is to be placed, are they to be equally in the dark about something so important as this?[9]

The orientation point to which Socrates was referring, is that for which human beings reach in everything they know and do, though it is itself beyond their grasp. It is the orientation point by which wisdom in life is promoted, and by that means intellectual, social and moral life is brought about. As one writer summarized it recently, '[Socrates] sought to promote wisdom in life by rational means — and not mere intellectual wisdom or knowledge.'[10]

---

8. Bruce Chatwin, *The Songlines,* (London: Pan Books, 1988), pp.2,16
9. Plato, *Republic,* ed. and trans. I. A. Richards, (Cambridge: Cambridge University Press, 1966), p. 114 (Book 6, 505).
10. Nicholas Maxwell, *From Wisdom to Knowledge,* (Oxford: Basil Blackwell, 1984), p. 120. For a specifically theological discussion, see D. W. Hardy, "Rationality, the Sciences and Theology," in *Keeping the Faith*, ed. G. Wainwright, (Philadelphia: Fortress Press, 1988), (London: SPCK, 1989), Ch. 12.

Another form of the same orientation-point was offered by the great philosopher/theologian Anselm. There is, he said, 'that than which nothing greater can be conceived', and this is God, the one to whom we should turn ourselves to do honour; for honouring this excellence is the basis of all knowledge and practice. If theology has to do with singing everything into existence as a hymn of praise to God the Creator, actually to do so — to honour God in all knowledge and practice — is the best kind of theology. It is God-focussed wisdom.

The New Form of Wisdom

Is such an orientation-point, manifest in wisdom — the creative use of our knowledge and practice — lost forever? Michael O'Siadhail's poem suggests not.

> Infinities of space and time. Melody fragments; a music of
> compassion, noise of enchantment. Among the inner parts
> something open, something wild, a long rumour of
> wisdom keeps winding into each tune: cantus firmus, fierce
> vigil of contingency, love's congruence.

So what has been lost is not the possibility of such wisdom, the possibility of a direction which can be the source for creative human understanding (poesis) and goodness, but the ancient form of wisdom. The form of wisdom itself has become more complex, as one would expect in a world grown much more complex.

It has been commonplace, if not popular, for a very long time to abandon any explicit orientation to wisdom, or to forego the honouring of excellence in that full sense to which Anselm was pointing. But this is not because people have no inkling of it. They do glimpse it, but only in fragments: 'melody fragments'. And the world in which they live is so fragmented, that they cannot have more than a glimpse of it. But that is not to suggest that the elements of this wisdom are not all over the place. If it isn't too odd for an American to recall an English national holiday, I can remember some marvellous bonfires, towering eight feet high at least, in the workers' yard of Durham Cathedral on Guy Fawkes Day. After a while, the fire collapsed into large glowing coals, glowing embers, on the ground. The fragments in which we experience wisdom are like those embers. Those isolated embers, the elements of wisdom which still burn with the heat of the fire from which they come, can still provoke great interest, but in their separation people forget that they do derive from the fire. This forgetfulness is due in no small part to the simple difficulty of conceiving this wisdom. We are simply not in the position of those who in earlier days could speak so simply and trustfully of wisdom. It is very difficult for us to say with the Psalmist,

> [Lord], how I love your law!
> I meditate on it all day long...
> How sweet are your words to my taste,
> sweeter than honey to my mouth!
> I gain understanding from your precepts;
> therefore I hate every wrong path.[11]

Neither the Lord nor his wisdom seem so clear or sweet to us now as to evoke such simple and trustful meditation. It is not that they are not as much present as ever they were. But our minds are clouded by other preoccupations, and they have become too manifold for us to trace their roots in the wisdom which is the excellence of the Lord.

But perhaps we make too much of this difficulty. The fire for which we seek is already among us, in all those isolated sparks of which I spoke, or — in O'Siadhail's words — there is music in the fragments of melody. Where these are drawn together in their interconnections, there is the 'long rumour of wisdom' of which he speaks. And that, as we saw before, is the issue — how in the interweavings of people, their cultures and nature — God is present. Where we can draw out these interconnections, we will be finding wisdom in practice; where our searchings converge, there will be a practical manifestation of wisdom. Wisdom will thrive amongst us where this convergence is achieved, where the bonfire, so to speak, is seen in the fire of all the sparks, or the music in the melody fragments.

I realize that such a thing is difficult to grasp. We are habituated to think of a wisdom which is compact, intense and accessible to us; and such a notion is attractive and reassuring. But, as I said, the form of wisdom seems to need to be rethought. Let me repeat the last stanza of the same poem.

> Infinities of space and time. Melody fragments; a music of
> compassion, noise of enchantment. Among the inner parts
> something open, something wild, a long rumour of

11. Psalm 119.97, 103-4.

> wisdom keeps winding into each tune: cantus firmus, fierce
> vigil of contingency, love's congruence.

Wisdom appears as hints and rumours, and its form is an open one through which there runs 'something wild', an excess of life entering all the contingencies which are all we know of existence. And this winds through each of the many tunes into which the melody of existence is now fragmented. Nonetheless, in its own 'nature', it is itself a cantus firmus.

The Needs of a Creative Poesis

But what is the character of the creative poesis which we need to find the wisdom by which people and cultures may be properly interwoven with each other and with the natural world? Michael O'Siadhail gives a hint of it. Amongst the fragments of melody — amidst the noise of enchantment — there is 'a music of compassion', and amongst the wild openness of inner parts 'a long rumour of wisdom'. Such a thing can only be found through a risky waiting in which may be found the 'congruence' brought about by love. This is the kind of braiding together of people, cultures and nature in which we will find the wisdom — with all its excess of life — which is present amongst them.

> Infinities of space and time. Melody fragments; a music of
> compassion, noise of enchantment. Among the inner parts
> something open, something wild, a long rumour of
> wisdom keeps winding into each tune: cantus firmus, fierce
> vigil of contingency, love's congruence.

So far as it goes, this is an answer to the questions we posed earlier.

But at the same time, it leaves uncharted the kind of congruence which we should expect in love, as well as the nature of the openness and risk which are needed for the flowering of compassion and love. Does congruence mean sameness? For if so the braiding together will sacrifice the distinctness of those so interwoven, whether they be individuals, peoples, cultures or nature. Do openness and risk mean openness to anything and everything, so that every kind of difference is legitimate? For if so, we will be back in that 'inclusion for the sake of inclusion' which we mentioned before. These are surely crucial matters if we are to find the proper braiding together of people, cultures and nature.

I suggest the fuller creative poesis which is really needed is actually to be found in the inmost structure of Christian faith, where it is seen what is the full congruence of people with each other and with nature, and how it derives from the presence and activity of God amongst them. There are many ways by which this may be shown, but I shall start from the Resurrection. For in the events following the Resurrection we can see the incorporation of Jesus' followers into an open and lifeful congruence by which they are interwoven one with another through the fulfilling presence of God amongst them.

Just how does this happen? We need to try to unravel the dynamics of the lives and relations of those who came after the Resurrection, and the dynamics of God's presence there amongst them. How was it that the Resurrection showed this new human dynamic, and led these people into the character of God's activity amongst them? And what did it show about the character of God?

A particularly interesting insight into these questions is found in the story of Philip and the Ethiopian Eunuch.[12] For there was Philip, told by an angel to go out to the Gaza Road outside of Jerusalem, and then told by the Spirit to go up to the chariot in which a Ethiopian eunuch was returning from worship at Jerusalem. As it happened, the Ethiopian was perplexed about a passage from the Book of Isaiah, and Philip answer showed him that it spoke of the humiliating sacrifice of Jesus and the new life which came from it for those who followed him. The eunuch immediately asked to be baptized — and afterward 'went on his way rejoicing'.

As scanty as the story is, it is clear that God himself, the Spirit, through Philip, gives the eunuch that remarkable insight into God which is contained in the narrative of the silent suffering of Jesus, the denial of a just trial, his death and his being taken up from the earth. And what was given was not a lot of information about what had happened, and how important it was, but the generativity of it, the creativity of it. The experience of the eunuch was that what had occurred for Jesus was still happening, through the Spirit, as others were drawn into that suffering, death and resurrection. The 'generation' of the Jesus who suffered, died and was raised was those who came after and, in the Spirit, were drawn into what had happened. The baptism of the eunuch enacted, implanted, this generativity in his very being, and he went on his way in joy, the joy

12. Acts 8.26-40.

of Easter. So that apparently simple story tells us how, following after the Resurrection people are drawn into God's activity in the trial, death and Resurrection of Jesus. It happens this way: through the witness of the Spirit, they — like the eunuch — are led into the suffering of Jesus, his death and his resurrection, and the activity of God's Spirit is confirmed in them so that they too may go on their way rejoicing.

Our first question is: *How did these events show a new human dynamic, the full congruence of people for which we are seeking?*

In our very individualistic society, we are well accustomed to the habit of declaring our concern for others while also withdrawing from them. In our early days in Princeton, my wife and I learned with what readiness and friendliness people would say, 'how very nice to meet you; we must get together for lunch — we'll be in touch with you this week!' The only problem is that the call never arrived, and there was no further meeting — unless we ourselves initiated it. This is not very much different from the supposition that God affirms his people with a resounding 'yes!' while at the same time staying distant from them. Nor is it far different from the idea that God sets in motion a drama of righteous love, played out in Jesus and those who follow him, while himself standing apart. But suppose God is involved in the suffering death and resurrection of Jesus in a different way.

Let me quote the words of a love poem, another of Michael O'Siadhail's:

> Nothing can explain this adventure — let's say a quirk of fortune steered us together — we made our covenants, began this odyssey of ours, by hunch and guess-work, a blind date where foolish love consented in advance. No my beloved, neither knew what lay behind the frontiers. You told me once you hesitated: a needle can waver, then fix on its pole; I am still after many years baffled that the needle's gift dipped in my favour. Should I dare to be so lucky? Is this a dream? Suddenly in the commonplace that first amazement seizes me all over again — a freak twist to the theme, subtle jazz of the new familiar, trip of surprises. Gratuitous, beyond our fathom, both binding and freeing, this love re-invades us, shifts the boundaries of our being.[13]

---

13. Michael O'Siadhail, "Out of the Blue," in *The Chosen Garden,* (Dublin: The Dedalus Press, 1991), p.71.

The poem gives two especially important hints of the astonishing relation of two people in love. On the one hand, it gives an idea how much such relations are — and remain — contingent and gratuitous. They occur in the overflowing richness of a complex world where things need not happen, but do; and where they do, they are fully graceful, drawing those involved into a fuller kind of life, 'binding and freeing' them.

On the other hand, the poem contains a remarkable insight into the nature of love. 'This love re-invades us, shifts the boundaries of our being'. For us who have such love, love means that we are not selves in the way we were before, nor need we be withdrawn and self-protective in the way we have come to consider normal. The boundaries of our being are shifted, and go on being shifted, as our love draws us more and more deeply together, more and more profoundly with each other, limited only by the quality of the love which gives us freedom to love. The boundaries of our being, whether as individuals, peoples or cultures, are constantly redrawn by the love shown each to the other, moment by moment. And that in turn makes us still more free, in all the extremities of life, to love and cherish each other. As love develops, so does freedom, the freedom to love.

I need hardly say that this is an astonishing development of the possibilities for the interweaving of human beings. For it makes clear that the boundaries by which cultures and contexts are divided may shift as — in love and compassion — peoples are drawn together.

But that does not bring us far enough. The Ethiopian Eunuch was not drawn primarily into overwhelming compassion; the 'generativity' which he found derived from being drawn into a particular form of compassion, that of the Jesus who suffered, died and was raised. The content of the new life which the Eunuch found was the generativity of being drawn into the life, death and crucifixion of Jesus. That tells us much more about the proper interweaving of human beings, that they find new life in their sacrifice for others, not simply in cost-free compassion.

Now, *what does this show about the dynamics of God's presence n the interweaving of peoples, and about the character of God?*

One answer is that these things of which we have been speaking, whether the compassion which 'shifts the boundaries of our being' or the generativity which comes from sacrifice for others, are simply aspects of a drama into which we enter, which shows rather indirectly the righteous love of God. There are those who would have us think that it is only this, a drama in which we — to quote one present-day theologian — 'project ourselves onto an ultimate plane that gives meaning, and thus we are given ourselves… surrender[ing] ourselves to something that transcends and gives meaning to the limited horizon of everyday life.'[14] And in such a drama as the suffering, death and resurrection of Jesus, they see a demonstration of God's righteous love — a righteous love which somehow stands apart from the drama itself. In other words, God is the author and producer of this drama of righteous love, where we are the actors. The author and producer have gone away, leaving this powerful drama by which we may recover ourselves.

It seems to me that that considerably understates the righteous love of God, and its implications for the way in which God draws us to himself. If love does 'shift the boundaries of our being', can it be any the less so with God? Can we really suppose that the drama of the suffering, death and resurrection of Jesus into which we are brought (like the eunuch) by the Spirit is a drama from which God stands apart? The truth is that the boundaries of being between God and us shift with each new expression of his love, and do so most of all in the drama of the suffering death and resurrection of Jesus as we are drawn into it by the Spirit. The Holy Spirit does not simply draw us into the drama of Jesus. The Spirit draws us into the place in which God's love is most deeply present, and in which God is closest to us. The only limiting factor is the degree to which we are prepared to respond in love. It is, therefore, *we* who insist that God is distant, and we who erect a barrier which keeps God in heaven and leaves us alone here on earth. Far from this, God is most God where in the utmost love he enters most deeply into our life, in the suffering death and resurrection of Jesus into which we are drawn by the Holy Spirit. There, as I need hardly tell you, God lives through the extremities of our life — our sin and self-isolation, and our death — and is still most near to us. Not even the boundaries which we erect to separate ourselves from God are barriers to this love; this love shifts all such boundaries.

Strangely, *the marks of this are found in the proper interweaving of people and their cultures.*

You recall the words from the First Letter of John:

14. Hans Urs Von Balthasar, *Theo-Drama*, (San Franciso: Ignatius Press, 1988), Vol. I, p. 309.

> We know that we have passed out of death into life, because we love the brethren. He who does not love abides in death. Any one who hates his brother is a murderer, and you know that no murderer has eternal life abiding in him. By this we know love, that he laid down his life for us; and we ought to lay down our lives for the brethren... Little children, let us not love in word or speech but in deed and in truth.[15]

For those who are drawn by the Holy Spirit into the suffering death and resurrection of Jesus, and thus drawn into the love of God, the chief mark of this 'new generation' is to be found in our 'love for the brethren', a love which includes 'laying down our lives for the brethren'.

The suffering death and resurrection of Jesus are not simply the illustration of some kind of ideal which should vaguely inform our actions toward others. When we are drawn by the Spirit into the suffering death and resurrection of Jesus, we are drawn into a new kind of life with each other. That may seem scary. Sacrifice for each other usually frightens us because it seems death-like, wasting ourselves for the sake of someone else; and we usually rationalize ourselves into believing that no-one else could be worth such sacrificial wasting of ourselves. And for that reason, we usually turn the suffering death of Jesus into a vague ideal for a kind of love which isn't really expected of us.

But these reactions are simply wrong. Far from being informed of a vague ideal, we are actually drawn by the Spirit into 'the truth', the awesome dynamic of God's pervasively boundary-shifting love, and it is in the dynamic of that love that we are to be interwoven with each other. Following that dynamic, we 'lay down our lives for the brethren', not in fear but in the realization that in such sacrifice God meets us most closely and — in our very loss — raises us up. As we lose ourselves for the brethren, so we will win ourselves. This is the mark that the Spirit has drawn us into the suffering death and resurrection of Jesus.

The dynamic of this love transforms the way in which we are with each other as peoples, cultures and contexts. It is 'gratuitous, beyond our fathom, both binding and freeing... [it] re-invades us, shifts the boundaries of our being'. We can embrace others, and be embraced, in ways quite beyond our imagining — and there continue to be enlarged by the nearness of God's love. That is the fundamental pattern by

15. I John 3.14-18.

which, in the interweaving of human beings and cultures, the presence of God is found. It is the way in which the love of God is continued amongst us who are so sharply separated.

We are at an end. What I have sought to show is the agenda of theology for the future — finding God's presence in the interwovenness of human beings, their cultures and the natural world. Secondly, I have suggested how this agenda is to be met in a theology which is a creative, intelligent, practical poesis by which peoples, cultures and contexts are interwoven. Thirdly, I have suggested that the fullest form of this poesis is found in the Resurrection of Jesus Christ and the generativity which followed from it. By such means, I suggest, we are led both to understand the proper form of the interwovenness of human beings and the way by which God is present in it.

To quote an American evangelist whom I hear on radio broadcasts occasionally, 'think about it'. But perhaps you should also do more, that is be interwoven with others in the way which God has made possible.

3

The Truth Looks Different from Here

or
On Seeking the Unity of Truth from a Diversity of Perspectives

Janet Martin Soskice

Gustavo Gutiérrez, in a recent visit to Cambridge, told his story about the Medellín conference of 1968. (This is my recollection of his story and not an exact quote!) Following that important gathering, the South American bishops received a letter from Rome. 'We can see' it read, 'that your circumstances are very different from those we experience here in Europe. To enable us to help you, please send experts on South American economics, politics, sociology and anthropology to Rome. But don't send any theologians, because we have our own theologians here.'

Despite the fashionable sound to the phrase, theology has always been done 'in context'. Augustine was no less contextual a theologian than Bonhoeffer, with each page attesting to the writer's particular education, formation as a Christian, pastoral concerns and so on. Does this alarm us? Should this alarm us? If we admit to, and even delight in, the diverse contexts for the doing of theology are we 'going soft' on any claim to a universally valid Christian message? How do we speak of the truth and yet speak from our particularity? These are the questions I wish to consider here, questions whose significance for contemporary theology, now a global and ecumenical enterprise, need not be underlined.

I would like to begin, however, at a place seemingly remote from our own- Europe in the sixteenth century. I should like to look at one of those Reformation debates which, while distant in time and sensibility from those of our century, have repercussions which all Christians to a greater or lesser degree must still feel. With some reflections on the controversies which rent western Christendom in the sixteenth century and of which we are still so much heirs. This is my first context for theology and the micro-context I choose. For reasons which I hope will become clear, I should like to begin this discussion of 'truth' with a look at an exchange of letters in 1539 between Cardinal Sadolet and John Calvin.

When the Genevans went over to the Reform, Cardinal Sadolet, apparently of his own initiative, wrote to that city's Senate and people urging them to kick out the reformers and return to the Roman fold. The Genevans asked Calvin to reply on their behalf. The two, avowedly polemical letters which have come down to us as a result tell us much of what was at issue between the reformers and the old guard of that day.

The substance of the letters is interesting, for although both writers touch on issues such as justification by faith, the place of works, the intercession of the saints and transubstantiation, they do more than 'touch on' them. These issues are introduced almost in passing, as the 'cat calls' of the controversy. They serve as bench marks for the respective positions of the antagonists but are not developed in any depth by either Sadolet or Calvin. The real energy of the discussion and the real subject of the letters in both cases is twofold: first, what is the true church?, and second, where can one find truth necessary to salvation? As to what divides the writers and their respective parties, I want to say that they are as much or more divided by the assumptions they share as by the doctoral positions on which they differ. In particular, shared assumptions about truth force them inevitably and violently apart. Let me fill this out with reference to the letters. And I would ask you to pay particular attention to the picture of truth and the 'true Church' that emerges.

Cardinal Sadolet, writing to the Genevans, warns them against subtle and crafty philosophers who boast of hidden interpretations of scripture. He promises himself to "set forth things which are bright and clear", such as "truth always is" (p.6).[1] The Genevans must above all, if they

1. All references to Sadolet are from James Sadolet, "Letter to the Senate and people of Geneva, (March 18, 1539)," in *Tracts and Treatises of the Reformation Church,* Oliver and Boyd, 1958. All Calvin citations are from

fear the loss of their eternal souls, fear "depraved worship" for God and forgive our many sins, but if we turn to "preposterous and false religion" we have neither God nor anchor to save us (pp. 12-13). It is more pleasing to God that we believe what was always and everywhere believed by the Catholic Church for more than thirteen hundred years, or that we believe the innovations of men in the last twenty-five years, men who are not the Catholic Church? And then Sadolet provides a definition; the church is that which "has been always and everywhere directed by the one Spirit of Christ in which the Church no dissension can exist; for all its parts are connected with each other, and breathe together" (p. 14). There can only be one body, one Church and as for the reformers, "they attempted to tear the spouse of Christ in pieces" (p. 19). Their action has given rise to sects and falsehoods for, Sadolet says, "Truth is always one, while falsehood is varied and multiform" (p. 19). Sadolet draws to a close by citing Christ's prayer for the disciples in John's Gospel, "that they may be one, as we also are one" (p. 20). "All the glory of God", says Sadolet,"both his with us, and ours with him, consists solely in this unity. " (p. 20). The Church, according to Sadolet, is one. There is one true worship. Truth is one, error is multiform. The alternative to Christ's one Church is man-made sects.

Calvin does not disagree. "Nothing" he says, "is more pestilential to souls than perverse worship of God." (p. 224) There is no salvation for those who violate the unity of the Church, he says, but the question is 'where is true worship and true Church to be found?' "When the Genevans, instructed by our preaching, escaped from the gulf of terror in which they were immersed and betook themselves to purer teaching of the gospel *you* (Sadolet) call it defection from the truth of God; when they threw off the tyranny of the Roman pontiff, in order that they might establish among themselves a better form of Church, *you* call it desertion from the Church." (pp. 227-8, my emphasis) Calvin insists that he is not deserting *the* Church and it is noteworthy that never in his letter does he criticise the Church, or the Catholic Church, but always describes those he variously styles as the "Roman pontiff and his faction" or some such title. From Calvin's point of view he is not rejecting but rescuing and renewing the one true Church which latterly, he says, has been "criminally mangled" by the "Roman pontiff and his faction" (p. 231). For Calvin no less than for Sadolet there is only one

John Calvin, "Reply to Sadolet (September 1, 1539)," in *Calvin: Theological Treatises.* Library of Christian Classics, XXII, (London: SCM, 1954).

true Church and she is in distress. "True worship" has decayed (p. 240) and the purity of the earthly Church has been corrupted by what he calls "human traditions" which crush Christian liberty (p. 240). This conviction that he is not deserting the Church but rescuing her is the key to some of Calvin's more violent images. Where the tyranny of the Roman pontiff prevails the Church, he says, lies half buried, "Nor should you think this absurd, since Paul tells you (II Thess. 2:4) that anti-Christ would have his seat in no other place than in the midst of God's sanctuary" (p. 242). Thus enters this powerful term of sixteenth century polemic still in use in the sectarian disputes of contemporary Northern Ireland, 'the Pope as anti-Christ'. Yet Calvin's logic compels him towards this position, for if the Church is one and holy and the leaders of it are not its true leaders then who can they be? They cannot be merely mistaken. They must be positively wicked. Against pope and false shepherds, against human institutions, Calvin poses the word of God and "true pastors" "to deliver the oracles which they have received at the mouth of the Lord" (p. 242). The Christian faith must not, he thinks, be founded on human testimony or human authority, but engraved on one's heart by the finger of the living God (p. 244). And as for unity, Calvin insists he has "burned for the unity of the Church provided truth were made the bond of concord" (p. 250).

Now there were certainly significant theological differences between the reformers and the old church, but let us continue to reflect on some agreements. I have said that Sadolet and Calvin are pushed into bitter division as much by the assumptions they share as the doctrinal matters on which they differ. They agree that there can only be one Church and thus that rivals must not only be in error but almost satanic. They agree that truth is one, clear and distinct, and that error is multiform. Neither would thank you for saying "the truth looks different from here". From Calvin's point of view God alone is worthy of worship and therefore any veneration paid to the saints must be idolatry. From Sadolet's point of view the Pope is the head of the one true Church which is without dissension and therefore divisive criticism must have the scent of heresy. Black and white, saved and damned, in no sense are the two men in this exchange agreeing to differ.

Recent studies in early modern history have enhanced our understanding of this tumultuous century. We can see more clearly than before some of the sixteenth century's continuities with the concerns of late medieval Europe and some of its discontinuities, for the sixteenth century was a time of change, and of social as well as personal trauma for many. [2] An old order was in decline, the new ideas of the Renaissance were blowing fresh through northern universities. Calvin was not alone in fearing as well as welcoming the changes. His language, like that of Erasmus and Luther, was replete with metaphors of pollution, contamination, defilement and confusion of order. For in no sense did Calvin or many of his contemporaries treasure disorder, uncertainty or lack of authority. Outside of the antinomian fringe of the radical reformation, the mainstream of the reform longed for order, authority and stability. If we're honest, probably many of the ordinary people of Geneva just wanted to get on with making an honest living without the costly interference of bishops, kings, wars, famines and plagues. For the reformers of the mainstream and for Calvin especially, lawyers as he was, "authority" was a positive term. The authority of scripture facilitated escape from the authority of the Pope and in some cases kings. We should note that both Sadolet and Calvin draw a distinction between "man-made customs", which they reject, and "God-given truths" which they happily appropriate to their own side of the argument. The rhetoric of the debate determines that, by contrast with "God-given truths", "man-made customs" are made to seem untruths or lies, or at least extremely unreliable.

Now this longing for absolute certitude and disdain for the man-made and merely probable sounds familiar, does it not? Are we not reminded of the philosophical obsession with certitude which dominated early modern western philosophy and lingered on into our own century? Descartes, indeed is very near at hand. For the early modern European longing for certainty, already evident in the exchange between Sadolet and Calvin, was not restricted to religious matters, and nor is this coincidence. The Renaissance humanism that informed both Calvin and Sadolet brought with it another potent discovery — or rediscovery — the rediscovery by northern Europeans of classical scepticism, with the terrifying prospect that nothing is certain. In Montaigne's formulation, "Que scay-je?" (What do I know?). As Michael Buckley documents in his suggestive study, *At the Origins of Modern Atheism* this scepticism and its implicit atheism has a corrosive affect on seventeenth century intellectuals in Northern Europe, Catholic and Protestant. It was this scepticism which fuelled Descartes' search for certainty, just as it was a desire for certainty in religion that informed the rigid orthodoxies of

2. See, for example, William Bouwsma, *John Calvin: A Sixteenth Century Portrait,* (Oxford: Oxford University Press, 1988), and Carlos Eire, *War Against the Idols,* (Cambridge: Cambridge University Press, 1986).

seventeenth century religion and perhaps, in its own way, the reaction to them that was the Enlightenment. For as Buckley points out, the Enlightenment was not indifferent to religion "It would be more discerning to say it was obsessed with it" and "irrevocably hostile to supernatural revelation and confessional beliefs".[3] As he points out, after the"fratricidal wars" and "endless dogmatic controversies" that followed the ruptures of the sixteenth century, a reaction of disgust was perfectly understandable. So, too, was the Enlightenment ambition to establish universal truths, not bound to claims to a special revelation, on which all "men of right reason" would amicably agree. Kant states his faith thus, "inasmuch as there can be only one human reason, so likewise there cannot be many philosophies; that is, only one true system of philosophy based on principles is possible..."[4] No one, so far, in this historical sketch would thank you very much for saying "the truth looks different from here".

By the eighteenth and nineteenth centuries secular and scientific verities are contesting and even recasting the religious ones. The new paragons are Newton, Lyell, and Darwin, and the quest is for the real and demonstrable behind the apparent. With the nineteenth century critiques of religions the churches, having failed to agree between themselves on *the* truth have now to meet the accusation that their truths were never more than fictions to start with.

Equally destructive to the Christian faith as the criticisms from without were the inconsistencies within. For if, as part of your argumentative strategy, you style your opponents' position as one of 'man-made constructs' by contrast with your own position as 'God-given truths' then you will have difficulties when confronted with the human component of your own settlement. This, I believe, happened to Protestantism in the nineteenth century when historical criticism forces conclusions about the human and historical composition of the biblical texts and similarly, in the Catholic church, when the modernist crisis compelled admission of human features of the God-given Church. Crudely, if your theory of religious knowing is that things are either

---

3. Michael J. Buckley, *At the Origins of Modern Atheism,* (New Haven: Yale University Press, 1987), p. 37.
4. Kant, Preface to *The Metaphysical Principles of Right,* (in *The Metaphysical Principles of Virtue*, trans. James Ellington, 1964, p. 5), Cit. Lovibond below. That it was still very much "men" of right reason whose agreement was solicited by the philosophers seems clear. See, for instance, "Kant" by Susan , in ed. Ellen Kennedy and Susan Mendus, *Women in Western Political Philosophy,* (Brighton: Wheatsheaf Books, 1987).

'man-made' or 'God-given', and thereby either bad or good, and if one then not the other, then you will be hard put to explain how the bible is in any way a human document, or how its interpretation by the churches is in any sense a human activity. Similarly it will be hard to acknowledge that the church is in any real sense a human institution and subject, as all such institutions are, to error.

I am aware of having moved at great speed over complicated terrain in trying to show the pervasive influence of a certain view on truth and human knowing. It is one which presents us with stark alternatives: either we know things clearly or we know them not at all. Either claims are objectively true or they are completely false; either they are from God or from men and women. In its extreme form it poses the alternative to absolute certainty as total relativism. The slogan of this position might be truth as direct correspondence, and the ideal for human knowing, whether that be religious or secular, is that the knower be solitary and free, unaffected by constraints of language, culture, custom and all such other human limitations.

This vision of human knowing and this version of truth as certainty, if long untenable, is now impossible to defend. Nowhere has this become more instructively apparent than in twentieth century philosophy of science. As physical science has grown more complex, it has grown more modest about its truth claims; not because scientists no longer care about "the truth" or "the world that is the case" but because scientists, working at both micro and macro levels, are aware of dealing with states and relations whose complexity not only transcends our present formulation but which will never be comprehended within any human formulation. (What might an adequate or "true" theory of what happened "before" the Big Bang look like?) It is, in part, for this reason that models are seen as so important in scientific theory construction, providing flexible means for describing "that which is the case", while nonetheless not claiming exhaustive knowledge. While not necessarily directly descriptive, the models employed in scientific theories are nonetheless regarded as reality representing.

The inescapable inference is that science, too — even the hardest of hard science — is a human and interpretive venture. There is a good deal of debate amongst contemporary scientists and philosophers of science as to how to characterise the scientific project in light of this epistemic modesty, but a general agreement that scientific theories do not give us 'the world' or 'the truth' neat can be reached. It is important to emphasise that this modesty does not mean scientists would no longer regard themselves as concerned with the world that is the case, but only with an ever shifting tissue of representations. The world informs our theories, even though our theories never adequately describe the world.[5] Or, as Hilary Putnam puts it in a recent article, "the world is both 'objective' and not 'objective'; we cannot ask what is the case without choosing some system of concepts (and no one system is uniquely fitted to describe 'the world'); but once we have a system of concepts in place, what is true or false is not simply a matter of what we think". He continues more cryptically, "The reality is objective, but the 'objects' aren't!"[6]

While culled from modern philosophy of science, the basic point I wish to make is not so very different from one made many centuries earlier by Thomas Aquinas. In the first question of his *Summa Theologiae* Aquinas considers the difficulty of claiming that theology is the highest of the sciences when it seems to lack certainty. Some of its premises seem open to doubt. In reply he says that "There is nothing to stop a thing that is objectively more certain by its nature from being subjectively less certain to us because of the disability of our minds."[7] Then citing a simile of Aristotle's, we are like bats who, in the sunshine, blink at the most obvious things. Now this is analogous at least, to Putnam's claim that the world informs our theories even though our theories can never adequately describe the world. We continue to be like Aristotle's bats who, in the sunshine, blink at the most obvious things. What may be objectively certain in itself may be subjectively uncertain to us, or if you prefer, "the reality is 'objective', but the 'objects' (humanly delineated) aren't."

The epistemological modesty of modern science is thus not only a useful compliment to the propositions of theology, which has always at its best moments admitted the human limitation in any of our efforts to talk about God, but also provides a foundation for theological perspectivalism — the thesis that 'the truth may look different from here.' The world is construed very differently under a Newtonian or an Einsteinian description, but nonetheless both theories are usefully taken as representing the world that is the case.

---

5. I have explored this far more thoroughly in *Metaphor and Religious Language*, (Oxford: Oxford University Press, 1985), especially chs. 6-8.
6. "An interview with Professor Hilary Putnam," in *Cogito*, Summer, 1989, p. 89, p. 90.
7. *Summa Theologiae*, Ia,1,5. Blackfriars eds, Vol. 1, trans. Thomas Gilby, O.P. (London: Eyre and Spottiswoode, 1964), p. 19.

To my mind, if we are to continue within what is recognisably Christian orthodoxy when we embrace a diversity of perspectives, we must cleave to the idea that it is 'the truth' that we are approximating, however inadequately, and 'the truth' that looks different from here. That is, a concern for 'that which is certain in itself but subjectively uncertain to us' will continue to be at the heart of the Christian message. What I have tried to show thus far is that not only is it perfectly acceptable, epistemologically speaking, to seek a unity of truth from a diversity of perspectives, it is often desirable to do so. A complex description is more likely to provide an adequate account of complex subject matter than a simple single view. We can see this in scientific theory construction and nearer to home we can see it in St. Paul. Paul uses a number of metaphors (or models) to give account of what God has done in Christ (that which we designate in English by the wonderful non-committal term, 'atonement'). He speaks of redemption from slavery, a military victory, a new birth, a price being paid. But we do not believe Paul uses a plurality of descriptions because he's not sure which is the right one! Rather the complexity of that which he undertakes to describe is such that it *demands* a number of descriptions, no one of which alone is adequate. No one description could be adequate to this saving mystery, and taking one description or model and privileging it so as to occlude or silence the others would falsify Paul's account. In this case, a reversal of Sadolet's dictum would be called for: truth is multi-form, error is one.

Perspectivalism is, in one sense, at the centre of contemporary theological concern, and not only because of the ecumenical movement but because of the newly heard voices of liberation, black and feminist theology, amongst others. All these theologies emphasise historical and social particularity, and stress their own contexts as the scenes of witness to God's redemptive love — we drink from our own wells, says Gutiérrez, or, we might say "the truth looks different from here". This is undoubtedly an extremely attractive and invigorating feature of the new theologies from which the world wide Christian community has much to learn. But it is this 'drinking from our own wells' that invites the question of 'how it is we can be certain that the truth we are approximating, the water we are drinking, in South America or South Africa or a women-church in Detroit, is the same as that drunk in Rome or Geneva or Canterbury?' How do we preserve the unity of faith from a diversity of perspectives? Now at one level we might say that the fearful and death laden circumstances in which some liberation theologians write makes the resolution of philosophical questions like this a low priority, and rightly so. Some, like Albert Nolan writing in the midst of the struggles of the mass democratic movement, deliberately bracketed speculations about universal meaning in favour of preaching the gospel in the place to which they have been called.[8] But is the same strategy open to me in Cambridge or you in Dunedin or Christchurch or Sydney? How do we continue in our concern for the unity of truth and faith that has characterised the Christian witness? Need we continue in it?

Siren voices are heard here, emanating from a mysterious and elusive new territory called 'Postmodernism'. These tempting voices say, Parochialism is all there is. We must free ourselves from the Enlightenment ideals of universalism. For too long the myth of universal reason and its "grand narratives" have silenced the small voices. Western logocentrism and phallogocentrism together collude to oppress and silence women and other marginalised groups.[9] There is no metaphysical certainty, and for those of you in the Reform tradition there is not textual certainty either. Texts and even readers of texts are no longer stable for as Roland Barthes says,

> "we know that a text is not a line of words releasing a simple 'theological' meaning (the 'message' of an Author-God) but a multi-dimensional space in which a variety of writings, none of them original, blend and clash".[10]

According to these voices we must free ourselves from the 'myths of presence' and step out proudly into a world of fragments, for that is the only world there is.

Maybe, but maybe not. Certainly anyone who either is or regards themselves on the side of the poor and the voiceless has cause to agree

8. Albert Nolan, *God in South Africa* , (London: CIIR, 1988). Nolan is critical of what he calls the 'universalising tendency' of Western theology, "the assumption that nothing is true or valuable unless it applies to all people, at all times and in all circumstances" (p. 15), but nonetheless his own distinction between 'content' and 'shape' of the gospel, the first changing and the second across time and place, is an attempt to say how Christian continuity is maintained while hearing the new voice.
9. See Toril Moi on the French feminist, Helene Cixous in eds. Ann Jefferson and David Roby, *Modern Literary Theory,* (London: B.T. Batsford, 1986), p. 211. An account of the post-modernist critique of Enlightenment ideals is given by Lovibond below.
10. Cit. Jonathan Culler in *Barthes,* (London: Fontana, 1983).

with the post-modernist suggestion that master-narratives and 'canons of judgement' are not neutral but weighted to the interests of those groups which, historically, they have served. In 1992 we need only to reflect that the claim 'Columbus was the man who discovered America' is not obviously true if you are a descendent of the Aztecs. By the time small (European and colonial) children are able to give the 'correct' answer to the question (viz. Columbus) they are already embedded in a language which privileges certain perspectives and powers and which, without thinking, hears only the dominant voice as 'true' voice. 'Voicelessness' in this sense is so substantially documented by anthropologists and social theorists are to be no longer regarded as a contested hypothesis.[11]

Any statement of a 'fact' is already the product of an explanation or a narrative which, even despite best intent, is not neutral. (As Paul Ricoeur says, "to narrate is already to explain".[12]) But to be aware of the reality of ideology in language, and the social embeddedness of knowing and speaking is only, in our linguistically informed day, to exercise a proper critical faculty. The further challenge of post-modern parochialism is to say that the abandonment of meta-narratives *means* the abandonment not only of iron-clad claims to 'truth' but of the search for truth itself. Must we then really, to be able to listen to the quiet, local and previously silenced voices, follow that pioneer of post-modernism, Friedrich Nietzsche, and distance ourselves those symptoms of the sickness of the Enlightenment that are truth, reason and morality?

Recent feminist philosophy makes an interesting case study here. While for a time post-modern parochialism, combined with its critique of phallogocentric master-narratives, exercised a fascination (particularly in feminist literary critical circles) the mood is shifting now. Many feminists do not want to, and some would say cannot, adopt a philosophy which makes moral judgements impossible. Feminists do not want to say, at the last evaluation, 'do as you please because we are free from master-narratives and 'Author-Gods'. They want more

---

11. For an anthropological account of the 'muting' of women see the Introduction to ed. Shirley Ardener, *Defining Females: The Nature of Women in Society*, (London: Croom Helm, 1978), p. 20ff. For a more philosophical account, Deborah Cameron, *Feminism and Linguistic Theory*, (London: The Macmillan
Press, 1985) and Diane Macdonell, *Theories of Discourse*, (Oxford: Basil Blackwell, 1987).
12. Paul Ricoeur, *Time and Narrative*, Vol. 1, (Chicago: University of Chicago Press, 1984), p. 178.

characteristically to say that some things, like gratuitous inequalities and oppressive structures, 'are wrong'. The Oxford philosopher Sabina Lovibond has pointed out that, in this moral sense, feminism as a movement stands within Enlightenment and modernist (not post-modernist) hopes that "sooner or later, arbitrary authority will cease to exist." It is difficult, she says, "to see how one could count oneself a feminist and remain indifferent to the modernist premise of social reconstruction."

> "What", she continues, "are we to make of the (post-modernist) suggestions that the project has run out of steam and that the moment has passed for remaking society on rational, egalitarian lines? It would be only natural for any one placed at the sharp end of one or more of the existing power structures (gender, race, capitalist class...) to feel a pang of disappointment at this news. But wouldn't it also be in order to feel suspicion? How can anyone ask me to say goodbye to 'emancipatory meta-narratives when my own emancipation is still such a patchy, hit-and-miss affair."[13]

Lovibond's argument is readily applicable to liberation theologies. For despite promising murmurs about the importance of local narratives and parochial truth, neither feminist nor liberation theology is to my mind likely to find an ally in some of the postmodernist theories currently on offer. Both will continue to want to make universal claims in the area of morals and for this reason both will need to find a way in which an emphasis on particularity and context is compatible with universal value, or the unity of faith. While theologically, socially and sometimes ecclesiologically innovative these new movements are fundamentally aligned to an old-fashioned moral realism. 'Some things are wrong', they want to say, and cannot say, globally, 'some things are wrong' if one has already ruled out universal claims.

The difficulty we face is that of seeking metaphysics without mastery and here, curiously, the theologian has the advantage over the morally embarrassed post-modernist. For if the latter has followed a familiar trajectory initiated by Nietzsche, then 'the death of God' has resulted in the death of man, the death of the subject as humanistically

---

13. Sabina Lovibond, "Feminism and Postmodernism," *New Left Review*, #178, 1989, p. 12.

conceived, and in turn the death of value including moral value. If the post-modernist recoils at the vision and wishes to reinstate morals they face the difficulty of doing so without reinstating a moral master-narrative. The Christian, on the other hand, holds fast to God who is the guarantor of value, but need not fall once again into repressive 'master-narratives' if they follow the strategy outlined in the first part of the paper and commonplace in historical Christianity. That is, the Christian cleaves to the conviction that 'the truth' inheres in God, while realising that all our approximations to it are just that — approximations, and thus open to bias and human error. The Christian can retain the idea of the unity of truth, grounded as that is in the divine, while embracing a plurality of perspectives. We are like bats who blink in the sunshine at the most obvious things.[14]

In fact I do not believe that either feminist nor liberation thought is much endangered, except in the most transient ways, by the extremes of post-modernism.[15] Curiously the danger might rather be on the other side; that these new movements may reinstate the older and unproductive stasis on truth and objectivity that I spoke of earlier. I give you one example — possibly apocryphal since it comes from California.

14. A more difficult question, but fortunately not ours to answer, is how the secularist and secular feminist will escape from the amoral vision of the future post-modernism holds out before them? It is interesting to find Lovibond speaking of "the epistemic equivalent of an article of faith, a commitment to persist in the search for common ground with others: in fact, something which could not be relinquished on pain of sinking into 'hatred or reason and of humanity' (Plato, *Phaedo*)" (p. 14). The French writer, Julia Kristeva speaks directly of the crisis of meaning in language in a world without God. After speaking of the quest for "an impossible truth, concerning the meaning of speech, concerning our condition as speaking beings" (ix), she speaks of psychoanalytic discourse as perhaps the only one "capable of addressing this untenable place where our speaking species resides, threatened by the madness beneath the emptiness of heaven" (xi). In her Preface to *Desire in Language: A Semiotic Approach to Literature and Arts*, ed. Leon S. Roudiez (New York: Columbia University Press, 1980).

15. In order to underline this moral quandary of post-modernist thought I have run the danger of appearing dismissive of some of the astute criticisms of power and language to emerge from this quarter. Theology has much to learn from these, as Rebecca Chopp demonstrates in *The Power to Speak: Feminism, Language, God,* (New York: Crossroad, 1989).

An academic theologian I met from that state said that enthusiasm for inclusive language had now reached such a pitch amongst his students that, not only would they not read contemporary works that failed to use sex-inclusive language, they were now rebelling against readings works of historical theology that spoke in sexist terms. When their teacher replied that one could scarcely expect Schleiermacher writing (in German) at the beginning of the nineteenth century to be aware of sexist language the students replied, "Well how could he be so great a theologian then if he failed to notice this great affront to human dignity?" What is amusing about this tale of undergraduate woe is that it is not really a position of moral high-mindedness which is displayed here, but a failure of moral vision — a failure to see how differently things could look. Many people, male and female, over the age of thirty have had the experience of becoming aware of sexist language and practice, and wondering why it had never troubled them before. Many Europeans and Americans may remember becoming conscious of racism or anti-semitism, and wondering why it never previously hit them in the face. Now it is not my intention to condone sexism or racism or anti-semitism, and I do not think perspectivalism commits us to condoning them. But the real moral and, I would say, theological failure embodied in the thoughtless condemnation of Schleiermacher as a sexist is not so very far from that for which I have faulted Sadolet and Calvin. It is the assumption that the truth is always and everywhere transparent and self-evident. It is the assumption that the right thing for a Christian to do is always obvious. It is in short the sin of pride. It is the presumption that says, 'we see things absolutely clearly and those who do not see things as we do are either willfully stupid or evil.' It is the naivety which assumes without question that, had I lived in Nazi Germany, I would of course have defended the Jews, which ignores the more painful and difficult possibility that had I lived in Nazi Germany I might well not have defended them.

In theological terms it is the denial of original sin, and of the extent to which are born into and caught up in languages and cultures which, whatever their excellences, have their dark sides — structures and truisms so built around injustices, so built into the fabric of language itself, that we may not be able to see the injustices as such. We can learn this lesson in a hundred places. One is the theological and Biblical justification of apartheid developed by some South African theologians, interpretations which fashioned from Biblical accounts like that of the confusion of tongues following Babel a justification for a social policy of separate development. Yet apartheid theology was Biblically oriented and had its base in a respectable theological tradition. Its interpretation of the Bible was eccentric, but not totally incoherent.[16] Indeed it had many features of a liberation theology, for the Afrikaners at least. Surely the insight we must take away from a study of that particular variant of South African Calvinism which read a racist message into the Bible is not 'weren't those people foolish and immoral' but, at least at one level, 'there but for the grace of God go I'? One of the painful lessons we have always to learn is that Christians, even in their Christianity, are not free from the sin which distorts vision (this by the way is what I take Calvin to have meant by total depravity).

The answer to our fears of distorted perspectives cannot be, as I have said, an attempt to clamber onto the moral high ground, or an attempt to find a theological language with an authority which, as Rowan Williams puts it, is "determined from an elusive elsewhere", mysteriously ahistorical, unaffected by language or culture and thus 'objectively true'. This is not to resolve our problem but to deny it.[17] Christian theology throughout its history is always tempted by the prospect of a 'theology done by angels', free from human limitation, but what we have in fact is theology done by men, and recently by women as well.[18] The solution must lie in the theological modesty we considered earlier. Truth may be one, but our apprehension of it is limited and perspectival.[19]

---

16. For a critical discussion of the exegesis of apartheid see J.A. Loubser, *The Apartheid Bible: A Critical Review of Racial Theology in South Africa*, (Cape Town: Maskew Miller Longman, 1987).

17. Rowan Williams, "Trinity and Revelation," *Modern Theology*, 2:3, 1986, p. 197.

18. For the limitations of theology 'done by angels' see Fergus Kerr, *Theology After Wittgenstein,* (Oxford: Basil Blackwell, 1986).

19. The approach to theology here developed is thus entirely different from that which T.F. Torrance credits to Karl Barth. According to Torrance Barth "set himself to think through the whole of theological knowledge in such a way that it might be consistently faithful to the concrete act of God in Jesus Christ from which it actually takes its rise in the Church, and, further, in the course of that inquiry to ask about the presuppositions and conditions on the basis of which it comes about that God is known, *in order to develop from within the actual content of theology its own interior logic and its own inner criticism which will help to set theology free from every form of ideological corruption."* (my emphasis) cited by Richard Roberts in Stephen Sykes, ed., *Karl Barth: Centenary Essays,* (Cambridge: Cambridge University Press, 1989) p. 147. For a very different view of what Barth's intentions were see Ingolf Dalferth, "Karl Barth's eschatological realism" in the same volume.

It may even be that, if in our differing moral and theological journeys, we are moving to the light, we are doing so not despite our differences but because of them. Christianity and Judaism are not, after all, religions to whose faithful the Deity at one moment in time lowered a compendium of truths from the sky. Instead God is disclosed through human history. God covenants to be with the people, Israel, and it is through their historical experience that they come to know what God is and how God acts. God discloses himself in human history and supremely through taking on a human history in becoming man in Christ.

We have not one gospel but four. The Bible discloses God to us through human history and from different perspectives, and these perspectives we must believe are not in default of one plain and uncontroversial text or set of propositions, but indeed required by the complexity of that which is revealed, God Godself. Like so many facets of a gemstone these particularities are the means by which we apprehend, even if we cannot comprehend, the glory of God and God's creative and redemptive act.

What then of certainty? How can we be certain we are right? The answer may be that we cannot. There may be clear signs, however, that we have got things wrong. The signs are evil and its attendant suffering; the suffering of our fellow men and women and the suffering of creation.[20] The other speakers at this conference have written eloquently of these signs of suffering. As long as there are these signs we, collectively as well as individually, cannot be certain all our answers are right. But is this kind of certainty what Christianity offers? Is this kind of complete certainty not something that early modern European philosophy first constructed as a fiction and then demanded as a fact? What we are promised as Christians is that we shall know the truth, not that we shall have the facts. Indeed there are two good reasons why epistemic certitude must not be seen as part of the Christian promise. The first, as Aquinas knew well, is the fact of the Goodness of God —

---

20. I take evil to be a prime correlate of suffering. Cf. Paul Ricoeur, ".. to do evil in this sense is always, either directly or indirectly, to make another person suffer. In its relational or dialogical structure, in other words, evil committed by someone finds its other half in the evil suffered by someone else." In eds H. Deuser, G.M. Martin, K. Stock and M. Welker, *Gottes Zukunft Der Velt: Festschrift fur Jurgen Moltmann*, (Munchen: Chr. Kaiser Verlag, 1986), p. 346.

the unutterable holiness of God before which all human speaking and all human theologising is as straw. The second is the pledge of the spirit and the hope of the kingdom — for the Christian story, like the Jewish one, is a story that awaits completion. The future, for us, is God's future and it is not for us to delimit the boundaries of God's grace.

We are limited creatures, even our speaking of God is limited. Yet for a religion whose central doctrine is the incarnation this should not be a problem. If God did not despise and despair of the limitations of the human condition, why should we? Why should we aspire to be philosophical angels when God became a man? Maybe this will mean, as Professor Metz has recently said, that we must acknowledge religious diversity to be not the work of satan but the will of god.[21] Truth may be one for God, but Calvin and Sadolet were misguided in thinking it one for us. We may know the unknowable God truly in the knowledge of love, but as far as our cognitive knowing goes, we know in part and we know in progress.

Gregory of Nyssa, in his *Life of Moses*, tells us that Moses came to learn that "to follow God wherever he might lead *is* to behold God".[22] We, too, must remember that ours is an eschatological faith, a religion of hope and future, of now and not yet. We must remember that the truth is what we seek as much as what we savour and indeed we must remember that the truth may look different from here.

---

21. At the *Concilium,* conference, Louvain, Summer, 1990.
22. I am grateful to Ann Conway for drawing my attention to this text.

Response by Jürgen Moltmann

This is the first fascinating and important attempt to melt modern, liberal and academic theology together with feminist and liberation theology under the roof of "theological perspectivalism". John de Gruchy has spoken elsewhere in this publication of the communication difficulties between the Western academic theology with its arguments and the theology of the third World with its experiences and witnesses.

I find the present discussion about religious pluralism and pluralistic theories of truth very interesting. But it only takes place in the old Christian and rich countries of the First World which can afford such pluralism. Only here in the "modern world" does one think about a possible "post-modern world". But the political theology and the liberation theology were originally theologies of the people, a rebellion of the victims of the "modern world", the voice of the speechless. The feminist theology also read the His-story from the underside as Her-story. Janet Martin Soskice has rightfully called attention to the indispensable "moral realism" and the vitally necessary vision of justice with which one must publicly say: "There is something wrong." But can one bring these two so different discussions under one roof?

1. I will begin with a thought out of the classics. For the Greek philosophers, the true, the good and the beautiful belonged together inseparably, so very much that one had to say: there is no truth in the evil and nothing good in the ugly. In order to develop Janet Martin Soskice's thoughts further, I want to emphasize the relationship between truth and justice. The statement "the truth looks different from here" is only acceptable on the basis of equality, that is for example, between Cambridge and Oxford, between Tübingen and Princeton and in the academic community. But it is not acceptable where inequality and injustice is prevalent, that is between the slums of the poor and the palaces of the rich, between the perpetrators and their victims, between the Concentration Camp murderers and their innocent victims. Where violence and injustice is prevalent, the truth is not at all to be recognized. The first victim in the Gulf War was truth. It was already jointly killed

in the beginning by Saddam Hussein and President Bush. All public statements in the Gulf War were conscious lies with the intention of disorienting the enemy, as it was said. The ends justify the means! Up to this day, we do not know the truth about the Gulf War. It was no different with the truth after the catastrophe of Chernobyl. The public statements were without exceptions lies with the purpose of the reassurance of the people who died as a result of the contamination and are still dying.

> I, therefore, maintain:
> The body of truth is justice.
> The soul of justice is truth.
> Only where justice and freedom kiss one another,
> does truth come into the light and there
> are different perspectives of truth,
> which can be developed in fruitful dialogue.

2. That God alone is the truth itself and that all human theologies can only offer approximations and fragmentary perspectives on to the divine truth is right, and must be said repeatedly by the theologians, male and female. It is the old traditional distinction between the *theologia archetypa*, that is the theology which God in the knowledge of God's own self has, and the *theologia ektypa*, that is the theology which humans as the likeness of God can have. The divine self-knowledge is one, the human knowledge of God many. The temporal distinction between the human *theologia viae* here on earth in the pilgrimage through the distance from God of history and the eschatological *theologia patriae* in the Kingdom of God, the eternal home of all creations appears similar. The *theologia viae* is as diverse as the humans in the different times and places; but the *theologia patriae* is one and common to all. These distinctions between God and human are, however, metaphysical and not specifically biblical, Jewish or Christian.

Only the distinction between a realistic *theologia crucis* and an illusionary *theologia gloriae* refers to the special Christian experience of God: to the crucified Christ who says of himself: I am the truth and the life. The metaphysical distinctions presuppose that the truth is always there but in heaven, or respectively in the ideal state, we humans in this earth are bound to location and time and therefore, can only develop different perspectives of the other worldly truth. Opposed to this, the Christian distinction presupposes that humans "suppress the truth" (Rm 1:18) and exchange the truth about God their Creator for a lie (Rm 1:25).

How is the truth in a world of lies revealed? Like the light in the darkness, so comes the truth of God into the world of lies and becomes the victim of violence and injustice. In the crucified Christ, God's truth meets us as a contradiction to the contradictions of this world. In Christ, the suffering truth of God looks at us.

3. The crucified Christ stands between the victims of world history. He does not stand on the side of the perpetrators, the murderers and the victors. From this, follows that the most important help to the recognition of truth about ourselves is the perspective of those who have become our victims. The suffering ones have a long memory, the perpetrators have almost no memory. And the "lies have short legs". Who are we Germans in the eyes of the victims and the Jews who survived Auschwitz? Who are we white Europeans in the eyes of South American Indians, the African blacks and New Zealand Maoris? Who are we men of the patriarchy in the eyes of women? Who are we humans in the eyes of dying animals and trees? This outside perspective is important for the recognition of truth because it destroys our personal and collective self-image. It is our victims who say to us: "The truth looks different from here!", come and recognize yourself and you will understand who you are in truth and if then you do not like yourself, change and become born again to a truly human creation.

Response by Sue Patterson

Dr Soskice, you have posed for us a problem which is central to the whole business of this Symposium. You ask: given the apparently undeniable fact that there are many Christian perspectives, or contexts in which we are Christian, is it rational for us to continue to hold to the seemingly incompatible Christian doctrine of the one-ness of divine truth?

You have eloquently and persuasively set out for us the need for an epistemological model which will allow us to reconcile these two seemingly irreconcilable things. As you say, the traditional understanding of truth as direct correspondence will not do, because this way of looking at things seduces us into thinking that there must be a direct and certain correspondence between what we say and the state of affairs in question. Of course, this is as you say, both false and dangerous because it locks us into a one-to-one link-up in which *our* view is the only possible view.

You show us a possible solution in the replacement of direct realism (truth as direct correspondence) with critical realism. This option holds with the notion of correspondence but disposes of the certainty requirement. It lets perspectivalism get a foothold on truth because now no *one* position can claim to be the whole truth and nothing but the truth. What we have instead is a cluster of partial certainties, which all represent, or correspond to — albeit imperfectly and progressively — the one reality which is the one-ness of the Truth of God. We cannot expect to know this Truth with any certainty as human vision, is both both limited and flawed.[1] We must accept that the unity of our

1. Dr Soskice does not consider the loss of what she terms *epistemic* certainty to be significant problem for theology; it is *moral* certainty which is important because absolute truth, or unity of faith, is here equated with universal value. It remains for here to show that we are at least able to achieve a unity of faith through universal moral certainty. However, it seems that moral certainty is also denied us because here also the tenets of

perspectives lies beyond the reach of our understanding in the oneness of the reality of God.

This model thus rests on the twin pillars of correspondence and uncertainty. As such it is, as you say, consistent with traditional Thomist analogical thinking and it succeeds accordingly, on these terms, in establishing that we can indeed have both a one-ness of divine Truth and a diversity of human successive approximations to that Truth.

However, I do have some questions concerning this critical realist model — in particular its twin presuppositions of correspondence and uncertainty. Dr Soskice, you appear to be rejecting the *exactness* of the correspondence theory without rejecting correspondence itself. This provides a way of dealing with the inadequacies of the traditional view by admitting the need for caution in the claims we make concerning our conceptions of reality. As you say, at best our representations of reality can be only tentative and provisional, always subject to revision, never simply a rubbing off a brass relief. I want to ask, is this indeed possible — is it possible to keep the correspondence without the *verification* of that correspondence?

And then I want to ask whether the reconciliation of the oneness and the manyness of truth can be resolved simply by ridding realism of its claim to certainty.[2] It is perhaps not so much the uncompromising explicitness of traditional realism that is at fault as its presupposition of a separation (as opposed to a mere distinction) between language and non-linguistic reality? It is, I believe, this presupposition upon which the correspondence notion is built which is the root-cause of the problem. I believe it also has something to do with the difference in philosophical

critical realism apply: at best 'we know in part and we know in progress' because the only moral certainty accessible to us is that reached by a negative path. We have no certainty regarding the positive rightness of our perspective because our vision is distorted by sin, but the presence of evil and suffering show us where our perspective lacks rightness (although I do not see how it is possible to subsume all evil within human culpability). We learn as we go which things are not consistent with Christian values. We thus have a partial and progressive knowledge of moral as well as epistemic truth.

2. For a more detailed critique of Dr Soskice's position, see my paper "Janet Martin Soskice, Metaphor and Theology of Grace," (in publication *Scottish Journal of Theology*).

and theological uses of the word 'truth' which is apparent in your paper as an ambiguity.[3]

This means that at bottom I want to question also the commonly held view of language and non-linguistic reality which underlies the idea of correspondence — the understanding which sees them as separate 'layers' in which one represents the other more or less accurately and explicitly. I want to question the way the 'layers' concept reduces the issue of truth to the issue of whether or not our words can indeed be shown to correspond to an extra-linguistic reality. This issue is important for our examination of the one-ness and the many-ness of truth.

The problem for me is that while this representation model may work well in science when we are dealing with things whose properties we partially know, it may cause us trouble in theology. Even without the stipulation of exactness, the implicit lingering requirement of verification still embarrasses us, because, without some prospect of this,

---

3. A Paper like this which combines philosophical and theological arguments also combines two different conventions regarding the use of the term such as 'truth'. 'Truth' as understood in philosophical circles has a narrower meaning than it does in theological circles. In philosophy,'truth' pertains to what we say - only statements can be true or false, never things or people or situations. By contrast, 'truth' is used in Christian theology (in scripture and tradition) with reference to persons as well as statements. There is no problem with theological talk about the truth of God unless we also, in the same breath, talk about the truth of our propositions regarding God and the world. This creates some ambiguity in Dr Soskice's argument, beginning as it does with the statement "The Truth looks different from here" and then proceeding with an epistemological argument implying (as must any argument which relies on a correspondence however uncertain between statements and states of affairs) a distinction between truth and reality. This has the effect of making the initial topic statement appear metaphorical, but further on, when the epistemological argument is again related to the theological, I find myselves asking, what does Dr Soskice mean by truth here? — having adjusted my sights, as it were, to the philosophical picture she has been drawing for us, and now needing to re-adjust to the wider theological picture. And this begs the question: if there are two different concepts of truth here, is it legitimate to infer from conclusions reached about one in order to make conclusions about the other? As this difficulty of terminology relates to the problems associated with the narrower philosophical definition truth as correspondence to reality, it tends to disappear once we find other ways of talking about the relationship between our words and the world that is the case.

our God-talk tends to reduce to such statements as: whatever that is that is out there, or whatever is the cause of this experience, is God.

So what this apparently helpful epistemic uncertainty in alliance with perspectivalism seems to allow us to say is that there is a unity of truth out there beyond the limits of our perspectives, only we do not know for certain what it is. And we must console ourselves with the thought that, in any case, it is inappropriate for Christians to concern themselves with desire for this sort of certainty.

This conclusion seems to leave us rather short, but at least we now know better to claim an unwarranted certainty in our knowing.[4] As a one-time professor of New Testament here at Knox was fond of saying, "If you leave here thinking that you know anything at all, this place will not have done its job!" Conducive as this may be to humility of theology students, it is not a solution to the problem of truth.

However, Dr Soskice, you reassure us that, in spite of the limits and flaws in our perspectives, we can be certain of the absolute reality and truth of God which makes our perspective one in a unity of faith. What I now want to ask is: How do we arrive at such knowledge? It seems implicit in your argument that this is taken care of by analogy: but can we indeed know by means of analogy that the correspondence is there? An argument from analogy requires correspondence, but how can we say that we have correspondence when we don't know to what degree

4. To begin with, Dr Soskice appears to have found a basis for certainty in moral realism. We may be critically short of epistemic knowledge; we may never be able to say conclusively what the truth of our perspectives is, even with the benefit of the combined explanatory power of all our contexts, but this still leaves our knowledge of moral truth to bind together our perspectives, because issues of 'what ought and ought not' seem to transcend contextual barriers in a way that issues of 'what is and is not' does not. To my mind, it is rather too easy to move from this rather unstable position into the sort of wholesale shifting of theology sideways into the domain of values to avoid the embarrassment of having to make unsupportable empirical claims for which theologians influenced by British Empiricism have been notorious, and which Dr Soskice herself, in her book 'Metaphor and religious Language', rightly condemns. But in the event such a separation and shift takes us no closer to a unity of truth in a diversity of perspectives. For, to be consistent, critical realism must also apply to the area of moral realism. And this requires that, far from possessing a trans-contextual knowledge of what is good, we have at best a partial and progressive knowledge acquired by a process of elimination. We are left, it seems to me, no better off than before this argument.

that correspondence obtains? This is why I have difficulty with the logic or theo-logic that our collection of local versions of the truth, however partial and progressive, are true by *analogy* to the transcendent reality of God.

Dr Soskice, I suppose that all this is by way of saying that the Truth looks different from *here* !

Because it looks different from here, I need to propose and alternative model. It's a model with two branches. Here's the first: the linguistic philosopher Ludwig Wittgenstein[5] developed a theory in which language is an inextricable component of our reality, of the practices of our living in the world. Wittgenstein turns our traditional way of thinking at right angles. Instead of operating with a 'horizontal layer' model of language and world, he 'slices reality up vertically' as it were into a multitude of language/world pieces. These he calls language-games because they are activities or practices which interweave language and world.[6]

This is a model which, starting at grass roots level, reworks the relationship of words with reality. Here certainty is not a matter of explicit statement or belief so much as as a matter of living according to patterns or axioms generated by our communal experience, the doubting of which would destroy that pattern because it would be to doubt the very stuff of our existence.

Now for the second branch: another philosopher, Michael Polanyi, while not addressing the language-world relation in the way Wittgenstein does[7], also considers certainty to be implicit in the practice of our lives. So, in place of the realist understanding of certainty as indubitable correspondence and the critical realist notion of the imperfect certainty of that correspondence, these philosophers both posit a tacit certainty which arises out of and is confirmed by our ongoing contact with the world — a certainty of practice which is itself ungrounded. But

---

5. The choice of this model and other aspects of Wittgenstein's philosophy does not necessarily imply a wholesale and uncritical acceptance of Wittgenstein's philosophical and theological views.
6. This exposition is unavoidably over-simplified. For a more comprehensive explanation of language-game theory see Merrill B. and Jaakko Hintikka *Investigating Wittgenstein*, (Oxford: Basil Blackwell, 1986), also my papers 'Word, Words and World,' (*Colloquium* May 1991).
7. *Personal Knowledge* and *The Tacit Dimension*, (London: Routledge & Kegan Paul, 1958 & 1966). For a discussion of the philosophers, see my papers 'Word, Words and World' (op cit.) and 'Gratuitous Truth: Metaphor and Revelation' (in publication, *Colloquium,* October 1991).

where Wittgenstein slices reality up across the grain, as it were, Polanyi turns it back to front.[8] Here it is not we who reach for a more or less objective reality so much as reality which reaches for us, engages us in mutual participation and provides the ground of our confidence in our dealings with the world.[9]

We know this process well from learning to drive a bike or a car or a tennis racquet. First the things drives us, then it becomes an extension of ourselves. We have learned to drive it. In this way, and at this tacit level of knowing, the traditional and critical realist separation between subject and object, knower and known, propositions and reality is breached. In this way we arrive at a certainty beyond words, which is lived in the practices of our lives.

Where Wittgenstein talks about certainty Polanyi talks about commitment. As we know from our own experience, a claim to certainty is inherent in any commitment that we make. We have to stand somewhere; we have, for the time being at least, to accept unquestionably the rightness of some stance, or we have no basis from which to evaluate anything else.

Now it is easy to see why direct realism has enjoyed such popularity. From where we stand it always looks like our Johnny is the only one in step. But, in step or not, according to Wittgenstein and Polanyi, we are, believe it or not, all going round in circles: experience gives rise to belief, belief orders experience. And so on. Such circles come in all sizes from simple superstitions to customs to entire world-views. Because they are what we live by (or from), the axiomatic certainties which are generated by and in turn regulate our actions, seem always to be context-free-eternal, absolute. They seem to be self-evident truths. Yet they can only claim this truth within the microcosm of their own circle — the context for which they are the rules. Beyond their own circles these truths are groundless.

---

8. However, Polanyi's theory of knowledge proposes 'layers' of a different kind in an ontological hierarchy. While I accept the overall logic of Polanyi's Higher Organising Principle, I am uncomfortable with some aspects of this theory, especially its extension into a specified metaphysical hierarchy. I have chosen to utilise some aspects of Polanyian epistemology without necessarily accepting all its tenets or the particular theological application presented by the author.
9. This process Daniel Hardy terms our 'noetic qualification by the object' ("Christ and Creation," in *The Incarnation,* ed. T.F. Torrance, (Edinburgh: Handsell, 1981), p. 97.).

The problem with commitment is not commitment as such, but the way we let it grant our experience, our beliefs, our world-views an indubitability not only for us to ride on but, we are tempted to believe, for everyone else to ride on as well. It is this *abuse* of certainty to which you, Dr Soskice, so rightly object — the reason why Calvin and Sadolet could argue so bitterly about the one true church and why we still have such arguments today. What you have called the sin which distorts vision lies not in our commitment as such, but in our failure to recognise that our commitment to a particular perspective is just that: a commitment to a *perspective*. It is not and cannot be the whole truth. We cannot avoid commitment because we have to stand somewhere, but, to mix metaphors, the fact of our commitment means we are constantly tempted to be one-eyed.

Of course, as I mentioned earlier, when we dispense with the notion of truth as correspondence we can no longer use correspondence or analogy as a way of relating the one truth of God to our perspectives. Also as we have seen, we have to adopt a different understanding of certainty. Does this in fact mean that we have to say goodbye to a solution to the problems posed to us? Is the only alternative to being one-eyed a plunge into the flux of total relativism, or are our many circularities of belief and experience not the dead-ends they seem?

I do no believe we need to draw the dead-end conclusion from Wittgenstein and Polanyi. What we learn from them about perspectivalism is not that there is no justification of human experience and beliefs, but that there is nos such justification to be found simply within *human experience*. From a traditional point of view, that is entirely the answer we expect. But how does this model make the connection between our perspective-boundedness and the transcendent truth of God?

I believe that it does so by establishing the necessity of grace. The circles of our beliefs and practices may pretend to be self-authenticating but this is an illusion, for as the mathematician Godel has shown us, that which a system as a whole depends must lie outside of that system.[10] Our human systems of experience are simply incomplete. Alongside that we may put Polanyi's observation that the whole is not simply

10. This grossly over-simplified is the Godelian theorem (and Aristotelian axiom) to which Polanyi adds his scientist's knowledge of the organisation of the components of material existence to form his Higher Organising Principle.

greater than the sum of its parts but is also the organiser to which the parts own their rationale.

In other words, not only the meaning of a system as a whole, but also the meaning of its components, depends upon a rationale which is outside the system, but which nevertheless reveals its organisational structure within the system. From our point of view here this means that the truth which orders human existence lies beyond that existence yet reveals evidence of its organising structure within the scope of our humanity.

I myself believe that this line of argument is the only way forward from here.[11] It is, I believe, consistent with a theology of grace. But more than that: as Dr Daniel Hardy has demonstrated, the Polanyian development of Godel's argument is consistent not only with a bare theism but with a Christological conclusion.[12] Our knowledge of the truth about our own particular context and about all of our contexts demands not only that the justification and judgment of all that is both world and human and judgment enter our context as self-gift. We can know the oneness of God's Truth only through the grace of Incarnation.

Two qualifications need to be made here: the first point. A full entry into our human context of that which is its justification requires that this entry be couched in human terms. It must come in person of the one who justifies, the one who judges. From Wittgenstein we get the rider that this entry of God's reality into our world is at the same time and inseparably the entry of God's truth into our language: God's incarnation into world is God's incarnation into the *word*-embedded practices which make us human.

The second point: what goes for our human context as a whole goes also for particular contexts: the justification and judgment of a particular context must come from outside of that context. As Dietrich Bonhoeffer tells us in his *Christology*, Christ, our justifier and judge, must come to us as anti-logos, as stranger — the One who is over against us and at the same time at one with, but not defined by, our style of humanity. Wittgenstein's related insight, one shared by Professor Moltmann in this Symposium, is that we can subject our way of life to a hard look only from outside, because in the very process of looking at it

11. It is an epistemological endpoint which is inherently theistic. Interestingly enough, as Michael Dummett points out, it may well be the only coherent endpoint for a realist epistemology (*Truth and Other Enigmas*, (London: Duckworth, 1978), p. xxxix).

12. Hardy, *op.cit.*

we distance it.[13] We have opened up what we are to questions and now cannot go back to where we were. To question one's own perspective is to have moved already to a new perspective. We have yielded to something like a persuasion and we have been converted. As Dr Hardy says,[14] the boundary of self has shifted.

This truth who is the bridger of truth, in coming to us as stranger, clothed in what we are not, converts our perspective by confronting us with that which we are not, so we can become what we are not, heirs by inheritance. By Grace we see ourselves as we are through the eyes of a stranger. This metanoia comes with personal encounter, not through the abstract discernment of universal values — the Truth is inseparable from person and particularity. It is in Christ that our vision becomes that of the other; it is in Christ that our view of our own particularity is transformed.

However, this is no cheap grace: it is purchased at a price: the price of a comfortable ride, the price of one-eyedness.[15] As you so rightly emphasis Dr Soskice, what keeps us from God's truth is the sin which distorts vision. If our commitment to the truth of God is primary, it will cost us those things about our context which are incompatible with the Gospel, things which are as natural to us as breathing and almost as hard to give up. As Dr Gutiérrez has pointed out,[16] not all customs are good ones. These incompatibilities are what we discover when our eyes are opened, when in Christ our perspective is transformed and we become strangers to what is ours.

I want to finish with a few brief comments about our New Zealand context. Dr Soskice has drawn our attention to the destructive legacy of Cartesian thought — the separation of mind from matter, knower from known (and I would add, language from world) — which has so permeated our society that we are quite unaware of the extent to which its presuppositions govern our thoughts and actions. One of the discoveries I have made through being helped to see my own culture,

---

13. *On Certainty*, # 595; for a discussion on this point , see Thomas Morawetz *Wittgenstein and Knowledge,* (Amherst: University of Massachusetts Press, 1978), p. 132.
14. In his paper "The Future of Theology in a Complex World," (published in this volume).
15. As Wittgenstein says, "Where the principles really do meet which cannot be reconciled with one another, then each man declares the other a fool and a heretic." (*On Certainty, op cit.* #611).
16. In his paper "Joy in the Midst of Suffering," (published in this volume).

however briefly and imperfectly, from a Maori perspective, is how much our New Zealand white pakeha culture is ingrained with aspects of Western world-view which are opposed to the Gospel — the way we separate the spiritual from the physical, the human from the rest of creation, our obsession with getting on, our looking after 'number one'. On the other hand, my small acquaintance with the (seeming) Maori preoccupation with hierarchies according to age, tribe and sex- has made me more appreciative of Western ideals of democracy and meritocracy. I can speak only from my own experience here, but that is all any of us can do.

A primary Christian commitment opens our context to the critique of the Gospel of Christ. We may, however, choose instead to make our context primary. If we do choose so, there are two consequences: the first, less radical, is that there will be some aspects of the Gospel which we will need to discard as incompatible with our context, because here it is the 'what we do' of our culture or race or sex which provides the ground of truth. If we in New Zealand take Maori or Pakeha or Women's or Men's

Spirituality as foundational, we may find ourselves having to look twice at texts like "In Christ there is neither male nor female, Jew nor Greek, slave nor free."

The second, more radical, consequence is that the Gospel of Christ simply drops out of the equation. Our God is the one to whom we make our primary commitment. By making our own cultural particularity primary, we make it our God; and by so doing we reduce the Gospel of Christ to just another, subordinate world-view. We are, as you remind us, Dr Soskice, never far from the days of Sadolet and Calvin because we are never far from making a local truth absolute.

But, as we have seen, that won't do. We may make our local certainties into golden calves but in the end they are shown to be dumb idols by Truth's entry into our particularity. The our eyes are opened and we see our Saviour, not in our contextual gods, but in our neighbour the stranger. Diversity is where we find ourselves; unity is what we are given.

Reply by Janet Martin Soskice to Jürgen Moltmann and Sue Patterson

I am very grateful for both those responses. There is more to agree with than with which to take issue, but perhaps I could go over some of the remarks that were made, starting first with Professor Moltmann's. I was struck by his comments on truth, justice and the 'killing of truth.' Quite right, the first victim of the Gulf War was the truth, but even in the midst of it, receiving what we knew to be censored and loaded media reporting, it remained important to believe that there were truths to tell, even though we might not come to know them.[1] 'Totally objective reporting' on such things is a human impossibility, indeed a dangerous fiction, even if one is making the maximum effort to be honest and disengaged. For even outside times of war we do not get 'straight truth' from George Bush in his day to day briefings from the White House, or from anyone else for that matter. This not through any ill will, necessarily, but through the human condition. The truth may have been the war's first victim but was already fairly poorly before the war began.

What I'm trying to do in this paper may seem an impossibility. I am trying both to embrace, as a reality we must live with, the limitation and inadequacy of even our best efforts at human knowing, while at the same time resisting an etiolating relativism,— a position where, since no one can provide the truth raw, there is no point in any attempts to seek truth. Let's not opt for this crude and dispiritng vision nor for its leaden alternative. We may sometimes be so frightened by the diversity of our world that we latch on to whatever tiny truth we have and we fight for it against all comers. What I'm trying to do by, as it were, bumping things up into the transcendent, is to provide some

1. A rash of publications since the war, by journalists frustrated during its course by censorship restrictions, seems to demonstrate that I was not alone in feeling that, while totally objectivity on so complex a situation will elude us, much more can be said to illumine our way than was said during the war itself.

Christian space to hold things together I think this is necessary not just for us as Christians but as a witness to our world. In this Decade of Evangelism one message we have to bring to the world is that truth must be sought, and must be grounded in God.

Our world is facing all kinds of disasters. Perhaps the more important are those of which we've already spoken; disasters of poverty and the degradation of the environment, but we face also the poverty and degradation of mind, the poverty of hopelessness and of nihilism. These feed the other poverties and feed from them. In Britain today there is great poverty. There are materially poor people but more than that there is desperation and hopelessness. The young people I see sleeping rough in England don't seem have those moments of joy Professor Gutiérrez described the poor in his country as having even in the midst of their pain. I do not want to valorise one kind of poverty or another, — no poverty is desirable but 'where there is no hope the people perish'. Along with everything else we do, we should hold firm to the idea that there is some sense in longing for, seeking after and 'knowing' the truth.

One of the ambiguities in my paper of which I am well aware concerns my use of the term 'truth'. Sue Patterson picked up on this. This partly intentional, I am not trying to enunciate or deliberate on particular theological truths, but rather to examine the way in which ideas about truth and certainly, usually ill-defined, function in ordinary religious life. The word 'truth' is not in fact very well suited to what I want to say, but on the other hand most of you got the drift when, after relating the story about Rome and the South American bishops, I said, 'the truth looks different from here'. One could say 'we see things differently', but whatever circumlocution we use we will find ourselves coming back to the same set of problems.[2] Despite the philosophers, it remains perfectly acceptable, to use the term 'truth' in diverse ways; for instance, to speak in the ordinary way of 'lived truths'. Even the so-called voiceless people are living those truths in their lives, and hearing these 'truths' of people isn't just listening to their words. The

2. Sue Patterson is quite right to point out the mismatch between the 'truth theories' of the philosophers and the way the term functions in common parlance. Yet the philosopher theories stem from the problem we all address in daily life. I am much more cautious in discussing these matters in the book she mentions, *Metaphor And Religious Language*, and the interested reader can pursue matters there.

difficulty is as much getting the hearers to hear, as the speakers to speak.

Professor Moltmann's second point was that God alone is truth and the crucified Christ the truth of God. Just one qualification here. He mentioned the metaphysical position wherein Truth is in Heaven, one and eternal, and our human actions turn truths into darkness. Whereas Professor Moltmann sketches a version of platonic realism, I was trying, in using a more recent form of critical realism, to move on from those static structure to facilitate a mobile and changing vision which nonetheless finds a place to speak of truth.

With the final point about the perspective of the victims, I shall just have to agree. Our perspective is not the only perspective. We are lucky when we have a chance in our lives to meet someone who makes us see, and sometimes to change our image of ourselves.

Dr. Sue Patterson, in her careful and critical response, puts her finger on a lot of difficulties with my paper which I'll now try to skim neatly over. One thing I would say, however, is that I thought some parts of her paper were more appropriate to my book, than to this paper. In particular I am not as much concerned in this paper with critical realism as with moral realism and the debates are quite different.[3] I would want to agree whole-heartedly with her that we cannot separate language and reality. No student of metaphor could think anything else. My citation of Ricoeur's 'to narrate is already to explain' and the example of Columbus, as 'the man who discovered America' were in part to emphasise this. We inhabit language like fish in water, so pervasive is the medium that we can't even see it. We are linguistic beings and our reality is linguistically constituted to a very great extent. This is why issues of language, say the issue of inclusive language, are not inconsequential — our world is formed by what we say. So I agree with Sue Patterson whole-heartedly. One of the important contributions of post-modern theory is its critiques of ideology in language. These have fruit yet to bear in theology,

---

3. With regard to her comment "Dr Soskice does not consider the loss of what she terms *epistemic* certainty to be a significant problem for theology; it is *moral* certainty which is important..." I would like to make the following qualification. If I am not interested in the former it is because I am not here interested in 'epistemic *certainty*'. I am interested in knowledge and truth, but I think it unhelpful to confuse either with *certainty* narrowly construed, as my remarks in the earlier, historical sections of the paper are meant to show. **Moral** *certainty* is thus not my objective here.

although I'm wary, as I said, of the moral implications of some post-modernist thought .

I would want to distance myself from a correspondence theory of truth, yet reiterate Putnam's point that reality is objective but the objects are not. There must be some sense in which our language is reality representing, but it is always a construct and, in that sense, I don't know whether correspondence is a particularly helpful term. When you ask, Dr. Patterson, "how do we arrive at such knowledge"? I have much the same answer that I understand you to be giving at the end. Because I'm a Christian I have hope that as a gift of grace, and against all probability, Christ brings us the truth.— even though we are not able to formulate that adequately .[4]

When considering such questions as, "how do we arrive a such knowledge?" it is important to examine the content of the "we". Now I think, in the English speaking world at least, by "we" one usually intends an individual. And thus, 'How do I, Janet Martin Soskice arrive at the truth', or how do you, Sue Patterson, arrive at the truth? This focus on the individual is confusing. I'm quite convinced that knowledge is a social possession and that the "we" who arrives at the truth is social. In the Christian context, as in any other context of knowing, we are going to arrive at the truth communally not individually. We need to get away from this atomistic, individual-centred epistemology with its unstated premise that the "we" of knowing is that Cartesian ego. Our knowledge is social, just as our language is a social possession. No one of us invented language, we learned it and to great extent learned the whole world with it.

Finally, I much appreciated your remarks about Polanyi and the entry of God's truth into our language, as well as your alternative model One thing I want to emphasise, however, is how very easy it is for Christians to be complacent when talking about the truth which Christ brings. A critical glance at Christian history is not very amusing. We must look at what we've actually done in the name of 'gospel truth', — that was the point of the apartheid discussion. Christians have to acknowledge honestly and openly the fact that we have sanctified various horrible set-ups within our own churches and within our own theologies as well. There is no room for complacency.

---

4. I am not saying, as is clear I hope from the paper, that Christians are given neat propositional truths about which they can have absolute certainty. It might be better to say we are, if we respond to God's gracious promptings, being drawn to the truth.

We have rather to be eternally vigilant. But again, I'd like to say thank you very much for the care that's been taken with responses.

4

Joy in the Midst of Suffering

Gustavo Gutiérrez

Introduction

I would like to present in this paper some points on joy in the midst of suffering, but trying also to keep in mind one of the themes of our symposium: salvation. Let me begin with three quotations.

Some years ago Desmond Tutu wrote that all liberation theology stems from trying to make sense of human suffering, when those who suffered are the victims of organised oppression and exploitation, when they are treated as less than what they are — human beings, created in the image of God. It is possible to make sense of suffering.

My second quotation comes from a Peruvian Indian of the latter part of the the 16th century. He was a Christian Indian of the first generation. His name was Huaman Poma de Ayala. He wrote "My God, where are you? Will you not hear me and help me, because I myself am helpless". He wrote this before all the injustices that were occurring. Injustices that were suffered by his brothers and sisters. When we hear this we recall Jesus' short sentence on the Cross: "My God, my God, why have you abandoned me?" I would like to say at the start of my paper that these questions are bigger than our ability to answer them. I think that before human suffering our first step, our first attitude, is to have respect, and to try to avoid explaining the human condition too quickly.

I have always had a great admiration for philosophers and theologians speaking about God as if they were having breakfast with God every day. Many things are very difficult to understand. The question is to take a position from faith. In some ways theology is an endless task, trying to make sense of, in the light of our Christian faith, the suffering of the innocent. Innocent means, here, persons who do not deserve their suffering. As human beings, we are all sinners. In this case innocent is not the opposite of sinful.

Third, and to complete my introduction, I would like to recall something I learnt from a woman in a Basic Christian Community in Lima. She made a distinction at a meeting, and I must confess that it was a new insight for me: suffering is not the opposite of joy, sadness and worse still, bitterness, are the opposites of joy. I agree this is a very simple statement, but as a theologian I am often a very complicated person, and this understanding of suffering and joy was new to me.

Moving on then to the main part of my paper, I again have three points. I always have three points. I don't know if it is my Trinitarian devotion, or my philosophical background, a Hegelian philosophy from Louvain, or simply because in the seminary I learnt to do my meditation in three points!

1. Doing Theology

My first point is to make some reflections on doing theology. We are here at a theological symposium, and perhaps it is useful to reflect a little on our theological concern. To explain this point maybe I can start with a key passage from Mark's Gospel. You will recall Peter's confession. Jesus asks his disciples "Who do people say that I am?", and more precisely, "Who do you say that I am." Peter replies: "You are the Messiah", and after that his refusal to accept the consequences. We have on the one hand, a correct opinion, and on the other, on the part of Peter, wrong behaviour. It seems to me that theology can be placed in relation to, and between, orthodoxy and orthopraxis. That is, right affirmation and right commitment.

Theology is perhaps the way to arrive at a degree of coherence between these two dimensions of Christian life. This hermeneutic is an interpretation of this relation, without forgetting another aspect of Mark's Gospel. After Peter's refusal, Jesus says, "Get behind me Satan." Some translations say "Out of my sight." It is not exactly the same. "Get behind me Satan": You are an obstacle to the will of God. "Get behind me" means take your place again as a disciple, because it is more or less a technical expression of the idea of being a follower of Jesus. That is to be behind Him — Jesus. The expression "Get behind me", this short sentence, seems to express at the same time an element of forgiveness on the part of Jesus. Peter has already received forgiveness from Jesus because Jesus is confident that it is possible for Peter to take up his place again as a disciple. Theology is important here also.

Theology is important as an interpretation of the relation between orthopraxis and orthodoxy, through recalling the will of God, the capacity of God to forgive, that is to affirm the permanent possibility of re-conversion, and of our beginning again, in-spite of our faults, the life of discipleship. Jesus is constantly, and permanently calling us to be his disciples, to accept the gift of the Kingdom of God and to put into practice the will of God.

In Acts, the Christian Church is called on several occasions "The Way." It is a very special expression. "The Way" is a classical image to speak about our relationship with God. We must walk in this "Way". Perhaps you have observed in the Bible, if you are familiar with it, there are always people walking and eating, because these two images are the images of life, only one who is alive can walk and eat. "The Way" is to belong to a Christian community and to walk with God. Theology is also a "Way", it is a "Way" to understand, but this way of understanding must be placed within the "Way" of being Christian, otherwise we do not really have theology, which is a reflection on faith. Theological method comes from the same word, *hodos* meaning 'way' or 'road'. Consequently, to do theology is to attempt to understand our faith. Theology takes place, therefore, within the context of grace and of our striving to be Christian, to be disciples. For this reason, theology must always follow closely the life of Christians.

Sometimes when I speak in this manner, people tell me that I have a utilitarian manner of understanding theology. I do not know why these people are employing a figurative word because I try only to have a useful notion of theology, and a theology which is in the service of Christian life. Theology must be a serious confrontation of Scripture with Christian tradition. This is what contemporary theology is. But finally theology is oriented, as in the first centuries, to the Christian life. All theology is in the last analysis a spiritual theology. We can perhaps keep this in mind when we deal with the subject of suffering.

I quoted earlier the intuition of the Peruvian woman on suffering and joy as being different to the relation of sadness and joy. I would like now to try and explain this a little further.

2. Poverty

Poverty is my second point. It is a massive fact in Latin America, and also unfortunately in other parts of the world. But, the consciousness of this reality has changed quite considerably in recent times. I would like to indicate a number of aspects of this more or less new awareness. First, we are more conscious today, not only in Latin America, but also in other places, of what is described as the eruption of the poor, that is to say the poor who were absent from our history, are now becoming visible. Physically they were there all the time, but they were absent, in the sense of being non-relevant. The poor countries, the poor people, the despised races, women, all of these were absent and they are more and more present, with maybe one little rhetorical sentence, which we call the "eruption of the poor", because they are now present asking the reasons for their poverty and challenging the powerful. There are many ways in which they are present, politically, socially, racially, and so on. In the Christian Church on my continent one expression of this eruption, is the appearance of the Basic Christian Communities — the "Communidades de bases." You know the Basic Christian Communities are not a new pastoral phenomenon, they are more important than that, they are an expression of a global fact, the new presence of the poor. After we understand that we can talk about new pastoral methods, but first it is important to understand this presence, this new presence. One immediate consequence of this new presence, is our consciousness, our knowledge, about the reasons for poverty, because it is not enough to say that there is great poverty in the world today. It is necessary to understand the causes of this poverty, and when we speak of causes we soon enter into conflict, because to speak of causes and reasons, raises the issue of responsibility: economic and social structures play a role in poverty.

I was not at the International Eucharistic Congress in Philadelphia, held, I think, during 1976, but I have heard a tape of the proceedings. Two big names in the Catholic Church were present (both are still alive today), and gave papers. The first I regard as a very saintly person and he said this: "I come from a poor country, you are rich Americans, please help us." People were very happy. After that Dom Helder Camara, the Brazilian Bishop, spoke and said: "I come from Latin America, we are poor because we are suffering social injustices, and you Americans have an enormous responsibility for this." People who were listening were not so happy! This is truly what happened. In the first address no reasons for poverty were given, no causes, only the fact that we are poor and the request for help. The second was trying to say that those listening were one element in the problem. When one speaks about causes one always comes up against problems!

My second point is the experience of poverty. I said yesterday that poverty ultimately means death. We are accustomed to seeing poverty as an economic and social issue. But in a more human and global perspective, poverty means death, an unjust and early death. Again I have heard an old woman in a Basic Christian Community say the following: "We, the old people, we are closer to death." A young person answered; "No, grandmothers in Peru today are not closer to death, but children are." It is true, it is absolutely true, and I think this is poverty; physical death, due to hunger and sickness, and due to the use of repressive means of stopping the re-vindication of the poor.

Some years ago I was very impressed by reading a short statement by a Christian Community in Haiti (Haiti is the poorest country in Latin America — Peru is very close to Haiti). This statement says "wherever we look, we see death." I think it is the ultimate meaning of poverty, and for this reason it is an enormous challenge to us as Christians, because we must announce life, the Kingdom of life. And the reality of death is exactly the opposite to the Kingdom of God. You see, I am not trying to say that poverty is not a socio-economic issue. No, I am trying to see the reality in Latin America and express the feeling as we people are confronted by poverty.

It is a cultural death as well. Anthropologists love to say that culture is life. When one culture is not respected, we are killing the persons who belong to that culture. When a race is despised, we are killing people belonging to this race; when we do not recognise women and give them full rights we are killing them. It is another kind of death from physical death, but it is death.We experience this on my continent and in my country, Peru, as well. Maybe you have heard the Latin American social lie that there is no racism, because it is a mixed culture. Fools! We have no racist laws, because laws are not so important for us. We have something far worse: racist customs. Latin America is a very racist continent. Poverty means the destruction of individuals and peoples. As a consequence when we deal with poverty we are not dealing only with a social situation or issue, but with a global human situation. The relation of the Gospel of Jesus Christ to poverty is not an indirect consequence, but goes to the core of the Gospel, because poverty here means death.

Moving on to the third remark in my second point: the world of poor. There is not enough talk about the "eruption of the poor", the reasons for their poverty, or poverty as death. I think that we must try and understand what we like to call the world of the poor. The poor are not isolated individuals, the poor belong to social groups, cultures and genders. The poor have not only deprivations, but they have many possibilities as well. It is very difficult to find a definition of who the poor are, but perhaps a good approach is to start with the following. The poor are "the non-relevant persons, the insignificant." They are the insignificant for many reasons: because of the socio-economic status, the colour of their skin, their language, or their sex, but also because they are insignificant, they are nameless. I am sure that all of you know names of some Latin American Christians who have given their lives as a Christian witness. For example, Bishop Oscar Romero, or the Jesuits in El Salvador. But, I am sure that you do not know the names of the peasants, women, and students killed for the same reasons. To be a bishop, or a priest, and a Jesuit in addition, is to be significant, but to be a peasant is insignificant.

Around forty people were also killed on the day of Romero's funeral. I know because I was there, and I saw thirteen bodies. We do not know the names of these people. My remarks are not against Romero, or the Jesuits, I am only trying to stress that there are many others who were anonymous during their lives and who are anonymous after their death, and that this is what it means to be poor. It seems to me that what is demanded of the Christian is to live in the world of the poor. To be poor is a way of feeling, knowing, reasoning, making friends, believing, suffering, praying, celebrating and loving. All these are aspects of poverty. To be committed to the poor means to enter, or to stay, in the world of the poor. It is not enough to try to help people, but to live with them. We, as members of the Christian Churches, must try to have our home in the world of the poor. When I say to live with the poor as the poor, it is possible to understand the physical aspects of their lives, but it is not only this. We need also to live mentally in the world of the poor. In general I think the Christian Churches, until today, have had their home outside of the world of the poor. They go to the world of the poor to work, and not to live. The consequence of their commitment to the poor is a source of so much tension because the work is always a source of tension. We are happy in our homes, but the Christian Churches do not have their home there because they are not physically present. Please do not not misunderstand me, I am not suggesting that everyone must go to Latin America, or to Africa, or, I do not know New Zealand well enough, but I am sure there must be some places with poverty here as well. No, this is too simple. No, I am trying to speak about a Christian home, a mental home, a theological home, as well. A commitment to the poor means to have friends among the poor, and not only to be committed politically to them. The latter is very important but it is not enough. Friendships suppose equality: "I do not call you servants any longer, but friends." I think it is the same for us, in our relations with the poor, to be friends is to share our lives with others.

Why is this so important? There are times when I am outside of Latin America, and speaking about these matters, and people say "I understand you. You speak so strongly about poverty because you are Latin American." My answer is always the same one: "Please do not understand me so quickly, because my first reason is not because I am Latin American, but because I am a Christian, and if we believe in the same God, the God of Jesus Christ, maybe the concrete ways will be different, but the demand is the same." Maybe because I am a Latin American, or African, or whatever, I have a greater possibility to understand this through my own experience, but this is not the question. The basic question is not this. If we are committed to the poor it is not because we know the poor well, or because the poor are good people, but because God is good. This is the reason. The commitment to the poor is a theocentric option. It is not the result of social analysis, or human compassion, or direct experience. All these are very good and important reasons, but they are not the ultimate reason. My ultimate reason for being committed to the poor is because I believe in the God of Jesus Christ. This is my reason and after that come many other reasons, but without this, it is impossible to understand the point of being committed to the poor in a Christian sense.

Some people, and I was speaking about this with somebody here at the symposium, need to have an idealistic idea of the truth in order to say "the poor are so good, so generous." You know when I hear this I say to myself, these people have never seen a poor person in their life. Never! The poor are human beings, they are sinners, both good and bad people. For example I do not advise you to walk around the neighbourhood of my parish late at night. They are poor people and they are not all good people. This idealism, then, cannot be the reason. The reason must be because God is good, and I believe in this God. Poverty is a global situation and a main source, although not the only source today, of the suffering of so many innocent people in the world.

3. Job

I will now move on to my third and last point. Let me go back to the book of Job. The large milestone in this book is the wager. The question is whether it is possible to believe gratuitously for nothing. This is the question in the beginning. Satan does not think it is possible. God thinks it is possible, and his servant Job is an example of this. Job believes in God for nothing. Job's friends are supporters of the doctrine of temporal retribution. That is to say, God punishes the wicked with poverty and sickness and rewards the upright with riches and health. The consequences of this are clear. Job in his second condition is sick and poor. Job is a wicked person. But this affirmation is too logical to be true, and Job refuses to accept this theology. His friends are good theologians, wrong, but good theologians. It happens quite often, and their manner of understanding reality is very clear. Poor Job has no other theology with which to respond. Theoretically he has the same theology as his friends, but he has a different experience from the theology they are presenting. He says that he is innocent. His friends reply, "If you affirm your innocence you are affirming that God is unjust, which is blasphemy." Job says "No, I do not want to say this, but I am innocent." Job is a very obstinate person. Little by little Job interpreted this contradiction between his innocence and the situation in which he found himself, as being not only his own situation, but also the lot of the poor.

Chapter 24 in Job is the most beautiful and cruel description of the poor that we have in the Bible. Job understands that his condition, his situation, is the same as that of many other people in the world. Recalling his life he affirms the necessity of solidarity with the poor. Doing that, he is convinced he is following God's example. God is called in the Bible the "Father of the Poor." Job is convinced God wants justice. God's reflection at this point is a prophetic language, leading God to the poor and to revindicate justice. At the end of the book God comes and in this speech God is revealed as both powerful and weak, almost a child, tender and ironical. I mentioned yesterday that I think the book of Job is the most ironical book in the Bible. Probably the second is John's Gospel. Job reveals above all a joyful and loving God.

As I recall in my paper responding to Professor Moltmann, the main idea of God's speeches is that in the beginning there is the gratuitous love of God. Ironically God is saying to Job, "I love you gratuitously." And, again ironically, God is asking Job "Where were you when I laid the earth's foundation?" Poor Job came rather late in history, as we ourselves have. In the beginning was the foundation of the earth and the reason for this was God's love. As Saint John says "God loved us first". The movement comes from God. God says to Job, "your revindication in the context of the gratuitousness, is in free and gratuitous love." But there is more than that, at one moment in the book Job says that human life is a chaos, not a cosmos, but that in the end Job recognised that God had plans. This world is a cosmos, and this idea is a very deep one. Remember Job's final answer: "I once knew you only by hearsay and now my eyes have seen you." To know God by hearsay is to know God through other people. I think this is important for us as well. We need to have an experience of God in view of our limitations as well, so that we too can say: "My eyes have seen you." We can refer to this as a contemplative or mystical way of speaking of God.

Prophetic language with justice as its centre, and mystical language with contemplation as its centre, are the two aspects of our God language.

Theology is precisely this, language about God. We try to do good theology, that is to say, to use good language. According to Job we have both of these languages and we need to keep them in a healthy balance. Without historical commitment to other people, especially the poor, we do not have Christian life. But also without worship, without contemplation we do not have Christian life. God has not accused Job of nothing. In a way God has spoken to Job as an equal, as a friend. In Job's final reply we do not have a retraction, but a renunciation in a lamentation, but even this is understood by God, through saying that Job was right in his attitude of lamentation. As Christians we have become too soft in our prayers, and what we do not like in the Bible is protest against God. How to be committed to the suffering innocent without protest, even to God, is a very Biblical question. Lamentation is one manner through which to pray, though it is not the only one. As Christians we are very shy and it seems this is almost a blasphemy. It is not true, and I think Job really believed in God and for this reason said that he wanted to discuss matters with God directly, and not with his friends the theologians. I think this has to be our attitude as well.

What Job has taught us from the speeches with God is this: justice is very important, but it is not the final word. Grace gives justice its full meaning. Love operates in a world not of cause and effect, but in a world of freedom in gratuitousness. The world of retribution is not where God lives, at most God visits it. God is not a prisoner of the give-me and I-will-give-you type mentality. Justice is very important, we cannot avoid speaking from, and about, the suffering of the innocent. But grace, gratuitous love, is the last word, not because the former is eliminated, but the full meaning of justice is in the context of this gratuitous love. Without contemplation prophetic language can narrow it's horizon. We need to keep together these two languages in order to speak correctly about God from the suffering of the innocent.

Conclusion

I had an introduction, normally I have a conclusion.

I have two final points. The source of our joy is the gratuitous love of God. It saves us, but this joy, which is very classic, is a paschal joy. It is a passing from death to life, from sin to grace, from suffering to joy. It is not an easy joy, but we must avoid suffering, sadness or worse bitterness. The temptation is big, and is daily. The announcement of the Christian message can be a way to avoid this because in this moment people are closed in on themselves.

And my second and final conclusion is about theology. I have said at the beginning theology is placed between orthodoxy and orthopraxis, and seeks to understand the relationship between the two. When we speak of social injustice, the suffering of the innocent, not everything is clear to us. But at least we understand that it is only in solidarity with the suffering, with the poor, that we can try to avoid the reproach of Job to his friends. At one moment in the dialogue Job says to his friends: "Sorry comforters you are." That is because they only have words, and poorly thought out theology as well. Job knows the suffering of the innocent, maybe not with any clear, rational explanation. Job is also looking for solidarity to fill the presence of the love of God in his life. Trying to do theology from the suffering of the innocent is a manner, a small and humble means, of avoiding the accusation from the poor: "You Christians, you theologians, you are sorry comforters." We want to avoid this reproach in order to be real witnesses to the victory of the resurrection of the Lord.

Response by John W. de Gruchy

What follows is not so much a critique as an appreciation, but hopefully in the midst of the appreciation Dr Gutiérrez may well discern some questions. In other words his task is going to be more difficult than mine.

What he has demonstrated is the necessary connection between academic theology and theology as witness. It is always a mistake to separate them. They are separated by those who say that theology has to do simply with experience and is a witness, and therefore who "write off" academic theology, and they are separated by those who are involved in academic theology and who do not take witness and experience seriously. It's a false dichotomy which we have to avoid with all the passion we have. One of the things that attracts me greatly about Dietrich Bonhoeffer is the way in which his academic erudition, his knowledge of the Christian tradition, the Bible, and indeed his understanding of philosophical debate, is continually related to the question "Who is Jesus Christ for us today", that is, to following Jesus today. Gustavo Gutiérrez has enabled us to see yet again the way in which these two dimensions of theology come together, and must necessarily do so for theology to be Christian and not degenerate into the theology of Job's comforters.

All of us were asked to produce our papers by the September before the symposiuum. Some of us did and some of us didn't! But having read the commentary which Dr Gutiérrez wrote on Job sometimeduring 1990, what he said in his paper did not take me, by surprise. Why should he change the message that he has always proclaimed? Why should he have to come up with something new as though the "novel" is really what we want or need to hear? What we really need to hear is the Gospel. We need to hear it in a way that speaks to us today. If we are always searching for novelty in theology, then we will miss the Gospel. A year or two back I was invited to give the Warfield Lectures at Princeton Theological Seminary and I chose as my theme 'Liberating Reformed Theology'. In preparing those lectures I went back and read a great deal of John Calvin, and I discovered that the people who understood Calvin best were actually Roman Catholic theologians. Not the Roman Catholic theologians then, but the Roman Catholic theologians now. By that I mean that Calvin is not as well understood by Presbyterians and Reformed theologians today, as he is by some Roman Catholics. Why? Because those of us in the Reformed tradition have grown used to the Bible, whereas in certain parts of the Roman Catholic Church there has been a rediscovery of the Bible, of its power, of its Good News. That is exactly what was happening at the time of the Reformation, Calvin was a Catholic theologian who discovered the Bible again. The problem was, and this of course is the big difference between what we have been hearing today and what has happened to the Reformed tradition, is that Protestantism has become so wedded to a middle class reading of the scriptures. But all of us, whether Catholic or Protestant, are called again and again to be pastoral, biblical theologians who understand the task of theology as deeply rooted in the life of the church and its witness in the life of the world. Gutiérrez brought together a profound academic ability and witness, like a good Reformed theologian who believes in sola scriptura. Gutiérrez is a theologian who lives out of the scriptures and without which he would not exist as a theologian.

The challenge to us today concerned the conversion of the privileged, because few of us can claim to be poor. What we heard today was the classic Reformed theme that you only understand the law when you've heard the Gospel. It's only when you have heard about gratuitous love that you understand the Commandment. We are not saved by law but we are by grace. Yet many preachers today try to convert their middle class privileged congregations by preaching the law. We do that by saying how bad you are, not how good God is. Again and again when we try to enable our congregations to change in terms of doing justice in the world, which is absolutely vital, we do it in such a way that they cannot change, they only feel more guilty, more impotent, and less joyful. Now, in Gutiérrez's paper prophetic theology and the theology of grace were brought together, and this was at the heart of what was said. The uniting of justice and grace, but understanding the priority of grace, struck me as being of central importance. We were more fundamentally challenged in our hearts and our beings by the graciousness of what was said today to us who are privileged, than if we had been confronted with our sins. That means that we actually heard today the Gospel, and paradoxically we feel very judged as a result, but see the possibility of freedom and change.

To move on to another observation, there is a danger that we could turn the poor into a category. This came through also, very clearly in Gutiérrez's paper. The poor are not a category, as Gutiérrez reminds us, they are people. Now it is very easy for those of us who are privileged to live off the oppression of others. It happens all the time. But there's a more subtle way of living off the oppression of others, and that's by writing and speaking about them. We all do it and it's understandable that we do it. All I am suggesting is that we be aware of that danger when we do it.

Earlier in this symposium, I was a little worried at one point when we were talking about the cosmic Christ. Not because I did not identify with what was being said. I appreciated the paper presented as well as the responses, and would want to affirm much of what I heard. But, I remember Bonhoeffer writing from prison and saying the problem with the church is that Jesus is disappearing from sight. Now I'm quite sure that that wasn't what was intended, but I was becoming bothered at that point. How do we relate the cosmic Christ to Jesus? It seems to me to be a fundamental theological issue we have to struggle with. It raises all kinds of problems. We all know the history of the relationship between Jesus and the Christ and the search for the historical Jesus, and I'm not suggesting we need to go through that whole debate again. But what we were confronted with this morning was an ability to see the relationship of the cosmic Christ to the Jesus who was crucified. The cosmic Christ inevitably starts with the resurrection which is where the New Testament starts. But the resurrection must always be seen from the perspective of the crucified one. We can only say Jesus is Lord if we first of all say Jesus, the crucified one, is the Lord. And therefore it seems to me very important that we do not lose sight of the Jewish Messianic person Jesus, in our discussion of Christ and culture.

I have only two further things to say. Has liberation theology a future? Well the sure sign that it has a future is the fact that it is so strongly opposed. It wouldn't have a future if it wasn't opposed because then it would just fade into insignificance. I'm not sure that process theology has a future because nobody really fights the process theologians! Maybe it has ! Has liberation theology a future? Well, if it doesn't have a future then the liberation theology that was presented to us doesn't have a future, in which case neither does the Gospel, or Christian theology. Defending liberation theology is not the point, it's defending what liberation theology is seeking to witness to, that is the point. We spend an awful lot of useless energy trying to defend liberation theology instead of doing what liberation theology is calling upon us to do. Then it doesn't matter what it is called, it is what it is seeking to be and to do that becomes far more important. As a movement liberation theology obviously is in the process of development, and we could have long discussions about that. But what we are talking about here, is in fact, theology.

My final point concerns joy. Let me talk about the lack of joy of the privileged. The privileged who do not care. That I think is the important qualification, those who do not care, and therefore do not feel deeply for those who suffer. Those people do not know joy because they do not know God. What do they know? They know guilt, they know fear, they know cynicism. It's not that they do not celebrate, but that their celebrations are not joyful. They celebrate often, perhaps they celebrate far too often, but their celebrations are not celebrations. The greatest iniquity of people who do not care is that they cannot stand the joy of those who do suffer. They can in fact live with the suffering but they can't live with their joy. Why I say that, is because so often those who suffer are prevented from expressing their joy. For example, people who are in jail, and who start singing. What do the jailers do? They shut them up. People who are arrested and who laugh on the way to the court-house. What do the police do? They tell them to stop laughing. So the ultimate act of dehumanisation I think, what I learnt this morning, is to rob people of their capacity to be joyous, even when they suffer.

Response by Stephen May

We come together at this conference as the family of Christ, as those who have been made so by God's action. The conference title is 'Christ and context'. How then does the title of this session, 'Joy in the midst of suffering' relate to that title? Is 'suffering' the context? Is 'joy' the reference to Christ? Are we then talking about the joy brought by Christ in the context of human suffering?

I would hope not! This would be to ignore the suffering of Christ! It would be to make Christ instrumental in the solution of our self-perceived needs.[1] Rather, I would argue that all that *we* experience is in the context of *Christ* — of *his* suffering and *his* joy. In other words, ever since the death and resurrection of Christ we no longer die, suffer or live alone, but Christ dies, lives and suffers with us. All we know of light and darkness is lit up by His Light, a Light that has won us for Himself by entering and overcoming our darkness. It is in His light that we can truly understand our own experience. *We* exist in the context of *Christ.* [2]

In considering this topic I will attempt to relate its two 'items', chiefly looking at them from the side of joy. I will endeavour to address the problem of speaking of joy in this world. Immediately, however, the problem of speaking at all on this topic confronts us.

---

1. D. Bonhoeffer, *Letters and Papers from Prison*, ed. E. Bethge, English trans., (London: SCM, 1986), p. 326.
2. I would see this as one of the principal insights of narrative theology. Cf. J. Moltmann, *The Trinity and the Kingdom of God*, English trans., (London: SCM, 1981), p. 5: "the individual self will be discovered in the over-riding history of God and only finds its meaning in that context." Cf. also K. Barth, *Church Dogmatics,* IV. I, (Edinburgh: T. and T. Clark, 1961), *passim.*

1. The Problem of Speaking[3]

There are a number of reasons why it is difficult to respond on this subject to speakers of the quality and integrity of Dr. Gutiérrez and Professor de Gruchy. They are not merely hearers of the Word but doers of it, true theologians. The authority with which we heard them speak derives not merely from academic theological excellence (significant as that is), but also from their own personal involvement with the issues — and the people — that are here the subject of discussion. What they say thus carries its own self-authenticating *exousia*.[4]

There are a number of other reasons for reticence. In the light of the amount of injustice and suffering endured by the native people of this country, I feel somewhat ill at ease being a Pakeha standing here. Moreover, what is my own personal experience of suffering as a human being? In addition I am a member of the First World, which, as we have been reminded, does not exist in a neutral relationship to much global suffering, but, in another sense, 'stands' — it stands responsible as 'the guilty party'. We are told to avoid guilt, yet it is easy to let oneself feel disabled by precisely that.

In response to all this one is tempted to take refuge in what Dr, Gutiérrez himself says is the first act of theology, namely silence. However, silence is not enough, for all that theology is impossible without it. As Bonhoeffer says, we have to speak out of a proper silence, but we have to speak.[5] It is not a question of personal desire let alone wilful unfeeling arrogance.

Moreover, there is too much history of people being reduced to speechlessness, particularly in our century, to ourselves succumb too quickly to this counsel of despair. To do so would be to collaborate with those oppressors who have dehumanised blacks in South Africa,

---

3. Joy and suffering are not the only problematic words. As E. Jüngel points out ("What does it meant to say, 'God is Love'?" in *Christ in Our Place*, ed. T. Hart and D. Thimell, (Exeter: Paternoster, 1989), p. 295ff.) the very word 'God' has a defiled, blood-spattered history.

4. Mt. 7.29. According to Mt. 28.15ff. (the Great Commission) Christ has been given all authority, and the Church shares in it as it proclaims him as Lord.

5. *Christ the Centre*, trans. E. H. Robertson, (San Francisco: Harper and Row, 1978,) p. 27.

Indians in Latin America, Jews in Nazi Germany.[6] We should beware those who try to silence us.

But how and what we say — that is a different question.

Let us examine further this command to speak.

In view of the immensity of suffering in the world, this can seem almost obscene. Is not mute silence the only possible response? The contemporary world witnesses daily one disaster after another. A quarter of a million killed in Bangladesh through floods and typhoon, Kurds in Northern Iraq starving and freezing to death, famine and Civil War in Somalia: the list of anguish seems endless.[7]

How can there be joy in a world like this? In view of all the suffering in the world how can anyone get to sleep at night? Is it surprising that people insulate themselves from their TV sets so as to preserve sanity, only occasionally being shocked through their protective shells? Should we not, in the words of Dennis Potter's Jesus, "gather at the street corners to be sick?" "Now that *would* be a meaningful sacrament," he continues.[8]

Is joy simply a part of life, as Blake suggests?

> "Man was made for Joy and Woe;
> And when this we rightly know,
> Through the world we safely go;
> Joy and Woe are woven fine,
> A clothing for the soul divine."[9]

We weep and we laugh, and both are parts of life, the warp and the weft of it. Are joy and suffering part of the 'package-deal' of life? [10]

6. At the conclusion of a course which I taught recently on Dietrich Bonhoeffer and the German Church Struggle members of the class reported that they had not pursued contentious issues through fear of the reactions of others. I find this ironic and a little sad in that the very subject under investigation, the rise of Nazism, was marked by the general failure of the Church and 'right-thinking' people to speak up against evil.
7. The problem is well expressed by J. Moltmann, *Theology and Joy*, (London: SCM, 1973), pp, 26-8.
8. BBC television play, "Son of Man".
9. William Blake, *Auguries of Innocence in Oxford Dictionary of Quotations*, (London: Book Club Associates, 1989), p. 85.
10. "The capacity for pain is the inevitable concomitant of the capacity for delight. Suffering is here shown as the twin-sister of joy." H. A. Williams, *The Joy of God*, (London: Mitchell Beazley, 1979), pp. 98-9.

Here we enter the problem of evil. Whilst I acknowledge the multiplicity of life, its 'shadow-side' as well as its light, I would repudiate the domestication of evil as part of life's fabric. This is to trivialise evil. I believe God says 'No' to evil, and that true joy emerges not from a resigned tolerance to suffering, but from faith in its transformation, in the overcoming (not the balancing) of pain and misery. Like Dr. Gutiérrez, I believe joy is not the opposite of suffering — but joy does suggest its obliteration. "I reckon that the sufferings of the present time are not worthy to be compared to the glory that is to come," says Paul.[11] Like Dr. Gutiérrez again, I believe true joy is Paschal Joy.

2. Cheap Joy

If real joy is paschal joy, we cannot leap prematurely to the end of the story. Full weight has to be given to suffering so it is taken seriously. Otherwise joy is not joy but escapism. Not all the theology of Job's Comforters is false, though some of it is. It says the 'right' thing at the wrong time, which makes it wrong.[12] Thus Jahweh says to Job's Comforters at the end of the book, "You have not spoken of me as you ought to have done, unlike my servant Job."[13] And Job was complaining and railing at God! I find Dr. Gutiérrez's suggestion that we should rehabilitate complaint as a part of prayer as very suggestive.[14]

In bereavement couselling, then, the first requirement is to listen.[15] Bonhoeffer writes: "Why is it that precisely in thoroughly grave situations... I often decide to adopt a 'penultimate' attitude, particularly when I am dealing with Christians, remaining silent as a sign that I share in the bereaved man's helplessness in the face of such a grievous event, and not speaking the biblical words of comfort which are, in fact, known to me and available to me?"[16] To do so would be to

---

11. Rms. 8.18.
12. D. Bonhoeffer, *Ethics*, ed. E. Bethge, trans. N. Horton Smith, (London: Collins, 1964), pp. 363-72, on "Telling the Truth". Speech occurs in a context of relationships.
13. Job 42.7.
14. *On Job,* trans. M. J. O'Connell, (New York: Maryknoll, Orbis, 1987), p. 111 n7
15. G. Gutiérrez, *On Job*, p. 24: "If (Job's Comforters) were to be silent and listen, they would demonstrate the wisdom they claim to possess."
16. *Ethics,* p. 126.

cheapen joy, to talk about it with 'pert loquacity'.[17] Remaining silent, says Bonhoeffer, "points all the more genuinely to the ultimate, which God will speak in His own time."

Cheap joy is marked by its failure to engage with the real nature of the world. Jesus said, "In the world you will have trouble. But courage! The victory is mine; I have overcome the world."[18] Similarly, Jon Sobrino writes: "The cry of Jesus on the cross and the cry of countless victims in history... do not allow us to nurture an ingenuous faith in God; it must be a faith that overcomes the world."[19] Such ingenuousness is found in many places, ranging from a Christmas nostalgia for the lost world of innocence to the upbeat endings to news bulletins ('happy news') that convinces no-one. It is the ingenuousness of the unreal 'happy ending'[20] So too are the desperate attempts of the prosperous and significant to drown from their ears the cries of the poor. One of the aspects of eschatology, of apocalyptic, is its pulling back of the veils so that the true nature of existence is revealed. A pattern of Easter services in which all too many Sunday worshippers move from Palm Sunday (the triumphal entry into Jerusalem) to Easter Sunday without going through the Crucifixion heightens the problem.[21] One can remain just on the surface.

3. The Gift of Joy

Eberhard Jüngel writes: "God — a word which causes joy! God — a word which makes us free! Wherever this is not the case, wherever 'God' is a word which instead of spreading freedom and joy causes fear and trembling or merely disperses boredom, then there is not proper talk of God himself."[22] Similarly he commended Karl Barth's

17. H.A. Williams, *The Joy of God*, p. 95.
18. Jn. 16.33.
19. Quoted by G. Gutiérrez, *On Job*, p. 132, n35.
20. H. A. Williams, *The Joy of God*, p. 105. Writers ranging from Graham Greene to Flannery O'Connor have protested against the artificial happy endings grafted onto televised versions of their stories that completely destroy their point.
21. Is the existence of Passion Sunday an attempt to address this problem?
22. "What does it mean to say, 'God is Love'?" in *Christ in our Place*, p. 301.

entire life and thought as a whole for announcing that "'God' is a cheerful word."[23]

What this means is that joy is not an option, a matter of choice. The Church is under the authority of its Lord to proclaim the Resurrection. Barth writes of paschal joy: "This joy and summons arise from these dark places, and what is declared from this centre is glad tidings." This joy which has passed through a 'catalysator' has "been destroyed on the one hand, and reconstituted on the other — and even raised to the level of a command."[24]

This joy is not passing, but is firmly rooted. It has a firm foundation not in our achievement or emotion, but in what Christ has done. It is like the peace of the Johannine Farewell Discourses: "Not as the world gives give I unto you."[25] A Taize canon has us sing: "My peace I leave you; my peace I give you. Be not afraid."

This is the eschatological act of God that has its fulfilment only at the end of time. For Barth joy on this earth has a provisional quality, expectation based on a sure hope.[26] The Farewell Discourses speak with double meaning of Jesus' departure and return, of the grief that will turn to joy "like a woman in childbirth who forgets her pain for joy that a baby is born into the world. So with you; now is your time of grief, but I will see you again and you will rejoice, and no-one will take away your joy."[27] "By this ambiguity John means to convey that the death and resurrection were themselves eschatological events which both prefigured and anticipated the final events."[28] This joy is not 'pie in the sky when you die' but encouragement to act now concretely to share God's mission to the world he loves.

This miraculous act of God is to be found in some parabolic stories. Tolkien develops the concept of what he calls *eucatastrophe.* In fairy story this is the "good catastrophe, the sudden joyous turn... sudden and miraculous grace; never to be counted on to recur. It does not deny the existence of *dystrocatastrophe,* of sorrow and failure: the possibility of these is necessary to the joy of deliverance; it denies (in the face of

23. *Karl Barth: A Theological Legacy,* trans. G.E. Paul, (Philadelphia: Westminster, 1986), p. 21.

24. *Church Dogmatics*, III.4, p. 375.

25. Jn. 14.27.

26. K. Barth, *Church Dogmatics*, III.4, p. 384.

27. Jn. 16.20-22. This whole chapter is subtitled "Grief changed into joy" in one Bible translation.

28. C. K. Barrett, *The Gospel According to St. John*, (London: SPCK, 1978), p. 491.

much evidence, if you will) universal final defeat and in so far is *evangelium*, giving a fleeting glimpse of Joy, Joy beyond the walls of the world, poignant as grief."[29]

4. Joy as Reversal

Joy overturns the pattern of the world, as in the Magnificat. It is thus deeply subversive and, as has been said, threatening to the powers that be. It signifies their overthrow. It is thus characterised by laughter. "Laughter takes away the seriousness of an attack and debases it. It displays an unassailable freedom and superiority, precisely at the point where the powers and rulers of this world have been reckoning with fear and guilt feelings."[30] Laughter is a sign of faith and hope for it declares that evil, suffering, pain is not the last word. (It is indeed not the first word either, for Christ, the Divine Word, is the Alpha and Omega.) Laughter, the divine *hilaritas*, is an affirmation of God's victory over evil. Dare we say that Easter is a gigantic joke at the Devil's expense?! Joy testifies to *ecstasis*, to our liberation by the act of God from the tyranny of others and ourselves. [31]

The command of joy frees us from anxiety. It is given to us. We are not left in the hopelessness of lonely despair, nor even the comfort of shared misery but in its overcoming. If some Church services tend to the triumphalistic, others, supposedly eucharists, seem like the funerals of a dead hero — come to the kind of end we would expect in

---

29. J.R.R. Tolkien, "On Fairy Stories" in *Tree and Leaf*, (London: George Allen and Unwin, 1975), p. 68. Tolkien's and C.S. Lewis' own stories embody this. Cf., respectively, *The Lord of the Rings*, "The Return of the King," (London: George Allen and Unwin, 1966), p.2 41, and *The Lion, the Witch and the Wardrobe*, (Harmondsworth: Penguin, 1950), p. 146ff. As an epilogue to his essay "On Fairy Stories," Tolkien makes explicit his Christian framework of understanding as he speaks of what he calls the greatest and most complete *eucatastrophe*, at whose reality such stories point: "the birth of Christ is the eucatastrophe of human history. The Resurrection is the eucatastrophe of the story of the Incarnation. This story begins and ends in joy" (p. 71). *Surprised by Joy* is the title of Lewis' autobiography, (London: Collins, 1970).

30. J. Moltmann, *Theology and Joy*, p. 174.

31. The joyless person is completely locked up in him or herself. However, "women and men are not liberated from their old nature by imperatives to be new and to change but they rejoice in the new which makes them free and lifts them beyond themselves," writes Professor Moltmann. (*ibid*, p. 63).

a world such as this! Such services pronounce the word 'joy' slowly, with a sombre tone.

Joy has no room for guilt. It addresses its recipients as friends. It cannot be achieved — only received.[32] Those who grasp at joy fail; it comes to those waiting in patient expectation.[33] It is a gift of the Spirit,[34] which blows where it wills. Accordingly, it cannot be earned or deserved by any activity or status on our part. However, we can close *ourselves* off to the possibility of joy by grasping at false joys, having our hands full, as it were, and looking and acting resolutely in the wrong direction. The poor 'know their need of God' and thus can be won for salvation (as in the parable of the Pharisee and the Publican[35]).

Conclusion

How may we now consider the relationship of God with humanity in suffering and joy? Since I agree with Dr. Gutiérrez that the first act of theology must be silence, it should not be necessary to dispel any anxiety that affirmation of the Divine Word disables the reality of human experience. One needs to listen both to God and humanity — as seriously and intently. Listening to God cannot be an *alternative* to listening to humanity. In fact, listening to the Divine Word should *enable*, not disable, listening to humanity. To take seriously Paschal Joy, one needs to give full weight to all three days of the Easter

32. Costly joy is not the same as conditional joy. For discussion of the pivotal distinction between cheap and costly grace made famous by Bonhoeffer, see his *The Cost of Discipleship*, (London: SCM, 1959), pp. 35-47. Dr. Gutiérrez's own *On Job* could be interpreted as suggesting conditional joy: i.e. that the rich cannot experience joy unless they identify with the poor (pp. xvii,13,17). This would superficially seem to contradict the gratuitous, undeserved grace of God and, perhaps requires clarification. Perhaps this is also the case with the distinction between orthodoxy and orthopraxis seen by Dr. Gutiérrez in Mk. 27-38: whilst this certainly has implications for discipleship, most commentators see Peter's failure as primarily misapprehension of the suffering required of the Messiah. Peter is thus tempting Christ from his chosen path and is rebuked accordingly (e.g. D.E.Nineham, *The Gospel of Saint Mark,* (Harmondsworth: Penguin, 1963), pp. 223-8).
33. K. Barth, *Church Dogmatics,* III.4, p. 378ff.
34. Rms. 14.17, 15.13.
35. Lk. 18.9-14.

narrative — the suffering of Christ on the Cross, the hopeless meaninglessness of Holy Saturday, the unexpected unbelievable joy of Easter Sunday. As Alan Lewis argues,[36] the real significance of Easter is incomprehensible without awareness of what it follows; yet the Crucifixion without the Resurrection would leave us in utter misery. *Both* are required. It is necessary thus to avoid both errors — on the one hand, a triumphalistic emphasis on the Resurrection that fails to take seriously human pain, sorrow and sense of abandonment; on the other, despairing, almost necrophiliac absorption in the mesmeric pit of evil. The former leans towards an Apollinarian or Docetic avoidance of the real pain of human existence, leading to churches where people feel unable to express their genuine concerns and have to put on a front of good cheer; the latter to an often self-righteous affirmation of a cheerless reality ('this is what life's really like'). Real joy comes not only in the midst of suffering, but from its *depths.* Otherwise it must always be escapist in the bad sense. Yet genuine escape is required! If God has 'touched base' with us in our sufferings then the joy we proclaim is a sharing in the joy of God at our redemption.

It has been said that Luke is a Gospel of Joy. There joy is normally opposed, not to suffering or misery, but to fear. 'Do not be afraid: rejoice' say the angels.[37] The Gospel begins in praise to God, the God who fulfils his promises, greeted with joy by those who have kept faith in God's faithfulness; it ends in praise and giving glory to God as the disciples return to Jerusalem "in great joy" having seen Christ's (temporary) departure.[38] The heart of this Gospel, it could be argued, is the Parable of the Prodigal Son. As Schweitzer puts it, "God's joy is the criterion by which all else is measured."[39] Lost humanity is won back for God — should we not rejoice like the woman who finds a coin, or a shepherd a sheep? As we share in the risen Christ, we have joy — joy at his pivotal reversal of the trend of human history, joy at the foretaste we have now of the reality in Christ that will be ours for ever at the end of time — the defeat of death. Poverty means death,

---

36. "The Burial of God: Rupture and Resumption as the Story of Salvation," in *Scoyttish Journal of Theology,* 40, pp. 335-362.
37. Lk. 2.10. Cf. also Mt. 28.8 ('the women hurried away from the tomb, filled with awe and great joy') and Mk.16.8 ('they said nothing to anyone for they were afraid').
38 Lk. 24.52.
39 E. Schweitzer, *The Good News According to Luke,* trans. D. E. Green, (London: SPCK, 1984), p. 247.

said Dr. Gutiérrez. It is true. Saint Paul adds, however, "death is swallowed up in victory".[40] The one who is Himself Life is at hand. To those who have ears to hear, or empty hands and hearts to receive, joy is come in the midst of suffering.

40 I Cor. 15.54

Reply by Gustavo Gutiérrez to John W. de Gruchy and Stephen May

Thank you Professor de Gruchy and Professor May for your observations. In reply I have four remarks. I am not a sectarian person, and so I will have four points on this occasion!

The first is about academic theology, and theological witness. I agree with Professor de Gruchy, we must try avoid any dualism between these two aspects. In liberation theology we try to do that, witness is very important, but I also believe in theology being a rational task, because it is rational, but I cannot do theology without, for example, confrontation with contemporary theology. I do not accept the affirmation that as I am Peruvian, and belong to a very poor country, that my theology is a voice. Yes, this is important, but theology is more than a voice, theology is a systematic reflection, and it is important that we link these two aspects. Bonhoeffer's example in this area was very valuable. He was a very big Christian and therefore also a very big theologian. For the same reason we have very few big theologians. Bonhoeffer has put this question to us: "How do we speak about God in an adult world". How do we speak about God? It is a pastoral question. Classical Christian language is a pastoral question. From pastoral questions we have new theologies, from theological questions we have new books. Bonhoeffer's is a very deep question, and so it is therefore a very deep theology. Our question in Latin America, and also in other parts of the world, is not exactly how does one speak about God in an adult world, because our world of Latin America is not adult in the same sense. My question is how to tell the poor person that God loves them. It is the question I and others in Latin America have, because the daily experience of the poor seems to be the negation of the love of God. The question is important. In order to reflect on this we need to try, at least, to do serious, academic theology. I do not like to distance myself from academic theology. It is true, I am not a professor of theology, but I have a great respect for academic theologians (though not all of them), and for their theological method, because I have learned much from them, and continue to do so. But, for me it is very important to keep together the two aspects: Christian witness and academic theology.

My second observation is very brief: grace and the gratuitous love of God. I said several times yesterday and again today, that these are central in the book of Job, and also in Paul and many other books. In the history of Christianity, or more specifically in the history of theology, there many authors who addressed this subject. I would like to mention only two them at the present time: St Augustine and Martin Luther. *Sola fide, sola gratia*, and *sola scriptura* are the same. I think it is a very deep intuition, that salvation is above all grace. This is central to Christianity. It is the only way to understand the meaning of our human acts: as our human response to the first movement which comes from God. Our human experience must be an answer to this first love which comes from God.

The third remark is about joy and preaching. It is for good reason that we as Christians must announce the Gospel. It seems obvious, but when we encounter another culture, and those who live in other cultures, the question makes more sense. Why? I will attempt an answer, to this question, which is for me the only answer. To announce the Gospel is to share my joy with others. I am joyful, I must be joyful, because God loves me, and I would like to share this love with others. Of course there are other reasons: to expand the church etc. But really, to announce the Gospel is to share, for it is very important for me to share this love with others, and this is the reason for my joy. My joy is a consequence of the presence of the love of God in my life. I am very impressed by the presence of joy among the poor. You probably know one important Spanish word: *fiesta, la fiesta*. People loving, and these people are poor, they are suffering. It is wrong to speak of the poor as those who are poor, suffering, and crying all day. Fools! Fools! It is not true, their suffering is the real question, but there is also joy. I think that when we speak about the Gospel in this way, preaching joy, the poor feel very close to the Gospel.

My fourth, and final remark is to do with the future of liberation theology. I agree with Professor de Gruchy's remarks, but at the same time, in treating this question, I would like to add, not to subtract from your point. Personally, I am more concerned with the future of the liberation of my people, or with the future of the presence of the Gospel in that process of liberation. As a consequence, I am concerned with the future of liberation theology. When it is said, within the framework of liberation theology, that theology is a second act, we try to say this seriously. Second acts are not relevant. Secondary acts come after. First is the liberation of the people and the presence of the Gospel. I never spoke about liberation theology until my forties, and I think I was a Christian. I was trying to be a Christian. If I was a Christian before liberation theology, I hope to be a Christian after liberation theology, because I don't believe in liberation theology, I believe in Jesus Christ. Liberation theology is not a new article of my creed, it is a tool, not in the pejorative sense. It is a means to understand my faith, but no more. But, really I am concerned with liberation theology, as Professor de Gruchy has said so clearly, the question is not the name of this theology, but the place of this theology. I am very concerned with the place. This place is oppression, injustice, marginalisation, the hopes, and joys of the poor. I am very concerned with this.

By way of a final word, I am not trying to distance myself from theology. To say that theology is not my concern is not true. It is a great concern of mine, I love to do theology, honestly. But at the same time, theology is only one section of my life. It is not my whole life, and theology for me is very important as a means, a tool, in order to reflect about my people, their faith, my own existence, and the gift of Christian faith. It is the place of this thinking. By consequence, it seems to me, the future of liberation theology, is linked to the two more important points: the liberation of people, and the presence of the Word of God in the historical process of liberation. Thus, I am really concerned with the future of liberation theology.

5

Christ in Feminist Context

Elisabeth Moltmann-Wendel

I. Can a Male Saviour Save Women?

The figure of Jesus and the belief in Jesus Christ has become a problem for many women over the last twenty years. The figure of Jesus is male and the question is, if this figure can still serve as a point of identification for women who today want to rediscover themselves and their history. And in the name of Jesus Christ, in belief in him and his dominion claims of power have been made on heathens, Jews and women which sometimes ended with death and annihilation. How can women live with this past which is still present for many? Church and Christianity are secretly, deeply penetrated with the presupposition that Christ is male. In the Letter to the Ephesians (5:21ff), the subordination of the woman under the man is legitimated with the example of Christ and the parish community. He is the example of the hierarchical social order in which the man dominates. Just as Christ is the head, and the community is the body, so the man stands over the woman. He loves and she must respect him. In the witch hunts, a part of the legitimation of the persecution of women as witches was drawn out of the maleness of the redeemer. The Witches' Hammer (Malleus maleficarum) bases its assumption that women are easier victims of the devil, that is become witches, among others upon the fact that the redeemer was a man and with that, has protected the male species from such misdeeds; a strengthening of the customary argument of female inferiority and the dangerous nature of women. And with that, we are in the present. In the Vatican Declaration of 1976 against the admission of women to the priesthood, it says that women can never be admitted to the priesthood because in the practice of his office the priest represents Christ, but the woman cannot be Christ's image: "Christ himself was and remains a man."

The Protestant Churches have never dogmatically committed themselves to a maleness of Christ. Instead, in their structures prevails a somewhat relaxed but dominating spirit of brotherliness which takes the image of Brother Jesus as its starting point and cultivates a type of male team-work, comradeship, brotherliness in which women have difficulty finding a place. The maleness of Christ is not felt dogmatically but socially.

The Christ images in the Protestant sphere are also similar to the contemporary male ideals: Christ the Pioneer (Visser't Hooft), the brotherly human. In the Reformation time, Christ was viewed by Zwingli as "Captain of our souls". He became "Superstar" in the modern Pop culture. He became that which men and perhaps also women dreamed of as exciting maleness. But can the redemption images of women be fulfilled in a historical male ideal?

Christology, the dogmatic expression of the Church's understanding of Christ, causes women additional difficulties Christological reflection about Christ's person and work concentrates for the most part on the understanding of Jesus' sonship of God and on the event of salvation: his death and his resurrection. However, the problem of God's sonship places the daughters of God rather off to the side. Jesus' death, understood in the tradition mostly as death of atonement for our sins remains unacceptable for many women today because they refuse a general and a fundamental understanding of sin. Christ's death being understood as a "sacrificial death" has legitimized the selflessness of women and their subjection. The theme resurrection is for many still so far removed because they are just beginning to unfurl healing powers for themselves and their present surroundings and for the problems of the world. The emphasized uniqueness of the event of salvation is for many an expression of the Church's claim to absoluteness. Therefore, the patterns of thinking of Christology appear to come out of a rather patriarchal context and are, at least for the present time, without existential access for women.

How can Christ in the context of women become alive again? Is it possible at all to relinquish the male context of the Christ event and the interpretation of Christ? What has been attempted up to now and what is still conceivable? For the American theologian Mary Daly, it was clear from the beginning that women's liberation would lead to "the loss of credibility for many christological formulas which reflect the idolatry of the person of Christ".[1] There have been many attempts to break up this "Christolatry" in the past years. With the help of psychoanalysis, Jesus is understood as the first mature man who has integrated his anima and who with that became the first to overcome the androcentrism of the ancient world.[2] In the matriarchal research, Jesus has become a hero who as a symbol for the dying and again resurrecting nature rests on the lap of the Goddess, an old recurring myth in which the woman is the origin of life and the man, the hero, serves her. Furthermore, Jesus has become the "anointed one of the women" who matures through women and the women cults to the work of his life.[3]

In the more theologically-oriented women's studies, Jesus is again seen as Sophia-wisdom. Much indicates that Jesus understood himself as the wisdom and the oldest Christology appears to have been a Sophialogy. Wisdom goes into the streets, calls her children to her, is repudiated but also sought for by them. She played before God, can be described in many other female images and with this, is a fascinating contrast to the titles of sovereignty and the brother ideologies.[4] Another widespread image is Jesus as liberator (Ruether) to whom community of the liberated who continue this process always corresponds. He can be seen as "liberated humanity", a notion which does not presuppose his image of individual perfection, but rather sees a process to human liberation being started with him.[5]

The American Rita Nakashima Brock goes another step in such interpretation of Christ: for her the community of women and Jesus is inseparable. It is the experience of "inclusive community in solidarity" in which those who are despised and marginal become certain of their dignity as daughters and sons of God. In this community, she sees the divine power incarnated which heals and makes whole. With this, she opposes the old model which saw divine power incarnated in Jesus as an individual and creates a new model, the messianic community, in whose relationships life-giving power is experienced. The consequences are then, for her, that the redemption has not happened in

---

1. Mary Daly, *Beyond God the Father,* (Boston: Beacon Press, 1975), pp. 69 ff.
2. Hann Wolf, *Jesus der Mann,* (Stuttgart), 1975.
3. Christa Mulack, *Jesus der Gesalbte der Frauen,* (Stuttgart: 1987).
4. Elisabeth Schüssler-Fiorenza, *In Memory of Her,* (London: SCM, 1983).
5. Rosemary R. Ruether, *Sexism and Godtalk,* (Boston: Beacon Press, 1983), p. 138.

Christ "once and for all" but rather it is experienced in the messianic community which she calls Christa-Community. The redeeming action is, therefore, placed in the hands of the humans. This christological interpretation of Jesus' history avoids the problem of the male redeemer by understanding the humans as the continuation of redemption.[6]

Such different attempts have helped women to find an identity in Christianity once again. They are attempts to rediscover buried feminine symbols to make space for them in theology, or to dethrone the maleness and to set the model of community in its place.

I want to attempt still another way: I want to return to the figure of Jesus, as we encounter it in the Synoptic Gospels and to liberate it from the patriarchal wrappings of dogmas, male wishes and dreams. Already in 1973, Mary Daly encourage this as she wrote: "If he (Jesus) is no longer condemned to the role of the redeemer perhaps Jesus can be seen as a free human. Only the pride and the self-assertion of women can liberate the memory of Jesus from its destructive use and make the freedom free".[7] And Ruether demanded ten years later "a new discussion with the Jesus of the Synoptic Gospels, a figure which is note-worthily compatible with feminism".

I want to take up this point. This means at the same time, however, that in a second phase of feminist theology, we should not only attempt to rediscover the feminine in theology but rather also the humanity which has been lost in patriarchal theology, the non-deformed maleness. Because it could even be that the feminine image is just as deformed and through that would become dominating just like the maleness! This means for the reconstruction of the Jesus figure that we attempt to discover anew the human Jesus or, like Daly, to understand the free human Jesus. But how can this happen? It is certainly difficult with Pauline theology and the Pauline Jesus who for Paul "according to the flesh", that is, in his mortal humaneness, was uninteresting. It is more likely with the Synoptic Jesus tradition. We are, however, still accustomed to receive the biblical stories handed over through the traditional perspective of men. Much of what women see today has not been seen in this. In the meantime, the humaneness of Jesus is being reconsidered by women in all the Churches of the world. But we must also ask: How can we find a rational method for our legitimate

6. Rita Nakashima Brock, *Journeys by Heart,* (New York: Harper Row, 1981).

7. Daly, *ibid.*

subjective and emotional proceedings? How can we substantiate our new approaches and make them understood to a wider population?

For me the psychosocial analyses of Anne Wilson Scharf have become important for what maleness and femaleness mean in our culture and for the criteria which result from this.[8] For the self-understanding of men and as criterion with which they judge others, according to this, two things are decisive the person and the work. For the self-understanding of women there is beyond this a third dimension: the relationship. A holistic understanding of the human can only be achieved when we include all three categories. Our Christology has, however, become a typical product of male self-understanding in that it reflects person and work, and the important category of relation is lacking. If we ask about its occurrence, then we next find ourselves in no-man's-land. Hardly anyone has taken it seriously. But if we ask about the biblical Jesus stories we make the amazing observation of how many relationships are told of. Relationships which allow human life to become and to mature, and if we were to forget them, only a hardened and abstract human image would remain. In the context of a feminist theology, Jesus, must be liberated from an abstract way of perceiving him to his whole person.

II. Relationship and its Consequences

1.

The relationships in which Jesus lived are those of family, the group of disciples and of the women. He soon had difficulties with the family in which he at first found closeness warmth and approval, and in which he also must have aroused certain expectations. They want to keep him for themselves, talk him out of his ludicrous way and declare him as insane (Mk 3:31). The mother, above all, must have experienced disappointments as almost all mothers with self-willed sons experience it. With becoming an adult, the network of relationships breaks up, but it certainly left behind its clear traces which are shown by Jesus in a type of basic trust and carefree behaviour. The next formative group consists of the disciples. At the beginning these male friendships are built on solidarity and joint acting, healing, preaching, baptizing (Mk 6:12f.). They become, however, increasingly difficult Jesus is

8. Anne Wilson Schaef, *Women's Reality,* (Oak Grove: Crossroad, 1981), p. 108.

disappointed in the friends, groans about them, is annoyed by their dreams of power (Mk 10:35ff.), misses their solidarity in Gethsemane. Out of this relationship must have grown in him the recognition of the loneliness of his way. The third relationship group is that of the women. Often only slightly noticed and — analogous to the serving women's role in the Church — degraded to the serving and the care-taking women of Jesus and the group of disciples, they have been rediscovered, through feminist research as a group of self-sufficient women.[9] Most of all, Mary Magdalene, the first woman Apostle. Women followed Jesus just like the male disciples, were partly through healing of illness called to follow him, influenced his life and way of the cross at decisive points and displayed solidarity with him up to his death and the grave. The Canaanite woman makes it clear to him that he is also the Messiah of the Gentiles. The woman who anoints him in a group of men shows him the way he shall go into death as anointed king and prophet. An old iconographic tradition shows women, Mary and Martha, as they sit with Jesus in Gethsemane. In the Gospel of John there is something of this activity of the women still to be felt in the wine miracle of Cana which through a woman, his mother, is initiated, and introduces the series of Jesus's miracles. The resurrection is first experienced by the women who follow him up to the grave — with that expose themselves to persecution — and without whose proclamation the Christian church is not conceivable.

Jesus lived in relationships, experienced in them closeness trust, separation and disappointment. We hear — most of all in the Gospel of Mark — of the feelings which accompany these relationships and which present to us someone different from the detached Son of God who has been mature from the beginning: a human who needs other humans, who is afraid, confused frustrated and can not be thought of in isolation. A human image based on a strong and independent maleness has left us in theology a corresponding image of Jesus which was formed according to the motto: a boy does not cry and a Jesus does not sigh. In the women's context, on the other hand, a Jesus encounters us who challenges the male and human image still based on the constant independence, strength and repression of feelings. A human encounters us who we have not seen before. A human who teaches us to see anew what incarnation is, that is to become human, not to become male and from whom there can be no church which is only

9. Elisabeth Moltmann-Wendel, *A Land with Milk and Honey,* (London: SCM, 1986), pp. 117ff.

shaped by ordained men. This human image — and this is important — certainly comes only out of the perspective of women, out of the category "relationship".

2.

And with this we are at the second important point: the influence of the women and the impossibility of imaging Jesus' path through life without these women. Women who were searching for their own identity, first of all saw how partnership was the basis of Jesus' relationship with the women. Nothing of the usual animosity of the era is to be felt within it! With no woman did he ever split up in conflict. There is no story of the rich young virgin! This open relationship must have caused women to behave in atypical ways: They entered into unknown houses and men's groups. They freely anointed his head and feet. They follow the enemy of the state to the cross and waited there, went to the grave and were witnesses of the resurrection — all dangerous actions which break through the old women's roles and which were combined with the danger of death. A noteworthy dynamic between Jesus and the women is to be observed In response to a woman's (Martha's) urging, Jesus raises Lazarus from the dead. The passionate struggle of a mother for her disturbed daughter changes Jesus' self-understanding from a nationalist to a healer, also of heathens. Are they the powerless of society who see before them a change of society in him? An old manuscript reports that Jesus was also accused because he seduced women and children to impurity (Lk 23:2). An embarrassment for earlier, prudish times which we can however today explain as socially offensive, unconventional contact with a group which is separated out socially and is seen as latently impure. A sign of the Kingdom of God which will reverse all values existing up to now.

The Jesus-women-story shows us with that a model of a new lifestyle: the model of mutuality, this mutual taking and giving in which each person maintains his/her dignity but is inconceivable without the relationships to the others. An attempt which failed between the disciples and Jesus but which succeeded between him and the group of women. "Mutuality" took over from the hierarchical life model of the ancient world, a model which however unfortunately came to life again, which shapes our churches up until today but should have actually been surpassed long ago: the waiting and listening to the voice of authority and the commands to those below.

In "mutuality", on the other hand, each person first perceives her/himself and takes her/himself seriously and in this way is made aware of the other. In mutuality, our personality is changed, we can develop autonomy and once again also give ourselves to the point of unselfishness, up to (real) sacrifice. In mutuality, we can receive from one another without giving ourselves up.

Mutuality can sound very harmless and liberal. The political and theological explosive power which lies in this concept is shown by the elite thinker Friedrich Nietzsche who considered it to be a "vileness" because it could encourage the intentions to the power of the weak, and the patriarchal theologian Karl Barth, who denied any "mutualism" because it challenges the superiority of God above humans.[10]

The mutuality which one can deduce from the Jesus story abolishes all thoughts of dominion, the thought of God's superiority as well as that of man's and other false authorities. It is the rejection of every religious and societal hierarchy.

3.

The relationship Jesus/women or women/Jesus becomes still closer when we include the most recent exegetical studies of the early New Testament writings. Already in the 1970's Elisabeth Schüssler Fiorenza showed that the word "to serve" (*diakonein*) is only said of the women and Jesus. In the New Testament, "to serve" has little to do with our gender specific female services. There it means to reject the domination and the hierarchical order. It is the characteristic behaviour in the new community and shows "the eschatological reversal of all power relationships". Originally derived from the table service in which the server was the one with the lowest social standing, "to serve" was used by Jesus in order to characterize his life (Mk 10:45) and it was then also said of women. Just as Jesus served, so served Peter's mother-in-law who was healed of a fever (Mk 1:31). The women who served also go up to Jerusalem with Jesus (Mk 14:41). The relation of following, serving, coming up to Jerusalem is never said of the disciples

A further parallel between Jesus and the women is shown with "arise" and "awaken". It has been researched that this word in the New Testament is used twenty-five times for Jesus' resurrection; it is also

10. G. Kaper, et al. *Eva Wo bist Du?*, (Gelnhausen: 1981), p. 15ff.

found in the pre-Mark healing stories, but only for the healings of women: for the healing of Peter's mother-in-law and for the awakening of Jairus's daughter. "At the level of the tradition of Mark", so says Monika Fander, "a closer relationship is established between individual stories of healing about women and the passion-story".[11]

Furthermore the expression "suffering" (paschein) is said of Jesus as well as of the hemorrhaging woman (Mk 5,26; 8,31; 9,12). This word later becomes a set term for Jesus' passion. Already Matthew no longer applies it for the hemorrhaging woman.

Suffering and becoming new are, therefore, in the early layer of the New Testament connected with women's fate in a striking manner. Also the distressing Jesus experience in Gethsemane, which are reported with the words "to be deeply distressed", "ekthambeistai", has a women's parallel: the amazement of the women at the empty tomb (Mk 14:33; 16:5).

The early Christians could still see more in the illnesses of women than physical suffering. They could see parallels to Jesus's suffering who takes our illnesses upon himself (Is. 53). They could, however, also see resurrection and becoming new in the healing of the women. They probably saw Jesus and the women as people on the edge of society, but filled with new passion to change the structures. And they had no fear to describe the collapse and the doubt of both with the same expression. The "dangerous" connection would soon be separated. Jesus' passion and resurrection was removed from the women's experience. They became the unique and singular story of Jesus Christ. This now had very little existential connection, in any case, not to women's stories. It was isolated and dogmatized. In the image of the crucified woman which arose in the early Middle Ages and continually inspired new concepts up to the present, has maintained something of this nearness of the passion and women's suffering, of the powerlessness under patriarchal structures.

Women's stories and Jesus' story are deeply intertwined with another, but they do not dissolve into each other, not even in a Christa community. They are not identical. The Jesus story does not coincide with the women's stories. In its uniqueness it contrasts with the women's stories. This is shown,in my opinion, by the parallel example of the "thaumazesthai", the deep fear in different situations: the women experience here as they come to the edge of their existence, the comfort

11. Monika Fander, *Die Stellung der Frau in Markusevangelicum,* (Altenberge: 1989), pp. 179ff.

of the young man. "Do not be amazed. He has risen!" Jesus, on the other hand, experiences no comfort. He must go the way of death and loneliness without support. His story is therefore unique for the New Testament. But not in the sense of a male/hero uniqueness but rather it is unique in that it does not need to be repeated. The way of Jesus opens our way which we can go with less fear.

The death of Jesus is therefore here not understood as a death of atonement. It is understood existentially, parallels to the women's stories of illness and healing, if dying and arising. It is not a symbol for the forgiveness of sins but rather a symbol of human suffering and resurrection, human powerlessness and divine experience of power.

The Jesus story seen from the perspective of women shows us the human Jesus, not the man Jesus. Furthermore, it shows a model of new life which replaces the old system of superiority and subordination: the life model of mutuality. And third, from this perspective the dogma of death and resurrection is opened up and becomes the existential experience of illness and health, of dying and becoming new which is oriented by the women's story.

III. Traces of a Feminist Christology

The great closeness of women to Jesus corresponds to the fact that first early and original confessions to him have been transmitted from them. The first christological confession in the Gospel of Mark is spoken by a woman, the Syrophoenician. Her address "Kyrie" is not a predicate out of politeness. A "qualified christology" is expressed in it (Kertelge). It stands even before Peter's confession and it anticipated the confession of the Gentile soldier at the cross. Through this, the Syrophoenician becomes "the prototype of the believing Gentile, a symbol of the church of nations and this symbol is female" (Fander). The feminine confession also stands in sharp contrast to the disbelief of the disciples who shortly before did not come "to understand" at the dividing of the bread.

In the Gospel of John two Christ titles and confessions which vary from the norm are noticeable and may disclose a special meaning of Jesus for the women. The Samaritan woman unfolds a large number of Christ titles in her conversation with Jesus at the well. "Jew", "Lord", "greater than our Father Jacob", "Prophet", "the salvation comes from the Jews", "Messiah", "Christ", "Saviour of the world". The last title is used by the Samaritans who believe because of the witness of the woman, and it is the most original one. It is found only one time in the First Letter of John (4:14). Instead of speaking of the people who are to be healed, it speaks of the cosmos, which is to be healed, this globe which is loved by God and which has rebelled against him. Here the healer of the cosmos concretely heals the religions and people that are torn apart. In correspondence with the first women's confession of faith in the Gospel of Mark, the healing power of Jesus which unites humans is also placed in the centre of the Christ experience here. Not the individual and his/her sins and forgiveness but rather the cosmos and the healing of its disunity is the women's concern.

Even more informative, it appears to me, is the Martha confession which Martha, the sister of Lazarus, makes in the story of the resurrection of Lazarus: "You are the Christ, the Son of God who has come into the world". We normally only know the Peter confession: "You are the Christ, the Son of the living God" (Mt 16,16). According to research, both confessions co-existed in the early history of the Church, that means there were communities in which the Peter confession became known and there were communities for which the Martha confession was central.[12] The Martha confession has an important addition which was long over-looked: "Who has come into the world". It refers back to Jesus' many sayings about himself in the Gospel of John in which Jesus understands himself as the one who has come into the world as light, as witness of truth, etc. Sayings of Jesus about himself are brought into connection with Martha which show this woman to be in great closeness and familiarity with Jesus. This addition is the "most important along side the two other well-known titles of 'Christ' and 'Son of God' because it most clearly expresses the breaking of the other world into this world" (Rudolf Bultmann).[13] This confession is in this form unique in the New Testament: into the world, the cosmos, the object of God's love, into the power which rebels against God, Christ has come. Martha therefore, pulls Jesus very deeply into this world just like she herself is very much in this world, practical and sober, she experiences the physical death of her brother ("he smells already") and,however, knows that in this cosmos there is already new life.

The Christ confession of the women in the Gospel of John have a particular dimension: they look beyond human beings to the whole

---

12. Raymond E Brown, "Roles of Women in the Fourth Gospel," in *Theological Studies,* 36/4 1975, pp. 692ff.
13. Rudolf Bulmann, *Das Evangelium des Johannes,* (Gottingen), 1952, p. 309.

earth, to the globe. They are not anthropocentric but rather cosmocentric, not oriented to the individual human only but rather to the cosmos. Here salvation occurs. Here, with the Christ who has come, the separating power of death (John 11) which tore apart sister and brother and the law of the religious divisions which divided Jews and Samaritans is lifted.

When we compare the history of the reception of the Peter confession — focused only on God's sonship — and the Martha confession — oriented on this world and its salvation — it is clear that Peter's confession has made Church history a Church history influenced by ordained men and women held quiet. Martha's confession which goes back to a woman and — as far as we see today — transfers women's interests, influenced a community of equality for only a short time before it was absorbed by the patriarchal institutional Church and its confession became forgotten. To tap into it and its confession anew could be the goal of a Church today which once and for all breaks with the patriarchal traditions. Out of the beginning times of Christianity, we encounter a Jesus who had a direct closeness to women and beginnings of a christology which is not yet influenced by claims of power latent maleness and dogmatizing of Jesus' death. Its content which takes the women's experience as its example is the illumination and healing of the cosmos through God who has entered into the creation. If the Johannine women's confession stresses the this worldliness of the Christ event, the thinking in Mark makes this worldliness concrete through women's experience. The consequences for a present day christology would be:

> 1. to return dignity and value to women's experiences in church and theology, 2. to let the figure of Jesus to again become alive in marginal groups, 3. to experience his life and his death in ever new concrete forms, 4. and through this, to comprehend anew and realize the this worldliness of God in the cosmos.

Response by Janet Martin Soskice

It is a great pity that, due to health reasons, Elisabeth Moltmann-Wendel was unable to attend this Symposium and, but she has given us a great deal to think in her paper. The topic she has chosen to address is one of the most important and difficult under discussion in contemporary feminist theology and poses a challenge for all Christologies. "Christ in a feminist context: Can a male saviour redeem a humankind of more than fifty percent women?"

I hope Dr. Moltmann-Wendel will forgive me for beginning with a disagreement, or rather a qualification. I believe she will, since it is one which strengthens her case. She asks, "can a male saviour redeem a humankind of more than fifty percent women?" I quote from a recent article in the New York Review of books by the eminent Indian economist, Amartya Sen, now at Harvard. He writes "It is often said that women make up a majority of the world's population. They do not. This mistaken belief is based on generalizing from the contemporary situation in Europe and North America, where the ratio of women to men is typically about 1.05, or 1.06, or higher. In South Asia, West Asia, and China, the ratio of women to men can be as low as 0.94 or even lower, and it varies widely elsewhere in Asia, in Africa and in Latin America."

Women outnumber men, he goes on to say, substantially in Europe, the United States and Japan, but "the fate of women is quite different in most of Asia and North Africa." In some places of course, female infanticide is still practised but this is really not a significant factor and nor is death in childbirth. Rather it is the persistent failure to give girl children and women medical care similar to that which men get, the failure to give them comparable food to that which the men get, and failure to provide equal access to what social services there might be. Where there is anything, boy children and men get it first . The title of Sen's article is a chilling one, *"More Than 100 Million Women Are Missing*", because 100 million is the figure by which, if we project on the basis of European and North American figures, there is a shortfall of women in the world population. One hundred million. "These numbers" Sen says, "tell us, quietly, a terrible story of inequality and neglect leading to the excess mortality of women." [1] A hundred million women missing. Sexism is not something that hurts women's feelings, sexism kills millions and millions and millions of girls and women each year. And yet the churches have been so slow to condemn sexism as a sin. Slower even than in declaring apartheid a heresy. Worse still, we are still told in many quarters that feminism is really not Christian, that it is 'anti-Christian', that it is a secular thing. It is even suggested that if you are a faithful Christian you won't have anything to learn from feminism, you would only teach the feminists perhaps. It's even said that feminism is just a middle class, white, preoccupation that distracts us from the real moral needs of the world today. What world are people who make these remarks living in?

Over the years, I have learned a great deal from the debates about the ordination of women. I myself have never felt a calling to ordained ministry. What got me engaged was not so much the fact that women were refused ordination in various denominations, but the grounds on which it was argued they should be so refused, and in some churches, still are. Looking at the Catholic tradition, which of course embraces far more than just the Roman Catholic church, one sees that the question of the ordination of women has never seriously been raised in centuries preceding our own. The topic was hardly ever broached at all, a non starter, no more was female suffrage, or whatever. But at the very few points where it has been mentioned, the answer is invariable. Women can't be priests because they are subordinate to men and so could not signify the deity. Of course in recent documents, this argument is not used. Instead we have a new argument, and let's be clear, it is a new argument, it is not the traditional argument. The traditional argument is the one about subordination. The new argument is that women are equal but different, and different in such a way that they could not be priests. Women, in this new argument, still can't signify Christ. Then of course we have the well rehearsed argument about 'why not?' Jesus after all was a young man when he died yet an eighty year old priest is still judged able to signify Christ. Jesus was a Jew, yet a Chinese man can signify Christ. What then is so over-ridingly important about being a woman, that this feature out of all others makes some people un-Christlike in the one relevant sense? We are still told in some quarters that this is a matter of divine

1. *New York Review of Books*, December 20, 1990, p. 61.

dispensation. This is the way God has ordered the world and God has ordered the symbolic reality. This is the way God has constructed both the order of creation and the order of redemption.[2] In this order women cannot be priests, but they can be mothers and nurturers. Their part indeed, in the symbolic order, is to be not-Christ. After all if everyone was Christlike then who would be the people who could be non-Christlike by contrast? The whole order of creation would be upset by ordaining a woman, we are told. It would be like, well like ordaining a pigeon or a bunch of bananas. (Such things and similar are said even in New Zealand!) In fact it might be better to ordain a pigeon since at least the Holy Spirit appeared as a bird at Christ's baptism. But the question can't be avoided. If women can't represent Christ, can Christ represent women? Is Christ only the saviour of men? Can a male saviour redeem women too? We are back now to Elisabeth Moltmann-Wendel's important question.

Susan Brooks Thistlethwaite in her book, *Sex, Race and God,* relates this story of one of her students. The student, a woman, was raped while taking her garbage to the dump and as she lay bleeding there on the heap of garbage, wondering if her assailant would come back to murder her,and afraid to move, she had a vision of Jesus as a crucified woman who said to her from the cross "You don't have to be afraid, you don't have to be ashamed, I know what you are suffering".[3] These kinds of visions, people never build shrines to. When we consider the global sufferings of women documented by Amartya Sen, their starvation, exploitation, and degradation; when we consider the specific cases like that of the prostitution and child prostitution trade in the Philippines, (just read that up if you haven't done so,) then we must ask as a very real question "Can Jesus be the saviour for women?" Are their sufferings and their dyings not caught up and mapped on the cross? With questions like this, many women are moving beyond questions of institutional reform in the churches.

Many women are moving beyond asking the question of ordination, to asking central questions about Christology and asking whether they can remain within the churches as they stand. Many women turn their

---

2. See for example the arguments in Manfred Hauke, *Women in the Priesthood? A Systematic Analysis in the light of the Order of Creation.* (San Francisco: Ignatius Press, 1988), and see also my review of that book in *The Tablet*, 11 Nov, 1989.

3 *Sex, Race and God: Christian Feminism in Black and White.* (London: Geoffrey Chapman, 1990), p. 93.

gaze now to the churches and see them not as sources of 'good news' and abundant life but rather as the validators of the oppression of women socially, politically, emotionally and symbolically. Sandra Schneiders, an American theologian and Roman Catholic religious sister, writes about with some feeling. It is not simply that women are excluded from Holy Orders, she says they have been made invisible in language and imagery, the impositions society and family put upon them have been given divine sanction and their emergence into the public sphere has been loaded with guilt, especially if they are working mothers. Yet, women do know Christ as their saviour. Perhaps it's a miracle of grace that they do. Schneiders says, that women's "experience as disciples of Jesus Christ makes them aware that what has been done to them in the name of God is contrary to the will of Christ for his follows."[4]

All this is by way of showing how very central is the question Elisabeth Moltmann-Wendel has chosen to address. In her paper, after tracing a number of ways in which Christ in the context of women might become alive again, including examining such symbols as Sophia/Wisdom and the Christa community, she advocates her own way, a return to the figure of Jesus as we encounter it in the synoptic Gospels. Jesus of the synoptics she sees as central to feminist self-understanding and also to a non-deformed maleness. But how do we rediscover this Jesus of the synoptics after two thousand years of patriarchal filters? As she herself mentioned, even Paul was not terribly interested in the mortal humaneness of Jesus. What method do we employ? She makes the suggestion that we start from an examination of self-understanding, and the differences between men's and women's self-understanding. Men's self understanding is largely based on person and work, whereas for women a third feature must be added, person, work, and relationship. Traditional christologies, the products of male theologians, reflect person and work but not, she suggests, relationship. Relationship, she suggests, is a subject on which women have a particular contribution to make. Dr. Moltmann-Wendel speaks of the influence of women on Jesus' life; serving, awakening and suffering. Jesus' life and witness and those of the women around him are intertwined. The stories of the women and Jesus intertwine but do not dissolve one in another for Jesus' death is unique, "not in the sense of a male/hero uniqueness but rather it is

4. Sandra Schneiders, *Beyond Patching: Faith and Feminism in the Catholic Church* (Mahwah, N. J.: Paulist Press, 1991), pp. 32-4, p.64.

unique in that it does not need to be repeated." She says, "The death of Jesus is therefore here not understood as a death of atonement. It is understood existentially, parallel to the women's stories of illness and healing, of dying and arising." (And here's an important sentence.) "It is not a symbol for the forgiveness of sins but rather a symbol of human suffering and resurrection. Human powerlessness and divine experience of power. The Jesus story seen from the perspective of women shows us the human Jesus, not the man Jesus."

I can see the force of Elisabeth Moltmann-Wendel's desire to ground things in the human Jesus, but my question is this: Will the rediscovery, the repristinisation, of the human Jesus be enough for beleaguered feminists and, more importantly, for the sufferings of those girls and women who may never in their life read a word of theology? What does it mean for those, more than a hundred million of whose numbers are missing? The relations of biblical women to the human Jesus are very important, but I want also to know more about what our relations can be to the work of the risen Lord.

In *Faith, History and Society,* Johann Baptist Metz makes an interesting distinction between Christian hope and secular utopian vision. It is something like this: Secular Utopias envision a time which will be marvellous for those lucky enough to live then, but offer little solace to those whose lives have been a means to this glorious end. But Christian hope looks to a time, God's time, when all will be well; when every tear will be dried, when all the suffering of the world through all its ragged and jagged history will somehow be made whole. And this must mean, for me anyway, this Christian hope must mean that Hagar will find her home and that wholeness will return to Tamar and the unnamed concubine in the Book of Judges, to the child prostitute killed by one of her customers, to the rape victim, to the mother who sees her children starve to death. Unless I can believe in a risen Christ who somehow — and I don't know how — will redeem these sufferings, as well as promise a better future, I can have no hope. Even if things changed now, overnight, to be wondrously egalitarian and good for women all over the world, how can we forget, what kind of amnesia would let us forget two thousand, four thousand, six thousand years of pain and death? We must practice 'not forgetting', in Metz's phrase, anamnesia. This anamnesia, this painful memory, is only redeemed by Christian hope because it is only God who can promise healing of the past as well as to our future. This is even more so if we hope for the renewal of the earth. I'm not quite sure how recalling the human Jesus alone is going to give us a Jesus who renews the face of the earth.[5]

Dr Wendel finds traces of a feminist Christology in the Christological confessions of the women in the New Testament texts. These are confessions indeed whose significance has been grossly and to my mind incomprehensibly overlooked by historical theology, particularly if we reflect on how much attention has been paid to Peter's confession. Alongside Peter's confession we must put that of the Syrophoenician woman, the Samaritan woman, and of course supremely, Martha. I would like, in conclusion, to add to Elisabeth Moltmann-Wendel's list Mary Magdalene, who met the risen Lord in the garden. But perhaps were Dr Moltmann-Wendel here, she would name Mary as well.

5 This is not to say we can relax about environmental issues because God will clean up all our mess in the eschaton. As with our work for justice and peace, we strive as members of the risen Christ for the coming of the Kingdom which is already and not yet.

Response by Veronica Brady

One of the interesting things about this conference is the way in which we have taken for granted a key issue, namely context. We have to speak from somewhere, but that somewhere is not innocent. Thus, I speak. I do theology as a white middle class Australian woman in a profoundly and enthusiastically racist, sexist, militaristic, consumerist society which also suffers from an advanced case of social amnesia. And yet I believe also that God exists, speaks and wills to transform us here, not elsewhere.

Christian existence is dialectical, it is about that speaking to and within a context. But it is also about God's challenging and, we hope, transforming that context. That raises questions, of course, and questions which cannot be answered glibly by saying that God speaks in history and/or in nature. But in what kind of history and whose nature?: God is also denied and profaned there, wherever and whenever people die of poverty, oppression, war or starvation and where and when nature is exploited and destroyed. The crucial question, then, is; where is God speaking?

Faith gives an answer to this, of course, but it is a cryptic answer, as Bonhoeffer suggests in his answer to the question, "Who am I?" concluding that:

> They mock me, these lonely questions of mine
> Whoever I am, Thou knowest, and God, I am thine!

What does this mean? It means, I suggest, that God speaks where he/she shows him/herself as the God who is both ground and yet in this world groundless, edged out of this world as Bonhoeffer puts it, on to the cross. If God speaks in history it is in history's underside. Official history, as J. B. Metz observes, is the history of the winners. But it is the losers, the poor, the oppressed and the forgotten, who speak to correct our amnesia, speaking from this dangerous memory to remind us of the God who was crucified in Jesus. The deeper one goes into this memory, the poorer it becomes in human terms, secret cities of the poor open out, filled with people whose names have never been heard except by the God who names them in Jesus and thus transfigures them then, and precisely there. There are millions of women among them but also millions of men. But the point is not their gender but their suffering.

All this is by way of introduction to my responses to Dr Elizabeth Moltmann-Wendel's provocative paper. But it is also a reflection on the topic of our Conference, "Christ in Context." After the large scope of previous papers is it not something of an anti-climax to begin, as the paper does, with what some would call "merely feminist" concerns? As they are set out in the first part of this paper, these concerns seem not merely ethnocentric but those of a small, privileged group of Western women, concerns which fade into insignificance in comparison with the creation which seems to be groaning around us in its agony of subjection. Granted that "the truth looks different from here", where women stand, are we not obliged also to see that "here" is situated in the "one world", not just in the already over-privileged and overly self-conscious first world?

Self reflection is a necessary starting point for theological reflection. But it can easily become self delusion since it is also to a greater or lesser extent, culturally conditioned. That is not to deny the challenge and scandal of women's oppression. That is an offence against the God in whose love there is no distinction between male and female, slave or free, Jew or Gentile, and doubly a scandal in the community which professes to live in his spirit and witness to his word. But to begin where the theologians the paper quotes do, by asking whether the figure of Jesus, a male, can serve as a point of identification for women today is to suggest that the human, indeed the biological, constitutes the only horizon of theological reflection. That is not to deny the importance of the biological to the contrary as we shall argue later, woman's body is crucial to her experience of self and thus of God. But it is to question the way it can be turned into an absolute and set over against — not the same as differentiated from — the male body, denying the inclusiveness of the new bodiliness and the new humanity which begins in Jesus.

Similarly, the objection that traditional "Christological reflection ... (which) concentrates ... on the understanding of his resurrection ... places the daughters of God off to the side" also misses the point of this new inclusiveness. The goal of christology is surely not to provide us with an image which corresponds to our felt needs but to discover to us new possibilities for our humanity. It is in this way that this image will not only "unfurl healing powers" for us as women, for our circumstances and our tragic world, but it will also be, as it were, ahead of us, challenging us, giving us to think, as a symbol does, speaking to us of the "so much more", the divine possibilities of our humanity. This is the way in which the humanity of Jesus will make us feel "good, whole and beautiful". But to see this only in terms of the body, indeed the "body beautiful" worshipped by our culture of consumerism, is not only to highlight the religious crisis of our time which Jürgen Moltmann speaks of but also to suggest that it is, in part at least, a crisis of the body.

The tendency to turn theology into a branch of anthropology or ethnology is a permanent problem for all theology, of course, but it is especially so for contextual theology. In the present instance, in the context of women's oppression, the objection to "male" images of Jesus surely confirms rather than undermines the binary division between male and female which is an aspect of the patriarchal system of domination and subordination and is therefore being contested. "It could even be (as the paper remarks, therefore) that the feminine image is just as deformed and through that would become dominating just like the maleness". It seems to me that what is wrong with the patriarchal paradigm is its tyranny, not its "maleness". The attempt to match God with needs created by this paradigm leaves us still within it, in a self-enclosed world, without grace, that is, without the possibility of interruption — one remembers Metz' remark that the best short definition of religion is interruption. We remain thus without real expectation, trapped in a world that is "human, all-too human", within the divisions which Jesus challenged, and within the rational confines of a culture without mystery, and are, in short, ideologically conditioned.

Theology is about the self-revelation of God. But that revelation occurs in a particular context and is mediated by language and symbols which in turn arise out of culture and tradition, the accumulation of thought, feeling and practice built up over centuries by the Christian community. Neither context nor tradition is innocent, therefore. As the paper's beginning implies, they shape and often distort even as they mediate revelation — hence, of course, women's difficulty with a Christology shaped by patriarchal culture, the difficulty with which the paper begins. But Feuerbach's shadow is a long one. Even theology, even feminist theology, can become merely the projection of emotional or social need. It, too, can become, in the words of Marx' critique of religion, a mere "generalized theory of the world, its spiritualistic point d'honneur". As Wittgenstein put it, when we think we are tracing the outline of something, we are often only tracing the outline of the framework through which we look at it. A picture can all too easily hold us captive.

Dr Moltmann-Wendel is aware of this, of course. That, I take it, is why, after this preliminary skirmish, she turns to Scripture, drawing from it an outline of the new, inclusive life offered to us there in Jesus. It is not entirely clear to me, however, how she bridges the gap between the concerns articulated in this first section and this new life. Hence, if it is not too impertinent, I would like to look at the hermeneutic involved, and then at the implications of her reading of this new life as, relationship, healing and awe. For, as I read this paper, the problem lies not, as some feminist theologians, Mary Daly, for instance, would have it, with Scripture, but with the traditional patriarchal reading of it. Apart from asking how to "find a rational method for our legitimate subjective and emotional proceedings ... substantiate our new approaches and make them understood to a wider population", however, the paper does not advert to this question of hermeneutics. But if we reflect on its conclusions it becomes clear that what it offers is a reading of Scripture which is more "poetical" than "scientific" — an unusual approach for theology which has for centuries allied itself with a Western rationality which does not see poetry as a form of knowledge. Indeed, many Christians, and not just fundamentalists at that, see poetry as irrelevant if not entirely useless, a form of language which — they say — operates at a merely aesthetic level, closed to the ethical, much less the religious. Therefore to read the language of Scripture as poetic, as having as the quality of relationship and thus as essentially dialogical rather than instrumental, to use Habermas' distinction, is also to challenge our present technocratic rationalistic culture which has conditioned so much of our theology.

As the paper sees them, the women in the Gospels respond dialogically to Jesus as to an appearing power, thus reading him symbolically rather than literally. He confronts them, as poetry does, with "a figured mode of being otherwise" — hence the emphasis on the "thaumazesthai", "the deep fear" they experience "as they come to the edge of their existence", hearing the words, "he is risen", at the empty tomb. There is thus, to use Janet Soskice's insight, an imbalance here between what is said and their experience. To put it another way, the rhetoric involved is what Ricoeur calls a "rhetoric of overturning" since its reference goes beyond anything they know to be the case. The women here model for us the kind of reading which Scripture properly demands, a poetic reading. As in reading poetry we enter a world projected by the text which is linguistic rather than "factual" the language of symbol rather than of sign, the world they discover is not immediate recognizable as their own but calls them to discover new possibilities of experience within it.

In this reading we preserve the necessary aporia of any talk about God, the sense of mystery, of the un-finished nature, of any thought about God something Professor Hardy has so helpfully insisted upon. The language of faith involves listening as well as speaking, receiving as well as giving, and prayer returns to its central position. Similarly, this rescues us from fundamentalism. Scripture is no longer a talking book, what Eberhard Jüngel has called "a ventriloquist's mask" which projects merely our own needs and interests, but a point of challenge and innovation. It may be written in human language. But that language witnesses to the fact that God has spoken, opening out new possibilities and Jesus becomes the great symbol of God — an Orthodox understanding, of course — or, the metaphor/model Janet Soskice writes about which allows us to express what we do not yet understand, advancing our understanding of it in the present.

The language of symbol, of poetry, then, involves the body as well as the mind, and this brings us to the next stage, to reflect on the possibilities Dr Moltmann-Wendel's paper also dwells upon. As she points out, Jesus in the gospel meets the women in their bodies, at the point of bodily need. In *Mark*, for instance, the word used for "body" in this experience of healing is the same word used for the crucified and risen body of Jesus. The body, the female body in particular, thus becomes crucial precisely because of its vulnerability, its subjection to force and necessity. This is a very different sense of the body, of course, from the one which prevails in our culture, the body beautiful, source of power and pleasure. This is a sense which privileges the male body even if it then proceeds to abolish bodiliness, turning it in effect into an extension of the machine, closed in itself, all but invisible, solitary, hygienically clean, imagined as immortal and invulnerable. Much of our theological reflection has been conditioned by this sense of the body. But this is not the way in which God meets us in Jesus.

The body of Jesus, as the paper insists, is vulnerable, open, given for us. The principle for understanding him is thus the hermeneutical principle Ricoeur articulates; "It is always through the fallen (and, I would add, the wounded) that the primordial shines through". In the mystery of the death and resurrection of Jesus we realise that a transfigured existence is possible, as Ricoeur put it, not through the triumph of reflection and rationality but through a felt appropriation of their limits. In this sense, the self becomes a goal rather than a given. Similarly the non-coincidence of self with self which is generated by oppression, exclusion and suffering points us in the direction of the economy of surplus and abundance manifested in the broken but triumphant body of Jesus. Fate and biology thus become occasions of grace, and Romans 8 takes on new significance with its image of the whole of creation groaning in its subjection, eagerly waiting for God to reveal to us the fullness of our life as sons and daughters, adopted into this largeness of life — the Greek word "adoption" is not merely a legal term but a term which is worked out in bodily terms.

We began to move, then, towards the Copernican revolution we have been looking for, a new paradigm which will enable us to overcome the tyranny of patriarchal Western culture dedicated as it is to control, exploitation and domination. Here the thought of the French feminist, Hélène Cixous, is helpful. She proposes two different economies. But, although she calls them the "masculine" and the "feminine", they are not biological categories. Rather they have to do with ways of being in the world. The "masculine" she calls the "economy of the proper" since it has to do with property, propriety, appropriation, with the technical/rational culture of exploitation characteristic of a Western culture today organized for the worship of what I like to call "the unholy Trinity", Mammon/God of money), Moloch (God of struggle) and Marilyn Monroe (ikon of human sacrifice to pursuit of mindless pleasure). The other, the "feminine", Cixous calls the "economy of grace". This economy has no sense of boundaries, its notes are generosity and movement-towards, and it essentially "pneumatic".

> If there is a 'propriety of woman', [she writes] it is paradoxically her capacity to depropriate unselfishly, body without end...She doesn't bid it over her body or her desire... Her libido is cosmic, just as her consciousness is world-wide... She alone cries and wishes to know from within, where she, the outcast, has never ceased to hear the resonance of fore-language. She lets the other language speak.

In this way the body becomes a point of inter-section not only between self and world but also between the world of objects and the world of meaning.

So the "Word made flesh" becomes also the World made experientially intelligible. The body is not to be separated from the mind, nor is it a mere distraction from the proper work of the mind. Rather it is the place of God's appearance and the means of our salvation, of healing, both bodily and spiritual. As the ultimate symbol, Jesus brings together body and spirit, fact and possibility, and does so dynamically, making our humanity new — the symbol gives us to "think" in a thinking done with the whole of ourselves.

This kind of knowing brings us much closer to other cultures, especially those of so called "primitive" peoples, the cultures that is, of most people on our planet, enabling us to receive the insights they have to offer us. It also expands the mutuality, sense of relationship, healing and wonder which the paper so rightly finds in the life of Jesus, and extends this life also to our relations with other living things. In turn, this enlarges the notion of community which is now seen not just in terms of action and ideas leading to action, but of existence, communion in life, and thus by implication in aspiration and suffering. The consequences for our models of church are obvious. The legal political model based on hierarchy and instrumental relationships gives way to one based on existing with, suffering with, rejoicing and hoping with the rest of creation. Nor does this community depend on geographical proximity or cultural identity. It can tolerate difference and is able to wait patiently in time, ready to receive the gifts of God in unexpected and unfamiliar places. At the same time, since God's power is manifest in the broken but healing, dying but living body of Jesus, a theology of this kind refutes the more nature-worship implicit in the emphasis some feminist theologians put upon the body. In this view, nature remains ambiguous since in his body Jesus is subject to the necessities which, Scripture tells us, are the consequences of our dangerous freedom which lead to suffering and death.

New models of God thus begin to emerge. As the paper reminds us, the experience of suffering and becoming new, of coming to the edge of existence in their experiences of birth, nurturing, vulnerability and death, gives women a peculiar access to the mystery of death and resurrection to the extent that manifests the relationality, openness and generosity of the life of the Trinity on the one hand and on the other of the vulnerability of love in Jesus a vulnerability which leads to newness of life, the body of woman becomes a particularly apt way of showing forth of the body of God. Instead of seeing Jesus, as Augustine does, as the virile male hero going to the cross as to his marriage bed, we may now see him, Nancy Klenk Hill suggests, in terms of a woman who died in childbirth. Woman's experience of birth, of being on the point between life and death, knowing and unknowing, the point of the risk and richness of love thus offers a special insight into the mystery of God in Jesus of life given for life. But the image broadens out, too, to become political in the widest sense, to include all those hungering and thirsting for justice and struggling for it, caught up in the one great act of giving birth throughout the world.

Woman's questions about the lordship of Jesus thus open out new ways of reading Scripture and of responding to the sufferings of our tragic world, and it is the great contribution of Dr Moltmann-Wendel's paper to have opened out these ways. It began with images of loss and oppression. But we conclude on the note of transformation with an image borrowed from Myra Jehlen which compares women with Archimedes, and, I would add, all the poor, marginalised, oppressed and despairing people of the world, trying as Archimedes did to lift the earth with a fulcrum, yet with no place from which to lift it. What the paper suggests, however, is that God's revelation to us in the mystery of the death and resurrection of Jesus offers that place and that that place may be found precisely in our bodies.

6

Christian Witness and the Transformation of Culture in a Society in Transition

John W. de Gruchy

Recent political developments have thrust South Africa into a state of social flux and transition. While the outcome of these developments is by no means clear or beyond doubt, there is good reason to believe that the end of apartheid is in sight, and that a non-racial and democratic society is in the process of formation. This sudden and surprising turn of events has raised the question of the role of the church and the nature of Christian witness in this transitionary phase, and in the new nation that is striving to be born. Even though responses of the past may still be relevant in some instances, they no longer seem as appropriate as they were. Yet given the present situation, which is full of contradictions and uncertainty, it is very difficult to formulate alternative responses which relate adequately to the emerging realities.

At the heart of the matter, theologically-speaking, is what H. Richard Niebuhr called the "perennial problem" of relating Christ and culture.[1] But this problem cannot be resolved theoretically on the basis of the models which Niebuhr describes, as though Christian witness and culture are static, pre-packaged entities. Indeed, culture in South Africa is itself diverse and contradictory, thus requiring different responses

1. H. Richard Niebuhr, *Christ and Culture,* (New York: Harper & Row, 1951).

even within the same historical context. Yet Niebuhr's concluding thesis holds, namely that faithful Christian witness, whether through confrontation or in solidarity with culture, contributes to its transformation in a way which points towards the coming of God's reign in Jesus Christ.[2]

Within South Africa two cultures, one European and dominant, and the other indigenous and subservient, have coexisted since the Dutch and British colonial powers and settlers gained control. Both the settler and the missionary church, with few exceptions, sided with the dominant culture. This has led to a compromised and ambiguous witness in which Christ has been made subservient to white interests. Yet there have always been some Christians who have confronted the dominant culture in the name of Christ and have affirmed the culture of the victims of oppression and exploitation. In more recent times, by far the largest number of Christians in South Africa have, in fact, been part of the oppressed, many of whom have sought to relate their culture to their faith, and their social expectations to the coming of God's reign in Jesus Christ.

Despite the ambiguity of the church's witness, the issues concerning Christ and culture have become increasingly clear, indeed, stark, especially during the past forty years of apartheid rule. The dominant Dutch Reformed Church theologically legitimated apartheid, thus making the gospel subservient to Afrikaner and white interests. At the same time prophetic voices within the churches proclaimed Christ against the dominant racist culture until eventually its underlying ideology was declared a heresy. In the process, especially for many black Christians, the gospel has become a means of liberation and social transformation, often in alliance with political ideologies. Now, as we enter an era of far-reaching change yet one full of contradictions, in which the old order fights desperately to survive and the new struggles to be born, the relationship between Christian witness and culture is becoming more ambiguous. Hence the need to discern the signs of

---

2. The 1989 Annual Congress of the Theological Society of South Africa was devoted to the theme "Christ and Culture Revisited" in which the work of H. Richard Niebuhr was re-examined in relation to the South African situation. See James R. Cochrane, "Christ and Culture: Now and Then," *Journal of Theology for Southern Africa,* June 1990, no. 71; D.J. Smit, "Theology and the Transformation of Culture -- Niebuhr Revisited," *Journal of Theology for Southern Africa,* September 1990, no. 72. See also Charles Scriven, *The Transformation of Culture,* (Scottdale: Herald Press, 1988).

God's judgment, grace and promise as these are becoming apparent in this period of transition.

Discerning the Kairos in a Period of Political Transition

When *The Kairos Document* [3] was drafted in 1986 South Africa was in social turmoil. Since the Soweto uprising ten years previously, which had been ruthlessly suppressed by the state, resistance and dissent had been kept in check by a national state security system of considerable power and influence. Nonetheless growing external and internal pressure forced the National Party government under P.W. Botha to initiate its programme of reform in the early eighties. But government reform did not mean any fundamental change in the structures of apartheid, let alone the sharing of power or its transference to the majority. Thus the new constitution and its tricameral Parliament instituted in 1983, which excluded the vast majority of blacks, triggered off an even greater campaign of resistance in the following years, leading to the declaration of a general State of Emergency in 1986, which was to last until 1990. Within that critical context of spiralling resistance, repression and violence, "the Kairos theologians" recognised a moment of judgment as well as an opportunity which called for direct Christian participation in the struggle, including acts of civil disobedience in resistance to government tyranny.

Since 1986 a series of events has dramatically changed the situation in South Africa, even though the National Party remains in power and the policy of apartheid and state security remain on the statute books. Indeed, the situation has become so fluid and full of contradictions that it is extremely difficult to analyse it without qualifications which befuddle clarity and prevent unambiguous prophetic and evangelical witness.[4] But the attempt must be made as such analysis is necessary for determining a culturally transformative Christian response.

---

3. *The Kairos Document: Challenge to the Churches, second edition,* (Johannesburg: Skotaville, 1986).

4. This paper had to be written by September 1990, nine months before its presentation. At the time of writing the situation in South Africa was extremely confusing, indeed volatile, so there is no certainty that this analysis will be accurate or appropriate in May 1991. This confirms the problem of relating "Christ and culture" in any static way.

Within the country the growth of the Mass Democratic Movement since 1986 kept up intense pressure on the government at a variety of levels, notably through labour and industrial action. Afrikanerdom, the power base of the National Party fragmented as more progressive elements within the Party pressed for more far-reaching and speedy reform, and began to speak of power sharing. The practical and political failure of apartheid, its basic immorality, and a growing awareness of the reality of the problems which it had created not only for blacks, but for the country as a whole, began to dawn on increasing numbers of whites. Economic pressure, partly through disinvestment and sanctions, together with an intensification of the liberation struggle by the African National Congress, especially at the diplomatic level, created severe problems for big business and the government. The long, drawn out conflict in Namibia and Angola, and some major military set-backs, made the war far too costly for South Africa in terms of lives, money and diplomatic relations. At the same time, it was also clear that the armed struggle of the liberation movements had little prospect of actually bringing about the downfall of the government.

The beginning of the peace process in Namibia, significantly aided by *perestroika* in the Soviet Union and the discrediting of communism in Eastern Europe, eventually led to Namibian independence and proved to be a catalyst which opened up new possibilities for change inside South Africa itself. This, coupled with a sudden change in National Party leadership which led to the election of F.W. de Klerk as State President, resulted in a series of government moves culminating in the unbanning of the liberation movements on February 2, 1990, the releasing of Mr Nelson Mandela from twenty-seven years of imprisonment two weeks later, and the beginning of a process of intense discussion between the government and the ANC to prepare the way for negotiations for a new non-racial and democratic South Africa. The decision by the ANC on August 6 to suspend the armed struggle is indicative of the speed and the extent to which these discussions have developed. Yet the ongoing debate within the ANC and other liberation movements on this very question indicates that unanimity has by no means been attained and there is considerable disagreement within the ranks. Hence the contradictory ways in which spokespersons have responded to them.

If there has been cautiously positive responses from the ANC to President de Klerk's initiatives, they have evoked strongly negative responses from the white right-wing, and unleashed a violent reaction from its more extreme elements. The significance of the right-wing, both amongst Afrikaners and a significant number of white English-speakers must not be under-estimated. At the same time, it must be recognised that the right-wing is not a new phenomenon, for the apartheid ideology it represents is precisely that which the National Party espoused and implemented since 1948. If anything, a significant section of the white electorate and the National Party has moved away from apartheid, while the Conservative Party and others to the right represent the traditional position of Afrikaner nationalism. The more the government and its former enemies engage in negotiations for a new non-racial and democratic society, the more its former supporters feel threatened and resist change. Within that equation it has also to be noted that many members of the security forces, especially within the police, are members of that right-wing or more conservative constituency. In other words, the right-wing can do and is doing a great deal to frustrate and thwart the birth of a new democratic nation even if it cannot prevent it from happening in the end.

Just as de Klerk's initiatives have sparked off a right-wing reaction, so they have also awakened far-reaching expectations amongst an increasingly impatient and frustrated majority black population. This can be seen in the escalation of strike action with the concomitant demand for higher wages, better living and working conditions, and a radical restructuring of education and health care in a country where the gap between rich and poor is enormous. Related to these demands has been a growing resistance to the privatization of the economy, and a call for a more socialist system. At the same time the legitimation of the liberation movement has led to an intensification of the struggle for power between the various groupings, notably the African National Congress (ANC), the Pan African Congress (PAC), the Azanian Peoples' Organisation (Azapo), and the Zulu nationalist movement Inkatha. This has erupted in a frightening spiral of violence notably in Natal and the Transvaal, some of it apparently tribal and ethnically based, some of it ideological and fueled by reactionary elements within the state security forces, but all of it rooted in the socio-economic ravages caused by apartheid.

The transitionary phase in which we find ourselves does not promise, then, an easy ride to non-racial, democratic freedom. The euphoria experienced on February 2, 1990, by liberals, progressives, and others involved in the struggle for justice and liberation, has been replaced, in the intervening months, by a new awareness of reality. While the emotional pendulum has swung wildly from moments of ecstatic celebration to frustrated and even fearful despondency, many have become aware of the long, hard road ahead of us. The wilderness journey en route to the Promised Land is strewn with obstacles and challenges which have to be met and overcome. Doctrines of inevitable historical progress are beguiling but dangerous, indeed, there are no guarantees that the transformation of culture will be a peaceful one. Developments after August 6, which should have signalled an end to conflict, indicate not only the fragility of the process towards negotiations, but even more the extent and depth of the problems created by centuries of oppression. To overcome three centuries of colonial and then apartheid domination overnight is impossible. At any point the process may collapse, and we may find ourselves embroiled in the violence of an all-out revolutionary conflict.

Despite this awesome prospect, certain things have happened which suggest that the process set in motion has already become irreversible. Whatever else may happen, it will be extremely difficult, indeed well nigh impossible, to return to the situation prior to February 2, 1990. In order to understand the reason for this it is necessary to understand why President de Klerk has risked his political future and that of his Party, indeed, white South Africa, in the way that he has. The simple answer is that not to do so entailed even greater risk and far more serious consequences for the country as a whole. Indeed, there is a profound sense in which de Klerk and Mandela need each other. Thus pre-eminent amongst the reasons for hope is the growing awareness within both the Nationalist government, the ANC, and many other groupings (though significantly not the PAC, AZAPO, and those of the white right-wing, including the official opposition, the Conservative Party) that the only way to avoid the violent destruction of the country is through negotiation for a new non-racial and democratic society. This represents a major shift of ground from the politics of domination, repression, confrontation and co-option, to the politics of negotiation. The tenacious commitment to the negotiation process which has been demonstrated thus far, despite severe strains, is indicative of the significance of what is taking place.

Thus, although the National Party remains in power and apartheid remains on the statute books, the government no longer appears to be the tyrannical regime described in *The Kairos Document.* Indeed, in a paper presented to the United Nations, Beyers Naudé and Wolfram Kistner, both strong critics of apartheid, spoke of the "interim legitimacy of the National Party government", thus justifying, from a Christian and theological perspective, the need for negotiation politics at this moment in time. But the question must now be asked concerning the role of

Christian witness in this hopeful yet fragile process. In order to discuss that, however, it is necessary that we examine the present location and role of the church within South African society.

The Church in South Africa as the Mirror Image of Cultural Division and Conflict

The Christian church in South Africa, which comprises the vast majority of the people, is not only confessionally and racially divided, but is itself a site of the larger social and political struggle. All the socio-political, cultural and economic divisions which stratify society, and which evoke different existential and political responses, are present within the church. Furthermore, each ecclesial group claims religious and theological legitimation for their varied and contradictory positions. Thus Christian witness is shot through with contradictions and ambiguities, trapped by its history and contemporary ideological struggles.

The obvious division which reflects this internal struggle within the church is the one usually drawn between the Dutch Reformed Church and those churches belonging to the South African Council of Churches (SACC). The Dutch Reformed Church has given apartheid its theological legitimation, while the SACC member churches have opposed the policy of apartheid and its implementation. The fact of the matter, however, is that the Dutch Reformed Church has itself become increasingly divided as white Afrikanerdom fragments, so much so that its more recent official position has been to withdraw from overt political comment and engagement for fear not only of exacerbating division within the church but also of further undermining Afrikaner culture and hegemony.

While the major parties in this Afrikaner fragmentation within the Dutch Reformed Church represent the conservative spectrum of white politics in South Africa, there are those who are also committed to a more progressive stance. In like manner, while the member churches of the SACC have all traditionally spoken out against apartheid, they have also been divided between those, mainly whites, who, though generally more liberal than their Afrikaner counterparts, have benefitted from apartheid, and the vast majority of their membership which, being black, has clearly been at the sharp end of government policy. *The Kairos Document* reflected these divisions within the DRC and SACC churches when it differentiated between "state", "church" and "prophetic" theologies.

Quite apart from the traditional divide between the Dutch Reformed and the SACC churches, post-World War II South Africa has seen the rapid growth of other more conservative and rightwing church groups, some of them Pentecostal and charismatic. In recent years they have, in fact, gained members from the mainline churches who have become disillusioned with their former church's political involvement. While all of these groups tend to be conservative in their political orientation, despite claims to political neutrality, some are actively right-wing. Indeed, the emergence of right-wing Christian groups in South Africa has become a matter of considerable concern during the past few years.[5] This was one of the main issues raised in *The Road to Damascus* document, the international successor to *The Kairos Document* produced by Christians in various "third world" countries in 1989.[6] In many respects, these groups have attempted to fill the gap created by the withdrawal of the Dutch Reformed Church as the overt legitimator of the state and its policies, especially during the reign of the national security system of the P.W. Botha era.

The church situation in South Africa is clearly more complex, then, than the traditional division represented by the Dutch Reformed Churches or the member churches of the SACC would suggest. By far the largest ecclesial group in South Africa is that designated as the African Indigenous Churches, whose membership is variously estimated between six and eight million. These Indigenous Churches are many and diverse, having considerable difficulty in working together as a unit, and there is considerable debate about their socio-political significance. But it is clear that they include within their membership a vast number of the socially uprooted black proletariat in South Africa, and that many are participants within the struggle for liberation within the trade unions and other bodies representative of the workers. Within that struggle the Indigenous Churches have sought to provide a means whereby African culture and Christian faith could be welded together, thereby providing an identity and structures of solidarity within the alienating environment created by the dominant apartheid, urban, and industrial society of twentieth century South Africa.

---

5. On "right-wing" Christian movements in South Africa, see the *Journal of Theology for Southern Africa,* no. 69, December 1989.
6. *The Road to Damascus: Kairos and Conversion,* a Document signed by Third World Christians from seven nations. (Johannesburg: Skotaville, 1989).

Many black Christians in South Africa nonetheless belong to the so-called mainline Churches, where they are invariably in the majority and, in recent years, have become prominent in leadership and in decision-making. By and large, in comparison with the Indigenous Churches, they tend to represent the better educated and, relatively-speaking, middle-class black community. Many of those who have provided leadership within the liberation struggle have their membership or roots within these Churches. Yet, having said that, here too the situation is a complex one, especially when we consider the extent to which blacks themselves are in ideological disagreement. The situation in the churches often mirrors the divisions one finds between the African National Congress and other charterist groups,[7] the Pan African Congress and its affiliates, the Azanian Peoples Organization (AZAPO), and Inkatha. In some instances, the tension between the groups has even led to situations where a minister or priest who shows partiality towards one position has had to flee for safety from his congregation, and in some instances, ministers have been killed. For reasons such as these, the bishops of the Anglican Church (Church of the Province of South Africa), decided in July 1990 that no ordained minister under their jurisdiction could belong to a political party. This very contentious decision did not mean that the Anglican Church was taking a neutral position on political issues, but that in such circumstances it could not fulfil either its prophetic or pastoral role if the clergy were card-carrying members of political parties.

It must be recognised that these ideological divisions, and the serious divisions which they reflect in the community and in the church, are partly but not only the result of apartheid. The strategy of apartheid has been to separate and divide people not only along white and black racial lines, but also in terms of other ethnic and tribal groupings. Those in power have sought to make political capital out of the ideological and tribal divisions of its opponents by exacerbating and fueling them. This is the reason why any discussion of cultural pluralism in South Africa is so fraught with difficulty. It immediately creates suspicion. The diversity of culture has been manipulated over many years in order to maintain white dominance. This abuse of cultural diversity should not

---

7. "Charterist" refers to the acceptance the Freedom Charter adopted by the African National Congress in 1955. Organisations such as Cosatu (Congress of South African Trade Unions) and the UDF (United Democratic Front) are Charterist.

blind us to its reality, but should rather make the church even more committed to the struggle for a non-racial, non-tribal democracy.

Christian Witness to the Promise and Hope of the Transformation of Culture

Thus far we have used the word "culture" without reflecting either on its meaning or its significance in the struggle for a non-racial and democratic society in South Africa. By "culture" is normally meant the social heritage of particular groups and nations which binds them together and gives them their identity. "Culture", in this view, is a social construction which is normally developed over a long period of time, a heritage of shared values, languages, customs, beliefs and worldviews. While this understanding of culture is undoubtedly important, it is inadequate and dangerous. When people try to preserve their culture as a static entity, it either dies and becomes an object of nostalgia, or it becomes a source of on-going conflict. Indeed, as a leader within the ANC, Barbara Masekela, points out: "In societies where social and political power is unequally distributed; where the dominant group has a distinct culture, that cultural pattern becomes hegemonic."[8] This means that other cultures are either suppressed or turned into "ethnological curiosities", but it also leads to the development of counter cultures of protest and resistance. Thus, in considering the Christian response to culture much depends upon whether we are speaking of cultures of domination, resistance, or the emergent culture of a nation in the process of being conceived and born.

Culture, truly understood, is not something which we simply inherit and pass on to the generation which follows us, rather it is a dynamic process in which its various elements, including such fundamental components as language and values, change and develop in response to new historical developments. Thus Buti Tlhagale rightly insists that culture need not just be a reflection of a "social heritage" but that "understood in its utopian dimension" it allows for "freedom and

8. Barbara Masekela, "We are not returning empty handed," *Die Suid-Afrikaan,* August 1990, p. 39.

creativity" and therefore the humanization of a new society.[9] Understood in this way, our various cultural heritages in South Africa only retain creative significance when they provide us with resources for responding to present challenges. Then they become sources of transformation which help us shape not only the present but also the future. In what way then, does this understanding of culture as dynamic process relate to our understanding of the gospel of God's reign in Jesus Christ?

Christian witness has as its fundamental presupposition the conviction that in and through the death and resurrection of Jesus Christ and the gift of the Spirit, God's liberating and reconciling power has become operative in the world as a whole in a new and decisive way which leads to human and social wholeness. Such witness does not take place in the realm of ideas, but is a witness of word and deed, of critical reflection and action, in which Christians engage the world in a transforming praxis shaped by its anticipation that God's liberating reign in Jesus Christ. Thus Christian witness introduces into society, and especially amongst its victims, a spirit of hope, indeed, a utopian expectation or a longing for change here and now in terms of the ultimate promise of God's reign.

All of this finds remarkable expression in the letter to the Ephesians where Christ is proclaimed as the destroyer of enmity between Jew and Gentile, and the transformer of their divided and competing cultures so that they can become participants together in a new social reality. Thus central to the gospel is that in Jesus Christ God has set us free from the bondage of closed, static cultures, and opened up the possibility for the birth of the new in which "Jew and Gentile, slave and free, men and women" can be united in one body. The church is thus called to be a penultimate sign of this new humanity, pointing to its ultimate fulfillment in the coming of God's reign. Such a confession of Jesus Christ is, however, inevitably a challenge to the prevailing and competing cultures, and is always in conflict with those dominant cultures which lead to the oppression of others. Such cultures seek to remain static, closed to the future, and therefore resistant to change which serves the interests of its victims.

The letter to the Ephesians also reminds us that the proclamation of the gospel of Christ crucified, at the same time as it reconciles, also leads

---

9. Buti Thlagale, "Culture in an Apartheid Society," *Journal of Theology for Southern Africa,* no. 51, June 1985, p. 33.

to an intensification of the struggle against the "principalities and powers of this world."[10]

Thus a genuine witness to the transforming and reconciling power of Jesus Christ within society will, like Jesus himself, encounter strong opposition, and those who engage in it will inevitably participate vicariously in the death of the old order and the birthpangs of the new. Precisely for this reason, Christian witness, and the hope which sustains it, does not assume inevitable progress; it knows only too well the reality of sin as this is embodied in the human will-to-power and vested interests. There will inevitably be many set-backs on the road to freedom, justice and peace. But it is of the essence of Christian witness that it nevertheless anticipates the coming of God's reign in the crucified Messiah, and therefore points through the suffering of the past and the present to the promised future.

In the light of this understanding of Christian witness, it should be apparent that the gospel addresses situations of transition with a peculiar directness. Situations of transition are quite literally periods "between the times" (*zwischen den Zeiten*), that is, more than at other more settled moments, they reflect the eschatological character of history. Indeed, the faithful proclamation of the gospel itself helps to create such moments of contradiction, flux and transition, as the old gives way to the new. In other words, from the perspective of the gospel, we must understand what is happening in society as related to both God's judgment and grace in history. It is therefore an opportunity for faithful Christian witness to point in hope beyond the inevitable confusion of the present to the possibilities which this historical moment promises for social transformation. How then are we to relate such Christian witness to the specific realities which have been thrust on our agenda in this *kairos* moment, not least by the gospel itself?

The Role of the Church as Bearer of Christian Witness in this Period of Transition

Since the beginning of the new period of political transition there have been various signs that some church leaders and churches which have been in the forefront of the church's struggle against apartheid, have begun to reassess their political role. One such sign was Archbishop

10. See Edward Schillebeeckx, *Christ: The Experience of Jesus as Lord,* (New York: Crossroad, 1981) p. 216f.

Desmond Tutu's announcement towards the end of 1989 that with the release from prison or the unbanning of leaders within the liberation movement, and, indeed, the unbanning of the organisations themselves, he would no longer need to fulfil the same political role which he had hitherto played in the struggle against apartheid. By this he did not mean that he would withdraw from prophetic involvement in the struggle for social justice, but that his role would be more pastorally oriented. A more controversial sign was the decision taken in July 1990 by the bishops of the Anglican church that no priest could belong to a political party. A further indication of the re-thinking that is currently taking place, and of possible serious disagreements in the formulation of Christian response, is the proposed Church Leaders' Conference planned for November 1990.[11]

Whatever re-thinking might be taking place on the political role of the church and its leaders, it is imperative that the redefinition of that role should in no way lead to a compromise in Christian witness for a just non-racial and democratic society. Indeed, in so far as the ending of apartheid as a form of legislated socio-economic domination and oppression based on race neither means that the social forces which produced it, nor the culture which it created have been overcome, the prophetic struggle against injustice must continue. The social transformation of South Africa from that of structured apartheid to a non-racial democracy requires not only the ending of white domination, but the creation of a new democratic and inclusive culture which will enable the building of a new nation. This means that the struggle against apartheid will and must continue not only until the constitutional birth of a new non-racial and democratic nation, but until the roots of apartheid are themselves eradicated. It is precisely for this reason that our focus is not simply upon socio-political change, but the transformation of culture itself.

---

11. After an initial resistance on the part of the SACC, due to the fact that the Conference was originally to have been convened by the State President, the Conference is now to be chaired jointly by the Revd. Frank Chikane, General Secretary of the SACC, and Dr. Louw Alberts, a lay leader within the Dutch Reformed Church and representative of more conservative evangelical and charismatic groups. As this paper was written prior to that conference it was not possible to determine its significance. What is significant, however, is the recognition of the need for the church in South Africa to engage in a process of consultation within its own ranks during this period of political transition.

Furthermore as the struggle against apartheid nears its climax, so other forms of oppression, and other issues of great importance for the well-being of society, become increasingly obvious. Although the oppression of women has always been endemic to society, and even more to an apartheid society, the struggle against apartheid has so focussed on the racial aspect that the gender issue has been suppressed to a large extent. From the perspective of the gospel this has never been right, and it is no longer possible for the church to remain silent. The struggle for a non-racial and democratic society means a society in which all are equal irrespective of race or gender.

Perhaps above all else, the struggle for justice in this period of transition, and therefore in the laying of the foundations for a new society, has to do with the restructuring of the economy and the equal access of all to the resources of the country. Apartheid has not only meant racial segregation, it has also meant monopolistic as well as a form of state capitalism which has virtually excluded black participation from its benefits. Apartheid has left a legacy of massive poverty, vast unemployment, and a lack of adequate or any housing and education for millions of people. The rapidly expanding population (fifty million projected by the turn of the century) of whom already seven million are squatters on the periphery of rapidly growing urban centres, will increasingly exacerbate these problems. Contrary to the gospel, the church generally has a dismal record in South Africa in relation to economic and labour issues. It is of vital importance that Christians ensure that the economic restructuring of the country does not favour the rich at the expense of the poor, but on the contrary results in a just distribution of wealth. In this regard it must be noted that the South African Communist Party has, since its unbanning, taken on a new lease of life — ironically when compared to what is happening in Eastern Europe — and that there is now an urgent need for Christians to enter into dialogue with Marxists in South Africa, especially on economic issues and those of human rights.

A final dimension of the ongoing struggle for justice is the urgent matter of the stewardship of the environment, and the need to relate this to matters of social justice and political restructuring. The South African environment, despite its natural beauty and resources, is in a critical situation, and there is every indication that the situation is worsening every year. Thus, once again, the urgent need for the church to insist on the development of environmental policies which maintain the integrity of creation, and not only ensure survival but also enhance the quality of life.

Throughout the period of transition, then, Christian witness implies continued resistance to what is unjust and false, and continued protest on behalf of what is just and true. At the same time, in so far as the present government moves beyond apartheid, and, hopefully, as a new democratic government comes into being, so Christian witness may mean critical solidarity more than protest and resistance. This shift in Christian witness does not mean that resistance may no longer be appropriate in certain instances within the process of transition, or even once a non-racial and democratic society has been established. On the contrary, critical solidarity means that the church remains prophetic in its stance towards the emergent new nation, but now on the basis of a shared commitment to the realisation of that new nation.

All of this suggests that there is not one model for relating the church and state, the church and politics, but that ways of doing so have to be continually worked out as circumstances and contexts change. In some historical moments the church as an institution might have to act in a direct, interventionist way, as has happened during the past decades in South Africa. The reason for this is that the political organisations representing the majority of the people have been banned, and their leaders imprisoned, killed or exiled. Thus church leaders like Desmond Tutu and Allan Boesak assumed a role which, in other circumstances, would not be their's insofar as they remain church leaders. But now that the African National Congress and other anti-apartheid political movements and organisations have been unbanned, and their leaders have become involved in the political process once again, we have a new situation. The church as an institution still has a politically prophetic and critical role to fulfil, but its participation in the shaping of policies and programmes may well be more the responsibility of its individual members.

What is of great importance, however, is that the role of the church in the shaping of a new nation is not understood in triumphalist terms. The church in South Africa does have a major role to play, not least because the vast majority of the population in the country claim to be Christian. But we must always become a little uneasy when we speak of the role of the church in nation building. There are far too many instances in the past when this has meant a denial of the gospel, a triumphalism which is the very antithesis of the message of the cross. The church and Christians have to recognise not only the rights of other communities of faith, but also that the way in which they participate in the political process has to be shaped by the gospel. Failure to recognize that has led to serious compromises in Christian witness, not least in South Africa.

The struggle is not one in which the church triumphally seeks to guard its own territory and claims, but concerns the transformation of society, the birth of a new culture of human solidarity, freedom and dignity which, in some significant measure, anticipates the coming of God's promised kingdom. Christians must share together with all other people of goodwill, moral commitment and faith, in ensuring that those values which have given humanity its dignity and freedom are protected and upheld both in the process of transition and in the building of a democratic culture and new nation.

A Witness to Humanizing Values in the Building of a New Nation

After a visit to South Africa, Eberhard Jüngel observed that since "the participants in the conflict are mainly Christians, and the Christian faith is therefore recognised as being vital to co-existence, church and theology have the chance (and therefore the task) of finding a *common* language that will serve coexistence by making it possible to deal with conflict." Jüngel went on to say:

> By such a common language, which should help truth come into its own, one could perhaps succeed in changing enmity into objective opposition. Without a common language to make a culture of responsible conflict possible, enmity will increase.[12]

The problem is, of course, that while the majority of South Africans claim to be Christian and therefore regard in some way the biblical narrative as normative for their lives, from what we have seen, the way in which they read and understand that story varies considerably. This derives from the fact that South Africans "live in different symbolic universes."[13] The way in which reality is perceived, and the way in which people respond to its demands, is different. The reason for these differences is complex, rooted as they are in very different cultural backgrounds and historical experiences. But they have been severely

---

12. Eberhard Jüngel, "Reclaiming the Word," unpublished paper, quoted by Dirk J. Smit, "Through Common Stories to a Common Language: Interpreting Biblical Narratives in an Ideological Conflict." Unpublished paper presented at the American Academy of Religion, Anaheim, November, 1989, p. 2.
13. Smit, *ibid.*, p. 13.

exacerbated by apartheid, by the ideologies which have emerged to legitimate or oppose it, and by the material interests of the conflicting groups.

Thus, while there may be a common biblical story to which appeal can be made in the interests of reconciliation and the building of a common culture based on shared values, this has to be understood in relation to the intense "hermeneutical struggle" which has been waged in South Africa during the past decades. In other words, by simply appealing to the gospel as a means to reconcile people, or by assuming that a common commitment to the normative narrative of Scripture, without getting to grips with the social and ideological forces which shape and determine the way in which the gospel is understood, is naive.

We have purposively indicated that the Christian witness we have in mind is engaged in the struggle for a non-racial and democratic society in South Africa. An underlying assumption and conviction is, therefore, that while a non-racial democracy cannot and must not be equated with the kingdom of God, it holds out the promise of a social order most consonant with the vision of the kingdom at this historic moment in South Africa. This clearly does not mean that it is only possible to be a Christian or the church within such a socio-political order; nor does it mean that the cry for life uttered by the oppressed can be fully met by the restructuring of society; and it does not necessarily mean that there is only one possible political structure which can embody the vision. It simply means that the human longing for dignity, freedom, equity and justice, which will find its ultimate fulfillment in the kingdom of God, can be penultimately best met in a society which strives to embody those values in its political structures. Which means that in South Africa the access to power and resources has to be open equally to all, and the use of power and resources has to be accountable to all.

One of Bonhoeffer's concerns in the writings which now comprise his *Ethics* was to stress the importance of Christians sharing with other people, irrespective of their religious faith and commitment, in the struggle to maintain values essential to the well-being of society. Apartheid has led to the subversion of fundamental human values, it has created a dehumanizing culture not unlike that which Bonhoeffer experienced during the Third Reich. Apartheid has led to a disrespect for law and authority, the cheapening of life, the destruction of the family, the subversion of the truth with lies, the manipulation of natural cultural differences, the abuse of human rights, the strengthening of the rich through corruption at the expense of the poor. The very values which, it was claimed, undergird "Christian civilization", and which we were supposed to be fighting for in the struggle against "godless communism", are the values which have been undermined if not destroyed.

As the drama of change unfolds in South Africa, so it becomes increasingly apparent how complex are the issues with which we have to deal. To speak of the struggle for a social order based on the values of equity and justice is necessary rhetoric, and it unites all who are engaged in the struggle for liberation; but to work out in practice what this means given the realities of the situation in which we find ourselves, soon reveals not only ideological but also analytical and strategic differences. These differences are certainly apparent amongst Christians and within the churches even amongst those committed to the struggle for liberation and justice. Thus we have to remind ourselves constantly of the gap between the rhetoric of democracy and the achieving of a democratic society; the rhetoric of utopian longing and hope, and the often harsh realities which confront us with different and sometimes contradictory options for action. This is not meant to decry utopian longing, on the contrary, for it is precisely such hope which gives direction and sustains both Christian witness and the struggle itself. But it does mean that we must recognise the enormous task facing those Christians who are actually engaged on the ground, those who are seeking to give embodiment to their hopes within the limitations of those resources and options which are available to them.

At the same time it must be recognized that "merely appealing to the practical power of the Christian story will not lead to a common perspective, praxis or language."[14] What is required is a fundamental change, a *metanoia*, which enables those who are guilty, those who have oppressed others, those who are privileged, to see things from the perspective of the victims of society, from the perspective of those who have suffered and continue to suffer as a result of oppression. Thus when we speak about Christian witness and the transformation of culture, we are speaking about Christian praxis in which the church identifies and suffers with and on behalf of the victims of oppression, takes their side in the struggle for justice, in fact, is a church of the victims; and yet a church which represents the oppressors, whether this means confronting them with the demands of God's justice, or vicariously accepting their guilt as the church's own.

---

14. Smit, *ibid.*, p. 19.

Identification with the Victims of Oppression and Representative of the Guilty

Paradoxically, partly because the church does represent a diversity of culture and ideology it also embodies the potential of enabling the reintegration and healing of society. Thus Jüngel's observations about the potential within the church for creating a common culture may be naive at one level, but they do also point to a "second naivete" which is essential to Christian witness, namely its "hope against hope" in the reconciling power of the gospel, the utopian vision of the promised Messianic reign of God, a message which always appears to be foolish and even a scandal, but which, for Christians at any rate, is the meaning of the crucified Jesus of Nazareth, and therefore the hope of the world.

Insofar as the church in South Africa is representative of the majority of the people, it is as much a representative of those who have been oppressors as it has been of the oppressed. This is part of the reason why the witness of the church has been so ambiguous and compromised. Yet it also is a reason why the church holds out promise for social transformation and the building of a new nation. The problem has not been the fact that it has included people from every sector of life, with their divergent interests, backgrounds and perspectives. The problem has been the way in which it has related to these divergent realities. Instead of identifying with the interests of the victims of oppression, the church has too often identified with the interests of those in power, the dominant culture. Or, when the church has been identified with the victims, it has been unable to relate to those in power.

Identification with the victims of society indicates that the church's relationship with those who suffer oppression of various kinds is fundamental to its witness. It must also be recognised that the victims of society change as society changes. In other words, we are not advocating any neutrality on the part of the church when we speak of its ministry to its total constituency. Commitment to the gospel of Christ crucified means, amongst other things, a commitment to the victims of society. This means taking sides with and participating in the struggle of the victims for justice, human dignity, and liberation. It means a basic commitment to human rights. The church has no other option if it wishes to remain Christian. But at the same time the church has a ministry to those within the dominant culture, whether they participate wittingly or not in the oppression of others.

This ministry has several facets other than critical confrontation. It is a ministry that has a necessary pastoral-evangelistic dimension, that is, a ministry seeking the conversion of those who dominate others, and a ministry which seeks to deal with their fear as well as their guilt. *The Road to Damascus* document was subtitled *Kairos and Conversion* precisely to indicate that the task of this critical moment is not only resistance to oppression, but the conversion of the oppressors. Indeed, the continuous conversion of all Christians.[15] The Institute for Contextual Theology, which was responsible for *The Kairos Document*, with this in mind, has now developed a programme of "ministry to whites" so that they too can participate in the birth of a new non-racial and democratic nation.

Fundamental to this process is the need to come to terms with and overcome the dominant and oppressive role which whites have played in history. This is a major problem, indeed, a major stumbling block en route to the birth of a new culture. Most whites have either uncritically accepted the dominant view of history, or they have become victims of a form of social amnesia in which the past is virtually blotted out of their consciousness. A large part of the reason for this is a suppressed sense of guilt, a phenomenon which also accounts to some extent for the violence of the extreme right-wing. But even the National Party which has now acknowledged the failure of its own policies, and is seeking a path to negotiation and reconciliation, has yet to confess its guilt for apartheid. There are signs that this is beginning, but the tendency amongst the majority of whites is to let "bygones to be bygones," an attitude which fails to deal with the immense hurt and suffering which apartheid has caused. It signifies a failure to grasp the extent of the oppressive suffering which has afflicted blacks in South Africa for such a long period, and which continues to do so even at this time of transition.

The transformation of culture requires a remembering of the oppressive suffering caused by apartheid, indeed, an awareness that that suffering remains very-much with us at present. The failure of whites to come to terms with their role in the history of oppression, and therefore their guilt, will actually prevent them from participating in the birth and development of a new nation. It will certainly mean a failure to recognise the justice of those calling for reparation and restitution, indeed, a failure to actually understand fully and heed the cry of the victims. There are remarkable parallels between this and the failure of Germany to come to terms with the Holocaust, even within the church. But as in that context, so in South Africa there is a fundamental need for

15. *The Road to Damascus*, ch. 4.

the church to bear witness to Christ's call to genuine repentance and thus a confession of guilt without which the deep hurts and suffering of the past cannot be healed.[16] At the very least, the church has to act vicariously on behalf of the guilty and point the way towards genuine reconciliation.

These two facets of Christian witness — identification with the victims, and representation of the guilty — are two-sides of the same ministry. Both are essential to the transformation of society. The birth of a new nation cannot simply take place at the level of constitutions and socio-economic programmes, it has to deal with the hurts and angers of the past, as well as the fears and anxieties of the present, both at an emotional, spiritual level, as well as at a practical level. Hence the need for the church to act vicariously and representatively on behalf of white South Africa in the process of confessing guilt for the sins of apartheid, repenting, and engaging in acts of restitution and reparation.

This re-orientation or *metanoia is* not an end in itself, but the beginning of that conversion, of which *The Road to Damascus* document speaks, which takes place within the context of the transformation of society itself. In other words, we are not saying that what is required is a personal conversion which will then lead to social transformation, but that within the struggle for social transformation, genuine personal conversion becomes a possibility, and that this in turn becomes fundamental to the creation of a new culture. Hence Christian witness means enabling people to see the evangelical implications, that is, the liberating possibilities of what is now happening in history, by discerning them from the perspective of the gospel of Jesus Christ, the crucified yet risen one.

Given the fact that the major stumbling block to the just transformation of society is human self-interest, and that in a period of uncertainty and transition there is an intensification of what has always been a high level of distrust, fear, hatred, frustration, with the consequent polarisation of factions and the periodic outbreak of violence, Christian witness thus has a crucial pastoral and evangelical role to play. No institution within society has the same pastoral access to people, oppressed and oppressor alike, the same confessed commitment to personal conversion, or the same resources, as the church to respond in

16. See John W. de Gruchy, "Confessing Guilt in South Africa Today in Dialogue with Dietrich Bonhoeffer," *Journal of Theology for Southern Africa,* June 1989, no. 67.

a transformative way to the human factors which bedevil the process of just social change.

If the struggle against apartheid has gone on for generations, all of this suggests, nonetheless, that the struggle for the development of a sustainable and just new nation will likewise stretch well into the future. Changing laws is one thing; changing the "habits of the heart" as well as the socioeconomic realities of the present, is another. The process is fraught with dangers and problems, and there is no guarantee of success. Certainly there is no easy way of circumventing conflict and suffering in the process because the nature of the change required threatens deeply entrenched attitudes and jealously guarded material interests, and evokes considerable uncertainty, fear and hostility. The powers of alienation, which have been suppressed and held in check by state security, are being unleashed as each step is taken towards negotiation.

Thus the new phase of the struggle is and will be no less demanding and costly than previous stages, at least in its initial phases, as has already proved the case. But the promise of the birth of a new nation holds out the promise that the oppressive suffering caused by apartheid, as well as the suffering of those who have been engaged in the struggle to bring it to an end, will become redemptive and thus not be in vain.

The *kairos* of this transitionary period is, then, essentially a moment of grace, an opportunity for transformation. If the opportunity is not seized, if the church fails in its witness, then it could become a terrifying, apocalyptic scene of judgment in which all hope is destroyed and the worst fears of many are fulfilled. Yet faithfulness to the gospel means being captive to the promise of a "new heaven and a new earth", and therefore an ongoing commitment to the struggle for the just transformation of society. For Christians, faith in the God of Jesus Christ also means hope for the world. As the pendulum wings between optimism and pessimism, as people grow tired and cynical, despairing of an end to the struggle for justice, so Christians "hope against hope", interpreting what is happening in the light of God's promise. Unless this hope is kept alive there can be no commitment to the struggle for a non-racial and democratic society, because without that vision and conviction it is not possible to witness to Jesus Christ.

Response by Daniel W. Hardy

First of all, I must thank John de Gruchy for a paper which I have found most perceptive and helpful, not only for the understanding of the nature and problems of Christian witness in South Africa, but also for the understanding and practice of Christian faith and life in places where comparable situations occur. And that means everywhere, for the range of issues and responsibilities which he discusses are found universally. While he does not universalize, such a truly particular view is surprisingly transferable to other particular situations, and almost totally so. That makes it all the more urgent for us here to work with him to refine his analysis and comment, for by doing so we aid both him and ourselves. It is in that spirit that I approach the task of discussing his paper.

It is worth adding that the task he undertook in his paper is astonishingly difficult. It is commonplace today for the Christian witness to fall into one of two traps, either to use Christian faith to bless — prematurely and uncritically — situations which have a purely secular provenance and prospect, or to use the authoritativeness of Christian faith as a substitute for careful consideration of situations and developing a fully Christian response. These alternatives might be called pragmatic liberalism and traditionalism respectively; popular as they may be, they are both inadequate. It is much more demanding, and much more rare, to find a genuinely Christian and theological reaction to a situation which is pragmatically derived; and that is what John de Gruchy has given us. For me to ask for it to be developed in some places, or modified in others, in no way detracts from what he has done.

As much as theologians would prefer it otherwise, human life and institutions are variable, constantly changing and highly contingent; and this renders theological response to them transitional. Yet there is a dynamic which can be found even in this variety and contingency. To it can be related the fundamental dynamics of Christian faith, and this — ongoingly corrected both by the situation and by Christian faith — is the Christian witness.

Following the first of these strands, that of finding the dynamic within the variety and contingency of human life and institutions, John de Gruchy traces the dynamics which led up to the present situation. I would like to start by making some comments about the descriptive analysis through which he finds the dynamic of human life and institutions in the recent history of South Africa. He rightly finds many factors — social, cultural, political, economic, religious — folded into each other; it is a complex dynamic. But there is one point at which it needs to be enlarged. It seems to me that natural factors need much more attention than this analysis provides. For example, land and the ability to derive benefit from it are not simply economic issues, but need to be regarded as important in their own right. But I will say no more about that.

That his analysis is so complex is due recognition of the complexity of an advanced society. But it needs to be seen that this very complexity is the product of cultural creativity. An important feature which is implicit in John de Gruchy's description, but which he does not explicitly recognize, is the *creative re-ordering by human culture* of the contextuality in which it (the culture) exists. Through culture human beings creatively re-order those factors which form their existence, but especially so where their own interests are at stake. In South Africa, this works both ways: whites culturally generate structures by which to secure and enhance their own privilege, and their culture continues to adapt them to serve their interests as long as circumstances permit. The blacks do likewise, but from a position of relative weakness, perhaps because they have neither the land nor (broadly speaking) the cultural expertise in the agricultural, social, cultural, political, economic, and religious techniques which are used by the whites to secure and enhance their position.

There is — or was — therefore an asymmetry between whites and blacks in the creative re-ordering of contextuality, by which the whites maintained their privileged position. What seems to have modified this asymmetry was the growing skills of the blacks in the creative cultural use of the factors by which a society is formed, despite counter-pressures by the whites, together with the pressures exerted by the well-developed techniques employed by other nations. The cumulative effect of these new cultural skills was a drastic limitation imposed on the creative adaptation by which the whites had secured and enhanced their position.

One of the most interesting effects of the asymmetry was the establishment of boundaries. What I have called 'the creative re-ordering of contextuality' by the whites, achieved through their use of the factors by which a society is formed, resulted in a society identified by its *absolute closure*. And the continuing use of the various means of cultural society-formation constituted the *repetition* by which the society achieved its stability. By all the standards usual in social analysis, the result would have been a static, sterile society, deprived as it was of the range of dynamic variation characteristic of a healthy society.

By this absolute, self-repeating closure, blacks were exteriorized (alienated), re-conceived (their ontological status re-defined as non-being, in the words of Enrique Dussel), and instrumentalized as sources from which energy could be drawn. The results were even worse, because — by various symbolical means — this alienation was implanted psychologically in the blacks themselves, with such efficacy that domination by the whites could be maintained with a minimum of force. Incidentally, this is one of the most injurious aspects of the legacy of *apartheid* which will require healing.

Conversely, the most interesting change which was produced in this asymmetry by black resistance was the change from absolute closure to a *relative closure*. The variety of social techniques by which they were 'socially eliminated' were 'undone', and the effect was to allow blacks (not only Mandela) stature, to such an extent that discussions needed to follow with the ANC. But more broadly, this produced the possibility of the ongoing interaction-in-diversity (the development of contextuality) which is required in a healthy society. And, interestingly, with the demise of absolute closure, social diversity (fragmentation) occurs on both sides.

Apart from these glosses, I do not wish to add to John de Gruchy's descriptive analysis. But the glosses are important, because they reveal a cultural dynamic of creative re-ordering, a *cultural history*, in which there is a move to absolute closure, and from absolute to relative closure, though still leaving scars which would need healing. It needs to be asked what significance there is in this. Is it, for example, a move into the sterility and damage — both to the self and to the other — which characterize sin? And is the move to a more healthy social diversity, occasioned by the black resistance, a sort of secular-social justification? And what is the motivating source of this dynamic? It is interesting that de Gruchy does not discuss these questions.

John de Gruchy's paper recognizes the importance of cultural dynamics; this is one of its most valuable contributions. Culture is, he says,

> a dynamic process in which its various elements, including such fundamental components as language and values, change and develop in response to new historical developments... [and] "understood in its utopian dimension" it allows for "freedom and creativity" and therefore the humanization of a new society.

If I am right, however, cultures do not simply 'develop in response to new historical developments'; they also produce them.

The interesting question, then, is whether the creative cultural dynamic which I have traced functions as something like a *preparation* for the engagement of the Gospel with culture which John de Gruchy then goes on to discuss, and if so how God is involved in the preparation. I wonder whether de Gruchy can explain these things.

De Gruchy's *theological* discussion begins, however, in the fluid situation of the present. He finds transitional periods, where there is fluidity and ambiguity, are the times which reflect the eschatological character of history, and those in which the gospel addresses us with 'particular directness'. And it is the task of the Church to witness to the 'promise and hope of the transformation of culture', relating 'what is happening in society... to both God's judgment and grace in history', based on the fundamental presupposition 'that in and through the death and resurrection of Jesus Christ and the gift of the Spirit, God's liberating and reconciling power are operative in the world as a whole in a new and decisive way' as anticipating the reign of God in Jesus Christ. In other words, we are to address culture with judgment and hope which draws on these Christian presuppositions, thereby to promote the opening and re-shaping of culture — and to reverse self-enclosed cultures. I want to address two questions in this connection.

Though it is a widespread practice, I am uneasy about the strategy of placing the fundamental dynamic of Christian faith — the death and resurrection of Jesus Christ and the gift of the Spirit through which God liberates and reconciles in the world — in the position of a premise whose effect is mediated through the witness of the Church. Unless I misunderstand, this confines the economy of God's salvation of mankind to the originative events of Christian faith, whose effects are then continued through the ongoing life of the Spirit in the dynamic of the history of the Church. This seems to limit the possibility of finding the dynamic economy of the Trinitarian life of God in cultural dynamics *per se;* instead, the Spirit forms cultural dynamics through the witness of the Church.

What is from my point of view a further problem arises in the *content* of the contribution which the Spirit makes to the development of culture. Fundamentally, the contribution is a prophetic one, as a struggle against injustice, through the formation of a 'new democratic and inclusive culture which will enable the building of a new nation'(p.10). But what is advanced as the means of forming such a culture are *principles for it* rather than the dynamic participation of the *Spirit in* the history of the culture. This is in itself problematic. It is not unlike the issue I mentioned last Sunday evening, where God stands aside and leaves us with a drama, but in this case principles, with which we with the Spirit are to work out our salvation.

Even if one accepts the necessity of principles (I do not, except as compressed statements of the divine interaction with us), the *kind* of principles offered seem to me to be problematic.

Firstly, the kind of inclusivity which is promoted in culture is an important matter. The most deep-running issue is the nature of the relationship between human beings which is advocated. Hidden beneath the suggestion of a society in which 'all are equal', it seems to me, is the supposition that human beings are related only extrinsically through the expectation of equality. There are two problems here. One has to do with the notion that human beings are primarily individual and related only extrinsically through voluntary agreement such as a social contract or a choice of the other. This is a modern liberal notion, and I strongly doubt whether it is a sufficiently strong notion of human relationships. The relation of human beings to each other needs to be seen as intrinsic to each, a relation which binds them together, within which bond individuality arises. The New Testament word for this is 'compassion'.

The other problem has to do with the sufficiency of the notion of equality, no matter whether it secures the position of races or genders or whether it refers to equal access to resources. I certainly do not think that anything less than this is permissible, but — given that human beings usually settle for the minimum — it is not a good foundation for a society. Furthermore, so far as I can see, 'equality' is not advocated by the Gospel, and does not mirror the action of God toward human beings in Jesus Christ. A much more radical ex-centricity is required, the ex-centricity of love, which 'shifts the boundaries of our being'. The New Testament words for this are such words as 'sacrifice' and 'generosity', which require a radical relocation of oneself for the other.

Alongside these two questionable notions must be placed two ambiguous notions, 'just distribution of wealth' and 'maintaining the integrity of creation'. Given the rapid increase of finance-driven life, these are particularly important areas, but the notions in question say little about what should be the content of the Christian witness in economics and ecology.

Having spoken about the content of the Spirit's witness to the dynamics of culture, I want finally to discuss the position of the Church. The division of the churches seems to loom so large for Professor de Gruchy as to vitiate any possible contribution which the Church as such might make. Its task seems to be collective witness, where that can be managed in a Church which 'is not only confessionally and racially divided, but itself a site of the larger social and political struggle.'

There are two issues, however. Can the Church witness of an inclusivity which it does not manifest in itself? That is to say, can its *act* of witness be separated from its *being* as a dynamic culture? This does not suggest, of course, that its own inclusivity should be based on a monolithic culture, which (like South Africa under apartheid) draws sharp boundaries of exclusivity. It does suggest the necessity of a inclusivity within which diversity functions importantly. Such a thing would be the most effective witness to democratic structure. (There is a direct correlation between the weakness of ecclesiology today and the Churches' inability to contribute to the crisis of democracy in the world.)

Nonetheless, such an inclusivity will be fluid, like the public culture which it seeks to aid. And, given the fluidity of public culture and of the churches, it makes very good sense to recognize

> that there is not one model for relating the church and state, the church and politics, but that ways of doing so have to be continually worked out as circumstances and contexts change.

That seems to me to be one of the most intelligent comments about church-state relations to have emerged in some time.

But the question remains, how does the Spirit of the Christ of God appear in the dynamic of the inclusivity of the Church, that of the State and that of their interaction? And what is the form of its presence? Is it only to be found in the *metanoia* of individuals or as a continuous conversion in culture, or perhaps as both, through which the promise of the future arises?

Response by Douglas Campbell

Introduction

It has been a challenging and also a profoundly uncomfortable experience to work out a response to the work of John de Gruchy (with specific reference to his symposium paper) — particularly when de Gruchy's remarks have reinterpreted, deepened, and sharpened, the words of one of his "uncomfortable" inspirations, Dietrich Bonhoeffer.[1] Particularly uncanny has been the relevance of de Gruchy's observations to the New Zealand context. It is, indeed, possible to view the work and words of John de Gruchy as suggestive of a *kairos* for our own nation at this point in its history.[2] In this sense, perhaps he has spoken words that we need not merely to listen

1. De Gruchy interacts with Bonhoeffer particularly in his *Bonhoeffer and South Africa: Theology in Dialogue,* (Grand Rapids: Eerdmans, 1984). References to most of Bonhoeffer's writings (both well and less well-known) may be found throughout this book. Cf. also his edited selection of Bonhoeffer's writings, *Dietrich Bonhoeffer: Witness to Jesus Christ,* (London: Collins, 1987).
2. De Gruchy refers to two very significant documents in the recent history of the church in SA, both of which point to something of a *kairos* or *status confessionis*, viz., *The Kairos Document: Challenge to the Church*, (2nd ed.; Johannesburg: Skotaville, 1986), and *The Road to Damascus: Kairos and Conversion* , (Johannesburg: Skotaville, 1989). He also recognizes the existence of such a critical moment earlier, in 1977, when the World Lutheran Federation declared the existence of a *status confessionis* in SA, and in 1982, with the declaration of the World Alliance of Reformed Churches that apartheid is heresy. *The Kairos Document*, de Gruchy tells us ("Christian Witness": 2), was edited after the declaration by the government of a general state of emergency in 1986 (which lasted until 1990). De Gruchy describes *The Road to Damascus* as "the international successor to *The Kairos Document* produced by Christians in various 'third world' countries..." ("Christian Witness": 6). Cf. also de Gruchy's "Bonhoeffer and the Relevance of Barmen for Today," in *Bonhoeffer and South Africa* pp. 123-43.

to but to hear, in the full biblical sense of that verb,[3] if the church in Aotearoa-New Zealand is to recognize the times and be an authentic witness to Christ. Certainly, de Gruchy issues a challenge to NZ: that of the reconciliation in Christ of a church and a context fractured by racial conflict.

This response to de Gruchy's paper, "Christian Witness and the Transformation of Culture in a Society in Transition," is structured in three parts: (1) Certain features of the SA context that bear a surprising relevance to NZ will be described briefly. These suggest that, at least in certain important respects, our contexts are converging, so that a challenge directed specifically to the one context may still nevertheless carry a pointed message to the other.(2) The basic thrust of de Gruchy's paper will be summarized, and a series of his insights briefly noted. (3) We will try, finally, in our last section to push further along the methodological and theological trajectory that de Gruchy has outlined, with particular reference to chapter two of Paul's letter to the Ephesians.[4]

---

3. Cf. Matt 7:21-27, 13:3-23, Lk 6:46-49, Jn 5:24, 8:47, 18:37.
4. We say "Paul's" letter advisedly: we hold the arguments against his authorship of Ephesians to be rather weak, and the widely (but not universally) held conclusion that the letter is pseudonymous to be an aberration of contemporary NT scholarship. Time unfortunately prohibits any detailed exploration of this question here. For further reading, an introductory treatment is given by Raymond F. Collins, *Letters That Paul Did Not Write: The Epistle to the Hebrews and the Pauline Pseudepigrapha,* (Wilmington, Delaware: Michael Glazier, 1988), pp. 132-70. A full bibliography and more detailed discussion may also be found in Andrew Lincoln's *Ephesians,* (Dallas, GA: Word, 1990), pp. lix-lxxiii - both these scholars argue for pseudonymity. The well-known, earlier proponent of pseudonymity, who integrates the question of Ephesians' authorship with canonical questions, is Edgar J. Goodspeed: cf. his "Ephesians, the Introduction to the Pauline Collection," in *New Solutions of New Testament Problems,* (Chicago: University of Chicago Press, 1927), pp. 11-20; his arguments are summarized in *The Key to Ephesians,* (Chicago: University of Chicago Press, 1956), pp. v-xvi. Particularly significant, however, is Ken Neumann's *The Authenticity of the Pauline Epistles: A Stylostatistical Analysis,* (Missoula, MT: Scholars, 1990), which exhaustively analyzes the use of statistics, style, and word-incidence, in Paul's letters concluding that no significant differences mark the ten-letter canon. For a brief introduction to the developmental reading of Paul that avoids many of the other problems raised for Pauline authorship by the foregoing see C. H. Buck and G. Taylor, *Saint Paul: A Study of the Development of His Thought* , (New York: Scribners, 1969), pp. 124-39.

1. A Disturbing Contextual Parallelism: New Zealand and South Africa

De Gruchy's analysis addresses a very carefully delineated context (this is a central principle in both Bonhoeffer's and his own theology[5]). But it is possibly a little disquieting for any New Zealander[6] to realize that the contexts of South Africa and New Zealand are now converging on a remarkably similar configuration of features and problems.

NZ and SA both share a colonial origin, which tends to generate a characteristic culture and equally characteristic problems — especially in relation to the ubiquitous quest of immigrant farmers for land.[7] Although SA is more heavily influenced by Dutch migration than NZ, both countries are also deeply rooted in British values, culture, and politics. But both countries seem to have had this legacy, once venerated uncritically, badly shaken, and are therefore seeking to emerge from something of a colonial infancy. Admittedly, it is only the indigenous population of NZ that has actually fought British imperial forces, while much of white SA culture also looks back on a bitter war against the Crown.[8] Nevertheless, both countries probably stand at present at an important moment in their post-colonial existence of "nation-building."[9] Substantial shifts in their underlying social, political, and economic configuration seem to have pressed upon them

5. See particularly de Gruchy's *The Church Struggle in South Afric,a* (Grand Rapids: Eerdmans, 1979), especially chapters one through four (pp. 1-193); and his *Bonhoeffer and South Africa*,pp. 3-10, 34, 40-41, 48-51, 58-59, 68-73, 106-14, 124-41 (and the comment in the foreword by Eberhard Bethge, p. vii).
6. Not to mention Australian or Pacific Islander - and particularly any Fijian.
7. Cf. especially the clearly Marxist, but still intriguing, analysis of Rob Steven: "Land and White Settler Colonialism: The Case of Aotearoa," in *Culture and Identity in New Zealand,* (eds. David Novitz and Bill Willmott; Wellington & Christchurch: CP Books, 1989), pp. 21-34. De Gruchy's comments on the origin of the Great Trek are also intriguing. He quotes Leslie Hewson: "Land and Labour! No one understands the complexities of the racial situation in South Africa until he has given due consideration to the significance of land and land hunger..." (*Church Struggle*, p. 20: cf. also p. 19).
8. Warfare as celebrated in NZ by Pakeha culture has generally served British foreign policy goals: cf. Jock Phillips, "War and National Identity," in *Culture and Identity in New Zealand*, pp. 91-109. The Boer war made this orientation effectively impossibly in SA.
9. A phrase used by de Gruchy ("Christian Witness,":p. 12).

a fundamental re-evaluation of their past identity, and a corresponding search for a new national direction.[10]

A major component in this pressure and in this new direction is, of course, race. Both countries have a history of co-existence and conflict with indigenous peoples. Both trace their European origin to rather cunning negotiations, and, failing these, to outright battles with such groups. And injustice has also been an undeniable component in the ongoing relationship between European and native over the century or so of their co-existence.[11] Furthermore, while the specifics of this distorted relationship have varied (and the differences are not unimportant), a present disparity in wealth and status is also closely correlated with the racial relationship.[12] This holds for virtually every conceivable parameter of social measurement in SA, but the correlation in NZ between race and other indices like life expectancy, infant

---

10. In NZ a reorientation taking place primarily at present in terms of the perhaps dangerously simple ideas of the New Right. It may be that in this respect NZ differs from SA, but one suspects that the New Right would find fertile soil in certain SA groups as well.

11. An injustice becoming increasingly apparent as some of these grievances are now being publically addressed in the wake of Maori agitation, particularly through the Waitangi tribunal, which draws on what is (arguably) NZ''s foundation document: the treaty of Waitangi. The accepted standard account of the treaty is by Claudia Orange: *The Treaty of Waitangi* (Wellington: Allen & Unwin, 1989). For an extremely interesting perspective on the Maori wars, and the churches position on native issues at the time, see John Stenhouse, "Science Versus Religion in Nineteenth Century New Zealand: Robert Stout and Social Darwinism," *Pacifica* 2 (1989) pp. 61-86; and also his "The Darwininan Enlightenment and New Zealand Politics," in *Darwin in the Pacific,* (eds. Roy McLeod and Philip F. Rehbock; Honolulu: University of Hawaii Press, forthcoming). Both these studies are further developments of his dissertation, *The Battle Between Science and Religion over Evolution in Nineteenth Century New Zealand,* (Ph.D, Massey University, New Zealand, 1985). Note, this is a rather recent experience and viewpoint for NZ, although not for SA. Until a few decades ago for academics, and a few years ago for much of the broader public, NZ's "racially oppressive" past was largely unknown. Its remembrance is a fairly recent - and painful - event, closely correlated with the production of the first university-educated Maori, and probably also stimulated by the controversial Springbok tour in 1981, which generated nation-wide division and protest over the racial issue.

12. Cf. Paul Spoonley, *Racism and Ethnicity,* (Auckland: Oxford University Press, 1988); and Ranginui Walker, "Maori Identity," in *Culture and Identity in New Zealand*, pp. 35-52, esp. pp. 40-44.

mortality, education, representation in the professions, and housing, is also quite well-known — and the correlation seems to be strengthening. So, to racial grievances we must add the linked and greatly complicating factors of poverty and constricted social opportunity.[13]

We should also note that, as the racial issue rears its once-forgotten head, many of the solutions offered in NZ (both by religious and secular organisations), like many of those already suggested in SA, are fundamentally *separatist* . That is, the problem of racial difference and/or conflict is perceived as resolvable largely, or even only, in terms of partition. In NZ such suggestions range from the "lunatic fringe" of radicalism that seeks a return to the pre-colonial situation (that is, to pre-European colonization), to the Anglican denomination's current initiative to separate its Maori, European, and Island, constituencies into distinct administrative entities, united in structural terms only at the level of its general synod[14] — and the bicultural initiatives of the

---

13. Cf. "Christian Witness," p. 11.
14. This characterization has been criticized as inaccurate, but a quick review of the relevant documents suggests that it is a fair summary. The various studies collected together in *Te Kaupapa Tikanga Rua/Bi-Cultural Development*, (N. P.: Provincial Secretary of the Church of the Province of New Zealand, 1986), and the new *Te Pouhere/Constitution of the Anglican Church in Aotearoa, New Zealand, and Polynesia*, suggest this quite clearly. "The 1984 Discussion Paper" quotes with approval the statement of Sir David Beattie, modifying the earlier statement of Governor Hobson: "I am of the view that we are not one people despite Hobson's oft-quoted words, nor should we try to be. We do not need to be" (*Te Kaupapa Tikanga Rua* : 18). Similarly, "The Report of the Bi-cultural Commission of the Anglican Church on the Treaty of Waitang"" states that "the Commission is convinced that partnership and bi-cultural development offer the way forward for a society ready to be enriched by its dual heritage... The Commission understands the meaning of the[se] terms... as follows: BI-CULTURAL DEVELOPMENT is the process whereby two cultures grow and develop within one nation in a spirit of mutual respect and responsibility. PARTNERSHIP involves co-operation and interdependence between distinct cultural or ethnic groups within one nation" (*Te Kaupapa Tikanga Rua* : 25). There were eighteen recommendations to General Synod, of which only two were not passed substantially as suggested (no. 6 was deferred, and no. 18 was referred to Standing Committee). Appendix D, "The Meaning of Terms," is particularly striking. It states at one point: "Applied to the Church, bi-cultural development means taking steps to ensure that the Gospel of Christ takes root in, and is expressed through two different cultural forms within the one provincial or national Church... [P]artnership involves co-operation and

Methodist and Presbyterian denominations, although they are not yet this developed, should also not be overlooked. This is not to obscure important differences between the separatist strategies of bi-culturalism vis-a-vis a strategy like apartheid.[15] The impetus for the SA separation of churches along cultural and racial lines (significantly, in the pre-apartheid period, and well-intentioned to boot[16]) was from the dominant, white cultures, while much of the NZ impetus comes "from the underside of history," that is, from the Maori. But *as strategies* they are similar, and the signficance of this should probably be pondered — even if it ultimately proves irrelevant for our present context.

There is a third, no doubt less important but nevertheless rather fascinating, contextual correlation between SA and NZ. As a direct result of our British colonial heritage, and also directly illustrative of racial and economic inequality, sport functions in both our countries as something of a national religion, providing entertainment, social cohesion, and also, undeniably, a vicarious sense of power and triumph (although this only really when one's team wins, of course). To adapt a well-known phrase: in SA and NZ, sport is the amphetamine of the masses. Furthermore, within the pantheon of sporting endeavour and achievement, for both the nations of SA and NZ, the central ikon is rugby.

---

interdependence between distinct cultural or ethnic groups within one nation" (*Te Kaupapa Tikanga Rua*, 34). The revised constitution, that arose directly out of the Commission, the report, and these recommendations (and intended for confirmation in May, 1992), in its first introductory proposal states "The new Constitution recognises three cultural streams (tikanga) within the Anglican Church in Aotearoa, New Zealand, and Polynesia." Its third states "[t]here is a General Synod/Te Hinota Whanui in which the three partners express their unity in the one Church" (*Te Pouhere* , iii). The suggested Constitution itself states in article 12 that "the principles of partnership and bicultural development require the Church to: (a) organise its affairs in each of the three tikanga (social organisations, language, laws, principles, and procedure) of each partner;..." (10), and so on. This is not to criticize these arrangements, but merely to point out that their strategy is clearly "partitive," arising out of a particular vision of New Zealand's future framed in terms of the concepts of "bicultural development" and "partnership."

15. Which *Te Kaupapa Tikanga Rua*, describes as "a distorted form of bi-culturalism inconsistent with the Gospel" (33).
16. See *Church Struggle*, esp. chapters one and two, pp. 1-101.

The question of a direct connection between sport and race remains somewhat contentious.[17] But there can be no doubt that the very question of their linkage has both connected and deeply disturbed both countries. The 1981 Springbok tour is a memory etched into the minds of most New Zealanders.[18] And one suspects that of all the boycotts introduced against SA over the last decades, the prohibition of international sporting contact and, in particular, the inability of the Springboks to play the (then) world champion All Blacks, has been one of the most painful, and hence most effective.[19]

The phenomenon of sport, particularly rugby — its quasi-religious status and function; its connection with disparities of race and wealth; and now its integration into lucrative marketing through an increasing professionalism (which raises further questions of economic justice) — is an additional contextual factor that characterizes both SA and NZ, and one that the gospel must confront. With the return of the Springboks to international rugby later on this year (1991), and perhaps touring NZ in 1992, it is also an issue that is far from dead.

In view of these correlations, both past and present, when John de Gruchy speaks of the contextualization of the gospel in SA, his

---

17. The correlation in SA was made well-known by a recent *Frontline* report (3/91) on TV One.

18. The NZ experiences of social unrest and police action were mild perhaps by comparison with SA experiences of political tension, but nevertheless traumatic for NZ, and at least partially analogous. It is also well, however, to acknowledge the sacrifices - however unwilling - that the rugby fraternity have since made in the cause of racial justice (and one should not forget those who have voluntarily, and often courageously, refused to tour SA; players like Chris Laidlaw, Bruce Robertson, Graeme Mourie, John Kirwan, and David Kirk). For literature on the tour cf. Geoff Chapple, *1981: The Tour* (Wellington: A. H. & A. W. Reed, 1984); also Jock Phillips, "Sport, Culture, and Identity" esp. pp. 111-12, 17-20, and nn. 1, 2, and 4 (pp. 120-21). For one perspective from the church cf. Christopher Nicol and James Veitch, "The New Zealand Churches, and the 1981 Springbok Tour," *Journal of Theology for South Africa,* 46 (1984) pp. 39-47.

19. But why has such a boycott not also been introduced, in the name of moral consistency if nothing else, against other Constitutionally racist nations — or against those that simply flagrantly deny human rights — such as present-day Fiji, or Argentina in the 70's? NZ has enjoyed and continues to enjoy uninterrupted sporting contact with these two countries, including the playing of rugby, which seems ironic when it steadfastly refuses to tour SA. One wonders who is the most morally repugnant in this regard: the NZRFU, for its amoral opportunism, or the protest movement (HART, CARE etc.) for its inconsistency.

analysis must carry considerable significance for the context of NZ as well.[20] His comments are directed at a country emerging from a colonial past and entering a critical phase of nation-building; a context also characterized by the attempt to redress, or at least to overcome, bitter racial conflict and economic disparity; and one worshipping false gods, particularly the Olympic god of athletic victory (although its dominant form is somewhat Anglified).

2. The Analysis of John de Gruchy

De Gruchy's study comprises a careful historical analysis of the contemporary SA situation and its church(es), from which a wealth of insights emerges concerning the problem of contextualising the gospel.

Viewed broadly, the balance de Gruchy holds throughout his study between realism and hope is impressive. To concentrate on either one of these extremes would be to negate the gospel — and the grim context of SA constantly tempts one to do just this. But de Gruchy succumbs to neither of these temptations, and so escapes charges of either cynicism or naivety.[21]

Also important is de Gruchy's careful attention to history and to its complexities — and it is perhaps this that in large measure is responsible for the peculiar richness of his analysis. He observes immediately — and correctly — that the entities "culture" and "church" are extremely complex, existing dynamically over space and time.[22] Because of this methodological subtlety, de Gruchy is also

20. Notwithstanding the important observation that no context really exists in isolation.

21. The maintenance of this balance is actually a conscious and consistent objective on his part: cf. *Church Struggle*, p. 198, & pp. 227-37; and de Gruchy's address to the annual capping ceremony at the University of Otago on May 11, 1991, which spoke primarily of a realistic hope.

22. On the issue of relating church and culture see the classic exploration by Richard Niebuhr (*Christ and Culture* [New York: Harper & Row, 1951], cited by de Gruchy in "Christian Witness," p. 1, n. 1). Much of the Newbigin corpus is also helpful here: see especially his recent *The Gospel in a Pluralist Society* (Grand Rapids: Eerdmans, 1989). One must recognize, however, that all such definitions are provisional. Anthropologists have written libraries on the notion of "culture" and admit that it still eludes them: cf. Diane J. Austin-Broos (ed.), *Creating Culture: Profiles in the Study of Culture* (London: Allen & Unwin,

able to propose the useful descriptive hypothesis that, at least in SA, the much-debated relationship between "church" and "culture" is best described in terms of the church *recapitulating* its context. Thus, for de Gruchy, the church functions, to put it simply, like a mirror: in it we see the face of its surrounding society "as a poor reflection" (1 Cor 13:12a), so that the political and social conflicts of society find a precisely corresponding ecclesiastical echo.[23]

Flowing from this basic approach and observation is a series of further insights, which we might loosely characterize as "the insights of historical realism" (we will concentrate here on six):

(1) De Gruchy observes that the churches witness is inevitably ambiguous. Because it embraces so many different sectors of society —sectors often in direct conflict with each other — the churches witness tends to be refracted and confused: its light is very much under a bushel rather than on a hill. Consequently, when analyzing –and attempting to realize — an objective like "the churches witness," its confused and clamorous backdrop must also constantly be addressed.[24]

(2) The danger of oversimplification. In the face of the complexities of historical reality, de Gruchy observes that simple analyses and their stirring rhetorics simply tend to break down. Often they do not grasp a context with sufficient accuracy to give reliable guidance within in it. Furthermore, as contexts complicate, previously reliable models become obsolete. This phenomenon of theological oversimplification and obsolescence may have a sinister accomplice: one can discern in the stirring language of certain apocalyptic or eschatological rhetorics a coercive tendency, the end-result of which is mere fascism.[25]

(3) The dangers of over-identifying with any particular social group. Lurking here, for example, in the initially rather glamorous notion of "nation-building," there is also a potentially coercive and triumphalist

---

1987); and David Novitz and Bill Willmott (eds.), *Culture and Identity in New Zealand.*

23. And often a corresponding hermeneutical struggle over the correct reading of the Bible and its social and political implications.
24. This observation clearly holds more for the post-Christian, Western world.
25. See John Stenhouse, "Science versus Religion": esp. p. 81 & p. 85; also Abraham Rotstein, "The World Upside Down," *Canadian Journal of Political and Social Theory* 2.2 (1978): 5-30; *idem*, "Lordship and Bondage in Luther and Marx," *Interpretation: A Journal of Political Philosophy* 8.1 (c. 1979) pp. 75-102; and *idem*, "The Apocalyptic Tradition: Luther and Marx," in *Political Theology in the Canadian Context* (ed. Benjamin G. Smillie; Waterloo: Wilfred Laurier Press, 1982), pp. 147-208.

theology and activity. A churches support for a particular group too easily leads it to ignore, or even to oppose, the needs of other groups with which it is not allied or in sympathy. In his *Church Struggle*, de Gruchy points out that it was (amongst other things) an over-identification with Afrikanerdom that contributed to the compromising of the gospel in the 1DRC.[26] So, in the NZ context, one must ask whether the church should throw its weight behind any one particular social group too strongly. Such support tends to blunt the prophetic distance that is necessary for the church to continue functioning as an authentic witness to Christ.

(4) The church must witness against various dimensions of injustice and oppression. At times a given church and context may focus overwhelmingly on one particular axis of suffering and redress (in SA, and probably in NZ at present, race). But this focus must not be allowed to smother a less popular or timely protest against other injustices — the injustices no-one has time for (particularly media-time). In the context of SA de Gruchy mentions the tendencies to overlook sexual, economic, and ecological oppression and, once again, that diagnosis seems uncomfortably appropriate for NZ.

(5) With traditional answers and models breaking down in the face of such historical complexities, de Gruchy avoids methodological inundation by repeatedly asking a simple but critical question: "What, in this context, constitutes an authentic witness to Christ?" He thereby reorients his discussion again and again to the churches relationship to Christ. While not necessarily providing complete answers, de Gruchy does consequently provide a direction — a *christological* direction: within a given context the life of the church still primarily depends, irrespective of that context, on Christ. Were this to cease, then (to paraphrase Bonhoeffer) the church would no longer be the church. This constant christological reorientation is perhaps obvious, but it remains of critical importance, if only because it is so often surreptitiously ignored.

(6) It remains for de Gruchy to make his basic christological axiom more specific. Consequently, he goes on to point out that, precisely because the church tends to recapitulate a context, along with all its ambiguities and dangers of partisanship, it must also automatically hold out the prospect of reconciliation. The healing of contextual fractures can therefore be inaugurated by, because it can begin within, the church. In particular, injustice may be dealt with through the

---

26. Cf. esp. chapters one and two, pp. 1-101.

churches offer of confession and forgiveness. This prospect of absolution perhaps comprises the only effective solution to the problem of guilt, and in turn creates a possible exit from the spiral of violence and anger that seem at least partially fueled by such guilt.[27]

De Gruchy combines the principle of christological direction with the theme of reconciliation by reflecting briefly on chapter two of Paul's letter to the Ephesians.[28] It seems appropriate, therefore, to conclude our discussion of his paper by further exploring that chapter, in the hope that by doing this de Gruchy's programmatic insights will receive further clarity and emphasis.

3. Further Insights from Ephesians

Verses 11-22 in chapter two of Ephesians contain Paul's famous discussion of reconciliation between pagan and Jew in terms of a new temple. But while this text has been much discussed, its theological presupposition has very seldom been isolated and clearly articulated. In part this is because Paul's imagery is unusual — even exotic — and his syntax is characteristically sprawling. Throughout this section, in elaborate chiastic constructions,[29] he combines various motifs from the book of Isaiah[30] with an intriguing series of architectural metaphors — one usually interpreted in terms of the Jerusalem temple, but more aptly read in terms of the magnificent temple of Apollo at Didyma in Asia Minor. This edifice was still under construction in Paul's time (cf. vv. 20 & 21), and possessed the critical architectural feature of "a dividing-wall."[31]

---

27. The spiral of violence clearly characterizes SA, but it is also present, in increasing measure, in NZ.
28. "Christian Witness," p. 9.
29. These have never really been articulated precisely, although various studies have made a beginning. Andrew Lincoln discusses (and dismisses) the suggestions of Kirby, Bailey, and Giavini (see *Ephesians*, p. 126). While not endorsing these specific analyses, we would hold to some similar resolution of the section's syntactical difficulties, but to argue our approach here is unfortunately impossible.
30. Isa 52:7 (cf. 9:6), 57:19, 28:19 (cf. 8:14), and the often overlooked, but critical 5:1-7.
31. The Jerusalem temple did not have a dividing-wall, except in the the Holy of Holies, and Paul's discussion does not really make sense with reference to this partition. The barrier surrounding the temple that kept Gentiles from setting foot

The basic thrust of Paul's argument is clear enough: the community of Christ constitutes a new sacred structure — a building of people — which embraces the old opposition between Jew and Gentile. Furthermore, the structural integrity of the growing building expresses the reconciliation and unity that Paul believes should characterize the people of God. Finally, the great "stone at the corner," whether that means the apex of the temple or its foundation,[32] is Christ.

So far the discussion seems clear enough. A critical question remains, however: on what basis does Paul argue for this shocking abolition of the age-old distinction between Jew and Gentile?, and hence for the abolition of any contextual barrier within the people of God, whether based on race or culture. Is it a pious aspiration?, something powered primarily by a vision of the future, that is, by hope? Or is it something more concrete?[33]

Paul's response to this important question is somewhat obscure (probably because it is so abbreviated), but we would hold that, given an appropriate prior analysis, it may be found in two critical comments. Paul states tersely in vv. 15 and 16 "...that the two [parts of humanity, that is, pagan and Jew] might be created in him [that is, in Christ — or, possibly, in the Cross] into one new person... through the cross, having killed their hatred in himself."[34]

---

in the sacred temple-area would be more appropriate semantically, but is most awkwardly — really impossibly — described with the word *mestoichon*. It was a small stone balustrade, and Josephus describes it consistently as a *druphaktos lithinos*. For further discussion of this point see Peter Richardson's "Architectural Metaphors in Ephesians 2:11-22," (unpublished paper given to SNTS annual conference, N. D.).

32. More likely the former, but the metaphor is probably not specifically architectural at all, alluding instead to an Isaianic text, and also possibly functioning within a catena of Messianic proof-texts based on "stone" used by the early church: cf. Isa 28:16, also Isa 8:14 and Ps 118:22, quoted variously in Rom 9:33, 10:11, 1 Pet 2:6-8, Matt 21:42, and Acts 4:11. Cf. also C. H. Dodd, *According to the Scriptures* (London: Nisbet, 1952; Fontana, 1965), pp. 41-43. The use of "stone" for Christ may have derived from a pun on "son," as suggested by Josephus' otherwise very puzzling statement in *War* 5.272.

33. Much of our discussion following is very close to much of de Gruchy's thinking in his *Bonhoeffer and South Africa*, and so should not really be opposed to his corpus or theology as a whole: these comments are merely a response to the emphases of his paper "Christian Witness."

34. The comments are in vv. 15b and 16b:....*hina tous duo ktisthei en auto eis hena kainon annthropon .. dia tou staurou apokteinas tein echthran en auto.*

Paul's argument is really only comprehensible if these comments are interpreted with a stark, even shocking, literalness.[35] Christ has, in some extraordinary way, drawn together a bitterly divided humanity within his own person, and has created a new person. This glorious act of creation has taken place, however, not in a divine play of light and dance with the Spirit as it did on the first day,[36] but on the Cross, where the old divided humanity, now present in Christ, has been put to death. Thus, in his crucified moment of suffering and pain, Christ has reconstituted humanity, executing the old, and thereby allowing the new person to be raised "in him."[37]

There seems little doubt that for Paul it was this reality that explained — and necessitated — reconciliation, in this specific instance, between Judaism and paganism. *Reconciliation rests on a christological reworking of being.* Insofar as one is crucified in Christ, the execution of enmity is therefore real and complete. Three aspects of this event now need to be highlighted further in the context of our discussion.

(1) Because reconciliation takes place in the crucified Christ, it is a personal event with ontological dimensions.[38] So it is language in terms of these dimensions that allows us to express and to communicate most accurately what happens "in Christ." Conversely, language that uses future and (or) political images is less appropriate or accurate.[39] A future orientation — although present to some degree,

---

35. The commentators seem reluctant, however, to embrace this reasoning: cf. the careful analysis of Markus Barth, which nevertheless comes up short in terms of fundamental theological rationality and continuity (*Ephesians*, pp. 1-3, 253-325, & esp. 295-311), and the sheer reticence of Andrew Lincoln, where the one "new person" seems akin at times simply to ecclesiastical unity, or to a new "sphere" (*Ephesians*, pp. 121-65, esp. pp. 159-62).

36. So Gen 1:1-5, Prov 8:22-31.

37. It should also be noted that v. 18b points out explicitly that it is the Spirit, specifically "the one Spirit," who incorporates us in this event.

38. It also exceeds the customary linear dimensions of time, recognizing no important distinction between past and present — or, at least, no significant temporal obstacle to the reworking of humanity.

39. De Gruchy summarizes the gospel succinctly in the fourth section of his paper: "Christian witness has as its fundamental presupposition the conviction that in and through the death and resurrection of Jesus Christ and the gift of the Spirit, God's liberating and reconciling power has become operative in the world as a whole in a new and decisive way which leads to human and social wholeness." But he goes on to qualify this definition (repeatedly) in terms of *political*

because the transformation in Christ is clearly not yet complete — is nevertheless not entirely sensitive to the past and present reality of life in Christ. There is a sense that what lies ahead is more significant than what is accomplished and presently real. Similarly, political characterizations suggest relationships of power and citizenship, and so again, although appropriate to some degree, do not convey with full sensitivity the intimate personal relationship between Christ and the believer in the Spirit. One might term such language "overly Synoptic," since in those gospels the notion of the future Kingdom of God dominates the sayings of Jesus (and the books themselves). But in Paul, and also more clearly in the gospel of John, we find familial, intimate, present terminology, and this is perhaps a more appropriate set of images for the description of what happens "in Christ."

(2) Paul's argument is clearly grounded in the Cross. The Cross is partially overshadowed in this text by gentler Isaianic motifs of peace and proclamation, and also by the grandiose facade of the new temple, but it is still present and is still fundamental to Paul's argument (v. 16b). The function of the Cross in Paul's argument here clearly implies identification through its embodying function. Thus the motif of the Cross should probably be understood in terms of its entire, incarnational trajectory — a trajectory Paul himself also embodies in his ministry to the Gentiles, which is described in chapter three of the letter (vv. 2-13). It should also be noted that this identifying incorporation is a painful act, because it means an identification of Christ with sinful and repulsive humanity, as well a bearing of their burdens — in this context, a doubly difficult task, because those burdens include the hatred of each group for the other. But it is this act of painful identification that creates the possibility of reconciliation and transformation.[40]

Thus, Paul's argument in chapter two of Ephesians is not an ethical exhortation, or an example we should follow. Neither is it primarily a hope, or a vision of the future. It is, fundamentally, a statement of fact,

---

imagery and *a future outlook* . In fact, his next sentence says "...Christians engage the world in a transforming praxis shaped by its anticipation that [sic. - "of"?] God's liberating reign in Jesus Christ" ("Christian Witness," p. 8). Similarly, much of the discussion in his final chapter in *Church Struggle* is cast in political and future terms, explicitly dependent on the Synoptic "Kingdom of God" motif, and its rediscovery by recent NT and theological scholarship (cf. pp. 195-237).

40. So we would argue that, albeit in muted form, Ephesians contains a *theologia crucis*.

and our exhortation, hope and future vision, are made possible only by the present reality it speaks of, and in dependence on that reality.

In this cluster of insights we may have a criterion that will further clarify the concerns that de Gruchy raises in the context of the churches witness in a divided context. A reconciliation through crucifixion, that is, a theology of the Cross (when understood in terms of the foregoing), speaks suggestively to situations of ambiguity; to over-simplification; to over-identification; and to the multiple dimensions of suffering and oppression.

(i) Ambiguity: the Cross clearly embodies costliness: the costliness of setting aside oneself and one's own context in order to identify with others, thereby bearing their problems, pains, and afflictions. This costliness cuts through much of the confusion surrounding the witness of the church. A costly, incarnational dynamic is not difficult to identify — although it is seldom apparent. In view of this, ambiguity can perhaps be judged by a theology of the cross. The more authentic expressions of the mind of Christ will bear the stamp of his incarnational and suffering life, just as Paul bore the marks of Jesus on his body (Gal 6:17).

(ii) Over-simplification: the Cross also embodies a kenotic self-emptying, as it identifies in love with the tragically divided context of humanity. In this event and act we also find a prototypical respect for context. Any given context is the potential ground of our incarnation through the Spirit. We cannot therefore dictate schematic solutions to it in advance — which would be a refusal to incarnate. Neither can covertly fascist solutions ever be appropriate. Identification precludes both oversimplification and coercion. A context is to be loved and entered into just as Christ engaged with our humanity. It cannot therefore be bludgeoned in advance and from without.

(iii) Over-identification: once embraced, however, a context yields up its fallenness. Incarnation encounters enmity, and bears it within, the ultimate solution to that enmity being crucifixion. Thus, inevitably, to bear a context means to expose its innate fallenness. When one experiences Christ's crucifixion and transformation of a context, it will probably become difficult to over-identify with any part of it, whether a present or an emerging principle. To do so would be to deify something under judgment — it would also be, in a sense, to exalt one's executioner.

(iv) The many dimensions of injustice: finally, one committed to identification to the extent of crucifixion should remain sensitive to the various dimensions of fallenness in any given context, be they economic, racial, sexual, or ecological. By definition, to be incarnate is to seek out dimensions of suffering. Thus, the incarnate one identifies with everyone, and experiences their every enmity. One who espouses a theology of the Cross and follows a crucifed God should therefore also be sensitive to oppression in all its aspects.[41]

(3) There is, however, a third, critical insight offered by Paul in Ephesians, that is, the model he himself supplies of contextual transformation within the crucified Christ. In Ephesians 2 Paul opposes the two contexts of Judaism and paganism. Paganism is described, as we would expect, in fundamentally negative terms. It is idolatrous and immoral: without God and without hope — an expression of death. But while Judaism is described much more positively,[42] it is plainly apparent that for Paul the new humanity, formed in Christ, transcends *both* the sheer negativity of paganism *and* the qualified goodness of Judaism. Thus, we can see that Paul the Pharisee has yielded to Christ's judgment on his own beloved culture — a culture originally initiated and sanctified by God — and has surrendered to its transformation in Christ.

So we too should probably expect today that the transformation of our context by Christ will both reconcile and change even that which we may perceive as good. This is because life in Christ cannot but be superior to the most cherished features of our old life and context. Certainly our cultural identity will not be obliterated: differences will remain. But the ground of our existence will no longer be cultural, or any aspect of culture. We are grounded instead in the person of Christ, through the Spirit.[43] In short, we now have the same ground as any

41. It is probably also worth noting at this point that the primary dimension of fallenness that Paul engages with in Ephesians is *thanatos*: death. Death may be present in any context or relationship, and it is death that remains the great enemy of Christ and the church. We need not specify that which we oppose beyond this. We are to bring life to those living under the shadow of death, and as we identify with those so living we will no doubt encounter death negating life and drawing it into dissolution and nothingness in many different ways. To define death more specifically than this, for example, as *ptocheia* (poverty) — as if one could define the essentially vacuous — may be to obscure one of its other hideous, mutant forms.

42. As possessing the covenants of promise and, by implication, hope and "God in the world" (2:12). In short, Judaism is "near" to God while paganism is "far away" (vv. 13, 17).

43. Paul's discussion in Ephesians also provides us with a pneumatological footnote to de Gruchy's discussion. De Gruchy makes the somewhat painful observation

other believer, irrespective of context, while our various contexts are constantly being judged and transformed by that ground.[44]

Such an understanding of Christ speaks just as powerfully to the context of NZ as it does to SA, with its increasingly bitter divisions of race, wealth, and power, doubtless replicated (at least partly) in the church. The fundamental reality of the church is a unity, worked out, often painfully, in reconciliation. A recognition of differences within this unity is no doubt healthy: it is only appropriate that the churches structure and form be conditioned by contextual variations. But a recognition of contextual differences *as fundamental* would amount to a negation of the work of Christ and exalt culture over the Cross. At the point when one's own cultural identity has become more important than the unity one shares in Christ with a fellow-Christian from another context, one has crossed, sadly, from the gospel to something else — something we often dub "cultural Protestantism."[45] This subtle border

---

(at least, to me) that Pentecostal and charismatic church groups, growing rapidly in SA since WW2, "tend to be conservative in their political orientation, despite claims to political neutrality, [while] some are actively right-wing" ("Christian Witness," p. 6). This observation does not hold in all cases, but is sufficiently accurate — and accurate also for the NZ context — to prompt the observation that, in terms of the pneumatology expressed in Ephesians, this is simply an inauthentic manifestation of the Spirit. The Spirit is defined there in terms of Christ, and therefore *must* create an incarnational and crucified human expression. Neither political neutrality nor right-wing activity seem appropriate expressions of this basic dynamic in SA (or in NZ?) - although one must also be wary of the Right-Left political dichotomy itself. Nevertheless, Pentecostalism and Charismaticism also stand judged by the incarnational, crucified, and hence, reconciling, christology and pneumatology of Ephesians.

44. The statements of the Barmen declaration, especially articles 2 and 3, are a timeless warning here: "We reject the false doctrine, as though the Church were permitted to abandon the form of its message and order to its own pleasure or to changes in prevailing ideological and political convictions" (a version of the declaration is printed on pp. 146-50 of de Gruchy's *Bonhoeffer and South Africa*).

45. De Gruchy has made a poignant observation about separatism as a possible solution for these sorts of problems in another context: "Separate development, like Marxism, does not only offer an analysis of the situation, nor does it simply propose a solution to the problem; it operates on certain assumptions about man and society. Because of this, the Christian critique has to probe the claims of ideologies at different, though inter-related, levels" (*Church Struggle*, p. 213). Later he also remarks: "For too long, the church [in SA] has been tied to sectional interests — the problems and aspirations of Afrikaners or English-

— a theological "line in the sand" — must be guarded vigilantly. Over it stands the placard, "There is one body and one Spirit — just as you were called to one hope when you were called — one Lord, one faith, one baptism; one God and Father of all, who is over all and through all and in all" (Eph 4:3-5).

---

speaking people, of whites or blacks. Its concern for people has been determined by the interests of its *own* people. But if the church is serious in its claim to be the community of the kingdom, then it has to break out of its ethnic straitjacket and become the church for all, especially for those who suffer... [And] in order for the church to be for all the peoples of the land, it has to rediscover its unity in Christ. It cannot do this through either cheap reconciliation or superficial ecumenism. It must recognize that the "middle wall of partition" has been torn down in Christ and that, above all else, this means that Christ has destroyed the barriers between black and white, Englishman and Afrikaner, rich and poor. The tremendous significance of this act of reconciliation has yet to be realized within the South African church..." (*ibid.*, p. 235).

Reply by John W. de Gruchy to Daniel W. Hardy and Douglas Campbell

I am very grateful to Professor Hardy for actually getting underneath my paper and looking at the theological issues, the meta issues if you like. We are operating at slightly different levels rather than in contradiction. If you compare the writing of Mark's Gospel at the time when the temple was being destroyed, an apocalyptic situation, with John working in Ephesus, or was it in Alexandria? You are in a different historical epoch, you are attempting to grapple with the same Gospel in a different way, but you are not necessarily disconnected. That is more or less what separates us, which is not to say that there are not underlying theological differences. Issues that are in tension with each other, and which need to be explored more fully. Perhpas it's too easy for us to get into a style of narrative theology, which in a sense is what I was doing, and not face some very complex issues that lie behind it. A narrative approach is attractive because people can respond to story telling, but they don't always want to get to grips with the hidden philosophical isues. We have got to be continually pushed to do that. I was very grateful for being pushed to do that, and therefore to be taken seriously — that's what we should be doing with each other. I was also delighted that my paper sparked off a bit of a New Zealand debate. We must get at the real issues, and the real issues are not, theologically speaking, only the obvious contextual ones but the premises, where we are you coming from. If we don't get at that these there will never be any coherence in the life of the church and its witness, and Dan Hardy is really asking the question of coherence and I think we've got to hear that very carefully.

Let me respond specifically to issues that have been raised. I did not deal with the land issue because I spent a great deal of time, or at least some time, dealing with the topic in my Public Lecture.[1] My paper actually reached it's climax on the land issue. It is fundamental. One

1. "South Africa Beyond Apartheid: En Route To The Promised Land," *Pacifica,* October 1992.

could say a great deal more about that. There is no possibility of any real reconciliation without the land issue being resolved. I fully agree with that, and therefore I was a little surprised that I was accused in my paper of not dealing with it because I saw the Public Lecture as somewhat complementary.

There are a lot of other things that I didn't deal with in this present paper. Some of them were rightly pointed out. I think somebody from the floor has raised the question of power and that is a crucial question in the relationship between cultures. But that's where I started in my paper, talking about a dominant culture and an oppressed culture. That's power language.

I don't want to get into the New Zealand debate, I want to survive this week and get home to the safety of South Africa! I've still got to fly on Dragon Air in China so... I think one very important point in Dan's response which I want to highlight was his emphasis on creative re-ordering from the various cultural perspectives, because that in fact is what is happening. I give you just one illustration. Much contemporary Afrikaner literature, poetry, writing, has got into the soul of the issues, and made an enormous contribution to what is happening now. That's taking the language of oppression, of Afrikaans, working with it, re-working it in a creative way, in a way that begins to identify with the oppressed and to niggle away at your heritage. In the same context we have the amazing outburst of black creativity, literature and drama — it's the most exciting place to live from a dramatic literary point of view. So yes, the situation has created tremendous creative energy but the creativity has also been a generating power for change. In that I think we see what you are calling for, an assessment of where the Spirit is at work. I may have sounded like an existentialist but I am not one, except in the sense that when you are in the process of actually being aware of making history, we are all making history, you cannot but think in terms of the moment. By I'm not meaning simply this moment, I'm talking about a transitionary moment which could be several decades, it could be several years, it could be shorter, it could be longer. And of course there's continuity with what came before and what came after, so I agree with that. I don't agree that I think in individualistic terms. I don't quite know how to respond to that except to say that I believe as I said in my Public Lecture that all of us in South Africa are in the wilderness together; de Klerk, and Mandela and everybody else, we're all in the wilderness together. We have to work it out in inter-relatedness. You can't leave Pharoah behind, in the South African situation. You've got to take him with you, in fact you've got to take all the Egyptians with as well, and the Egyptians have to actually move along with all the slaves. You've got no future unless you can work it out together. Sorry I've gone over my time, I've a few other things I wanted to say but I'm going to have to stop here.

7

Christ in Cosmic Context

Jürgen Moltmann

1. Christ After Chernobyl

No context without text: My text is the biblical tradition of the creation wisdom, the wisdom-messiah and the cosmic Christ.
No text without context: My context is the ecological crisis of the Earth-system, in which we live and move and have our being. This is not the particular context of certain self-interests, but the global context of life. If there is not a living and life-giving Earth-system anymore, there will be no humankind either, and where there is no humankind anymore there is no Christ, no "God incarnate" either.

The cosmic interpretation of Christ's death and resurrection takes us beyond the bounds of christology in the framework of human history and leads us to christology in the framework of nature. Unless nature is healed and saved, human beings cannot ultimately be healed and saved either, for human beings are natural beings and part of nature. Concern about the things of Christ, therefore, requires us to go beyond the christology developed in modern times, which was christology in the framework of history, and compels us to develop a christology of nature. Like the patristic church's doctrine of the two natures, the cosmic christology of the epistles to the Ephesians and Colossians was dismissed by modern Western European theology as mythology and speculation. Anthropocentric christology fitted the modern paradigm "history", and itself unintentionally became one factor in the modern destruction of nature; for the modern reduction of salvation to the salvation of the soul, or to authentic human existence, unconsciously from one to another; for the glorification of creation through the raising of the dead is the perfectioing of creation, and creation is aligned towards the resurrection of the dead. The statements about creation do not "serve" redemption, and redemption is not merely "the restoration" of creation, whose original order has become deranged.

The light of the resurrection appearances, then, was already identified very early on with the light of the first day of the new creation; and if this is so, then the One who "appeared" in this light as the first in the resurrection of the dead is also "the first-born of all creation" (Col. 1:15). "First" does not mean the created being who is first in the numerical sense; it means "the image of the invisible God" who "is before all creation, and in whom all things hold together" (Col. 1:15, 17). According to Heb 1:3, this "first-born" is "the brightness of his glory and the express image of his person, upholding the universe by his word of power" (Heb 1:3). The same is said about the divine Logos in John 1:1-3. This is a reference to the Wisdom messiah through whom and for whom God has created all things. According to Prov. 8:15, "Wisdom" is God's "comrade in creation". She is not yet called "first-born", but she is "before all things, from eternity" (Ecclus 1:4). All things owe their existence to her, for they have come into being through her mediation. The creator "makes fast" the universe through the immanent presence of his Wisdom in all things. The Christ who annihilates death in his resurrection from the dead reveals himself in the dimensions of this creation Wisdom, and was already understood in this sense very early on.[1]

The practical result was that in those multi-religious cities of the ancient world the Christian community no longer came forward as yet one more religion, devoted to a hitherto unknown deity. Instead it acted as the peace-giving and unifying community of the Creator and Reconciler of all things. Its missionary task was not to enter into a competitive religious struggle. The purpose was integration into the reconciliation and peace which was the eschatological horizon of the cosmos. The Christ proclaimed to the people of other religions — "the heathen" — is "the Christ *in us,* the hope of glory" (Col 1:27), and according to the Letters to the Ephesians and Colossians, this hope is the expectation of the cosmic Christ through whom heaven and earth and all things will find peace.

The church must be seen as the beginning of the reconciled cosmos which has arrived at peace. The church is the historical microcosm for

---

1. Cf. G. Strachan, *Christ and the Cosmos*, (Dunbar: 1985

the macrocosm which has become God's temple. It is the cosmic dimensions of the church that are meant, not the "churchifying" of the world. As "the body of Christ", the church is always already *the church of the whole creation* here and now. It points away from itself to the glory of God which fills heaven and earth: "The Most High" does not dwell in houses made with hands; as the prophet says, "Heaven is my throne, and earth is my footstool. What house will you build for me, says the Lord, or what is the place of my rest? Did not my hand make all these things?" (Acts 48f.; Isa. 66: 1f.). God is to be adored and worshipped in the temple of his creation: that is the meaning of every church and every cathedral built by human hands. It is only as the church of the whole creation that the Christian community is anything more than a sect or a religious society.[2] If God is not worshipped in creation, God is not properly known in the church either. The true church of Christ is the healing beginning of a healed creation in the midst of a sick world.

2. An Outline for a Differentiated Cosmic Christology

Previous cosmic christology has shared the one-sidedness of the traditional doctrine of creation. That is to say, it understands by creation only creation-in-the-beginning (*creatio originalis*) but not continuous creation (*creatio continua*) or the consummated new creation of all things (*nova creatio*). Creation and redemption then cleave apart and become two separate things. Creation is 'down-graded' into being a preparation for redemption, or redemption is reduced to the restoration of creation-in-the-beginning. In order to acquire a comprehensive concept of creation, we have talked about a unified creation process, which begins with creation-in-the-beginning, continues in the history of creation, and is perfected in the new creation of all things.[3] In a similar way we shall interpret Christ's mediation in creation in three separate strands or movements: 1. Christ as the ground of the creation of all

2. Cf. G. Schimanowski, *Weisheit und Messias. Die jüdischen Vorausetzungen der urchristlichen Praexistenzchristologie*, (Tübingen: 1985); also W.L. Knox, *St Paul and the Church of the Gentiles*, (Cambridge: 1939).
3. Cf. my *God in Creation. A New Theology of Creation and the Spirit of God*, (San Francisco: Harper Row, 1985), Chapter VII: The evolution of creation, pp 185ff.

things (*creatio originalis*); 2. Christ as the moving power in the evolution of creation (*creatio continua*); and 3. Christ as the redeemer of the whole creation process (*creatio nova*). By proceeding in this way we are really taking up the old Protestant doctrine of Christ's threefold office (*officium regium Christi*), developing it in the context of today's recognitions: Christ rules in the kingdom of nature (*regnum naturae*), in the kingdom of grace (*regnum gratiae*) and in the kingdom of glory (*regnum gloriae*).

This integral viewpoint makes it possible to avoid the one-sided stresses which have hitherto hampered cosmic christology. If Christ is described only as the ground of creation, this world, which is often so chaotic, is enhanced in an illusory way, and transfigured into a harmony and a home, which it is not. If Christ is described solely as the "evolutor" (Teilhard de Chardin's term), the evolutionary process itself takes on redemptive meaning for the initial creation; but the myriads of faulty developments and the victims of this process fall hopelessly by the wayside. If, finally, we look only at the coming Christ who is to redeem the world, we see only this "fallen world" in its need of redemption, and nothing of the goodness of the Creator and the traces of his beauty in all things.

A. Creation through the Spirit and the Word

If all things (*ta panta*) are created by a God, then a *transcendent unity* precedes their diversity and their historicity. It is not a matter of many worlds belonging to many gods or powers. This is *the one* creation of *the one* God.

If all things are created by the one God *through* his Wisdom/Logos and are held together in that, then underlying their diversity in space and time is an *immanent unity* in which they all exist together. Their unity does not come into being in a subsequent process, emerging from their relationships and the warp and weft into which they are bound. All things have their genesis in a fundamental underlying unity, which is called God's Wisdom, cosmic Creation or Word. The fellowship of all created beings goes ahead of their differentiations and the specific forms given to them, and is therefore the foundation underlying their diversity. If God withdraws this foundation, everything disintegrates and becomes a nothingness. If God lends it fresh force, their forms are renewed (Ps. 104.29f.). The Jewish and Christian doctrines about Wisdom or the Logos as mediator in creation are in direct contradiction to the atomism of Democritus. The beginning was not the particles. The beginning was "the symmetry", the concord. "The elementary particles embody the symmetries. They are its simplest representations, but they are merely a result of the symmetries" (W. Heisenberg).[4] Jewish and Christian doctrines of creation have therefore always maintained the idea of "the unity of nature".

If we look back at the creation story told in the Priestly writing, we find the immanent *unity of creation* expressed in two formulas: 1. In the formula of *creation through the divine Word*: "God said, 'Let there be light'; and there was light" (Gen. 1:3). 2. In the presupposition for creation through the Word, a presupposition which has received too little notice *the vibration of the present Spirit of God*: "The Spirit of God hovered over the face of the waters" (Gen. 1:2). The Hebrew word *ruach* is better translated as "wind" or "breath" than Spirit. The Hebrew word *rahaph* is generally translated "hover" or "brood". But according to Deut. 32:11 and Jer. 23:9 it has rather the meaning of vibrating, quivering, moving and exciting. If this is correct, then we should not think only of the image of a fluttering or brooding dove. We should think of the fundamental resonances of music out of which sounds and rhythms emerge. In thinking about "creation through the word", we should not therefore think primarily in metaphors of command and obedience. A better image is the song of creation. The word names, differentiates and appraises. But the breath is the same in all the words, and binds the words together. So the Creator differentiates his creatures through his creative Word and joins them through his Spirit, who is the sustainer of all his words. In the quickening breath and through the form-giving word, the Creator sings out his creatures in the sounds and rhythms in which he has his joy and his good pleasure. That is why there is something like *a cosmic liturgy* and *music of the spheres* .

B. The Securing of Creation

The second aspect of mediation in creation is the *securing* and preserving of creation. This idea leads over from creation-in-the beginning to continuing creation. *Conservatio mundi* can be understood to mean that God sustains what he has created and watches over his once created word in order to preserve it from the chaos that

4. W. Heisenberg, *Physics and Beyond*, (London and New York:1971).

unremittingly threatens it. But *conservatio mundi* can also be understood as *creatio continua* . In every instant the creative God reiterates his primal 'yes' to his creation. But both conceptions are related to creation-in-the-beginning, and are therefore one-sided. They do not permit us to think forward to the consummation of creation. Neither idea about the preservation of creation expresses a positive relationship to the redemption of all things. The regnum gratiae is cut off from the regnum naturae or potentiae and unrelated to it. But this obscures the grace which is already shown in the preserving and sustaining of creation, human sin and cosmic disorder notwithstanding God preserves his creation from corruption because, and inasmuch as, he has patience with what he has created. His patience creates time for his creatures. His longsuffering leaves them space. His patience, which is prepared to suffer, and his waiting forbearance are the virtues of his hope for the turning back and homecoming of his creatures to the kingdom of his glory. The God who preserves the world endures the self-isolation of his creatures and puts up with their contradictions, keeping their future open for them through his suffering and his silence, and conceding them the opportunities for conversion which they neglect. *Conservatio mundi* does not belong only to the kingdom of nature. It is already part of the kingdom of grace. In the preservation of the world, nature and grace are so closely interwoven that it is impossible to talk about the one without talking about the other.

C. The Renewal of Creation

If we think about the aspect of the preservation of the world which is orientated towards the future, then *creatio continua* is not merely the securing of the original creation because God holds it fast. It is at the same time already *the anticipation of the new creation* of all things. Continuous creation is creation's ongoing history. In this historical creation God "renews the face of the earth" (Ps.104 :30), looking towards the final new creation of all things.

The divine creative and redeeming activity experienced in this way in the human world has its hidden correspondences in the world of nature. What we see in the world of nature is not merely God's activity as preserver, but his activity as innovator too. The history of nature displays not merely the preservation of species but also their evolution. Continuous and contingent happening marks the historical process not merely of the human world but of the natural world as well. This means that it is possible to discover even in the history of nature parables and true symbols for the future of creation in its completion and perfecting. In nature's preservation and development, God already prepares the consummation of his creation, for his grace thrusts forward to the revelation of his glory. Paul sees this in imprisoned nature's "sighing" and "longing" for liberty in God's glory. The men and women who in faith experience "the first fruits of the Spirit", recognize the same longing of the Spirit as the driving force and torment in everything. The mediators of creation — the Spirit and the Word — wait and strive in all things for the liberation of them all. So "creation in chains" is not merely in need of redemption. It is also consumed by hunger and thirst for the righteousness of God.

3. Christ — Evolution's Driving Force or its Victim?

It was Teilhard de Chardin especially who interpreted the continuation and completion of creation through Christ with ideas taken from the theory of evolution. In fact to a considerable degree he identified the two processes.[5]

Faith in God and faith in the world coincide in faith in the universal Christ, who drives and beckons the world forward to its perfecting. Karl Rahner adopted this viewpoint in his famous essay "Christology within an Evolutionary View of the World", in which he elevated the concept of 'self-transcendence' into the fundamental universal concept for ongoing creation, for the unique character of human beings, and for the nature of Christ. My purpose here is neither to give a detailed account nor to enter into a detailed discussion of these evolution christologies. Our concern is simply the limited question of how the elements of truth they contain can be absorbed into a differentiated cosmic christology.

A. Christus Evolutor ?

Teilhard took up the vision of the cosmic Christ from the Epistle to the Colossians, wishing to expand the church's one-sided presentation of *Christus redemptor* through that universal completer of creation whom

5. Teilhard de Chardin, *Christology and Evolution*, (London: 1971), pp. 76-95.

he called "Christus evolutor." If the Christian doctrine of redemption is related only to original sin, it offers no perspectives for the completion of creation through a gathering together of all things under the head, Christ, and through their entry into that fulness of God which will one day be 'all in all'. But Teilhard discovered "the creative side of redemption", and saw this discovery as the step forward to a new theology. The completion of creation in the divine unification is higher than the redemption of the world from its sins, and is redemption's goal. "The *Christus redemptor* completes himself in the dynamic fulness of a *Christus evolutor* without in any way diminishing his suffering countenance."[6]

In the interests of this view, Teilhard transferred salvation as it was understood by Christian faith to the history of life and the cosmos, understanding this history of nature as evolution from the simple to the complex, from what is individual to what is shared, from the lifeless to the living, and to ever more complex forms of living awareness. For him, salvation history and the evolution of life coincided. He saw the appearance of human beings in the framework of the evolution of life in general.

"Evolution saves Christ by making him possible, and at the same time Christ saves evolution by making it specific and desirable".[7] But in his firm faith in progress Teilhard does seem to have overlooked the ambiguity of evolution itself, and therefore to have paid no attention to evolutions victims. Evolution always means selection. Many living things are sacrificed in order that" the fittest" — which means the most effective and the most adaptable — may survive. In the way higher and increasingly complex life systems, which can react to changed environments, undoubtedly develop. But in the same process millions of living things fall by the wayside and disappear into evolution's rubbish bin. Evolution is not merely a constructive affair on nature's part. It is a cruel one too. It is a kind of biological execution of the Last Judgment on the weak, the sick and "the unfit". If men and women adopt the same way of doing things, what we very soon have is "euthanasia" — "the killing of valueless life". Teilhard can therefore never have taught "universal reconciliation" of all things in whatever form, for that contradicts the whole idea of evolution.

When the first atomic bomb was dropped on Hiroshima on 6 August 1945, Teilhard was filled with enthusiastic admiration for the

---

6. *ibid.* p. 147.
7. *ibid.* p. 155f.

scientific and technological advance which this achievement of a scientific super-brain acting in teamwork had brought humanity. He believed that the control of atomic power would promote the evolution of humanity and the consciousness in a hitherto unheard-of way. Here Teilhard gave no thought to Hiroshima's hundred thousand dead and the people there who are still dying today from radiation damage. He also took a purely positive view of the hydrogen bomb tests in Bikini saying: "For all their military trappings, the recent explosions at Bikini herald the birth into the world of Mankind both inwardly and outwardly pacified. They proclaim the coming of the Spirit of the Earth".[8] Trusting in "life's planetary instinct for survival", he brushed aside the possibility that humanity could ever suffer a nuclear catastrophe: "The earth is more likely to stop organising and unifying itself."[9] He was incapable of recognising the possibility of an atomic apocalypse, about which Günter Anders, Albert Schweitzer and Karl Jaspers were talking even in 1958, because his confidence in the world made him incapable of considering humanity as a whole to be mortal.

For Teilhard, the perspectives of evolution were evidently so vast that while he was no doubt able to join together the remotest points of their beginning and their goal, he found it difficult to perceive what was close and closest. "We still have several million years in front of us," he wrote from Peking in 1941, thinking of the stage of evolution next to be reached in the socialization and totalization of humanity. He did not see that time is running out, because the ecological catastrophes which this very socialization and humanization are producing could very well put an abrupt end to any further evolution on humanity's part.

B. The Counter-Movement

Is it conceivable that this future of creation will be teleologically achieved by way of evolution or self-transcendence? No. It is not conceivable, because the process of creation takes place in time, and 'becoming' inevitably involves transience. There is no evolution without selection. It is true that we can say that all the lower forms of life are still inherent in life's higher forms. But this is true only of the form itself, not of its

8. Teilhard de Chardin, *The Future of Man*, (London and New York: 1964), p. 124.
9. *ibid.* p. 152.

individual examples, and does not lead to their immortality. Even the individual contribution to the evolution of the whole brings the individual no eternity. Teleologically, a perfect being at the end of evolution is certainly conceivable, but not the perfecting of all created things.

The perfecting of the whole creation, extended over time in the creation process, is only conceivable *eschatologically*. The teleology of creation is not its eschatology. What is eschatological is the new creation of all things which were and are and will be. What is eschatological is the bringing back of all things out of their past, and the gathering of them into the kingdom of glory. What is eschatological is the raising of the body and the whole of nature. What is eschatological is that eternity of the new creation which all things in time will experience simultaneously when time ends in eternity. To put it simply: God forgets nothing that he has created. Nothing is lost to him. He will restore it all (Rev. 21.5).

What has to be called eschatological is the movement of *redemption*, which runs counter to evolution. If we want to put it in temporal terms: this is a movement which runs from the future to the past, not from the past to the future. It is the divine tempest of the new creation, which sweeps out of God's future over history's fields of the dead, waking and gathering every last created being. The raising of the dead, the gathering of the victims and the seeking of the lost bring a redemption of the world which no evolution can ever achieve. This redemption therefore comprehends the redemption of evolution itself, with all its ambiguities. In this redemption, evolution turns and becomes revolution, in the original sense of the word. The linear time of evolution will be carried into a unique and then final eschatological cycle: into the return of all the pasts in the eternal aeon of the new creation of all things. Eschatological future is to be understood *diachronically*: It is simultaneous to all the times, and in being so it represents eternity for all things.

The *Christus evolutor* is the *Christ in his becoming* But the *Christus redemptor* is the *Christ in his coming* .

For cosmic christology this means that it is only the reconciliation of all things, whether on earth or in heaven (Col. 1:20), and their redemption from the fetters of the transience of the times which leads to the gathering together of all things in the messiah, and therefore to the completion of creation. The evolutionary series in the history of nature and in human history are the outcome of *continuous creation* The redemption and the new creation of all created things can be expected only from *the coming of Christ* in glory. The *recapitulatio mundi* presupposes the *resurrectio mortuorum*, for the cosmic Christ will not only become the Lord who fills all spaces of creation with "the messianic intensity" of the divine peace (shalom). He will also become the Lord who fills all the times of creation with the messianic extensity of redemption. In the Epistle to the Colossians, the spatial picture of the cosmic Christ is dominant, in Paul the temporal picture of the eschatological Christ (I Cor.15). The two images must complement one another if they are to comprehend the risen and exalted Christ in his spatial and temporal dimensions: his messianic extensity pervades the times of creation to their furthest origins.

This universal eschatology of redemption provides the foundation which then makes it justifiable to discern and acknowledge tendencies in the evolution of nature and in human history as being also parables and hints, anticipations and preparations for the coming of the messianic new creation. The active self-transcendence which is at work in these processes really does point beyond the historical present and beyond history itself to a future which fills it and brings it to rest. But the hunger for this future is not in itself this future's realization.

Only as a whole (*Ta panta*) will creation be reconciled, redeemed and recreated. Without the redemption of nature and the raising of the dead, even successfully realized, human self-transcendence into the divine life remains a fragment, and is at best a glimmer of hope for this unredeemed world.

Let me finish with a few remarks on the political and spiritual consequences of the cosmic Christ:

Some say the concern for the environment is a typical "First World" concern, while the concern of the Third World is hunger and cholera of the poor people. I see that the two concerns are intertwined, because "poverty is the worst pollution" (Indira Gandhi). How?

1. Poverty leads to overpopulation, because there is no other life insurance for the old but children who take care of them. Overpopulation leads to undernourishment and to the consumption of not only the available food but also of one's own basis of life. You have to sell not only the apples, but also the apple tree. We have the fast growing destruction of nature in third world countries along this logic.

2. The world market forces the poor countries into cutting down their rain forests and to the planting of mono-cultures which destroy their original subsistence economy. The world market forces those countries into allowing dangerous industries as in the Indian Bophal factory and into taking the poisenous garbage from the industrial nations as in West Africa.

3. In countries with great social injustice recklessness against nature is nothing special. Violence against weaker human beings justifies violence against the weaker nature. Where there is no social legislation there is also no economic legislation.

4. The terrible experience of the pest-epidemics in the Europe of the fourteenth century which killed one half of the whole population was one reason why Europeans became so aggressive over against the rest of the world. If one is in the unfriendly hands of "natural forces" without defense, one feels as if one is engaged in an ongoing "battle with nature". Poverty and epidemy are the worst destructions of nature. What happens today in Latin America (poverty and cholera) is our problem, because we are the problem of the people there.

And for the spiritual dimension let us hear the unknown saying of Jesus according to Logion 77 of the Gospel of Thomas:

> I am the light that is over them all.
> I am the All: the All has come forth from me
> and the All has attained unto me.
>
> Cleave a piece of wood: I am there.
> Raise up the stone, and ye shall find me there.

Does not follow from this the commandment: you shall love the Lord your God with all your heart, with all your soul and with all your strength — and this Earth as yourself?

Experience the creative power of Christ in the spring of nature, in the fruits of the earth, in love, in art and worship and poetry, and in the children! Sanctify natural life, because life is sacred! Christ is in it!

Response by Alan J. Torrance

Professor Moltmann, in a letter you wrote to Karl Barth 26 years ago you apologised that it took you so long to reply to a letter he had sent you adding that it (and I quote) "keeps looking at me questioningly as I go on with my work". Let me say that your paper which you were good enough to send me some time ago has been looking at me questioningly for some months now. A truly worthy response to a paper of this stature would take even longer than I have had — one suspects it might even be an eschatological enterprise! Several features immediately stood out for me when I read this paper. First, Professor Moltmann's refusal to use Christ to ratify or baptise some prior ecological, anthropological or ethical agenda — a temptation which so much contemporary theology falls into in a pragmatic world.

Second, his refusal to put eschatology to one side when engaging in contemporary concerns where again the onus on the theologian is to be seen to be being relevant to the present, to the here and now. The general thrust of this paper reflects Professor Moltmann's commitment, as we have come to know it well through his books, to rethinking our interpretations of God and of Christ in such a way that our reality is addressed by Christ's Reality in its cosmic dimension and significance. What has always impressed me has been your commitment to being a Christian theologian and your refusal to find cover under the umbrella of some foreign philosophy. We see again and again from your writings that, far from making your theology less relevant this makes it that much more relevant to the challenges of the age.

Having said this let me now engage with three themes in relation to which I should like to pose questions to Professor Moltmann. These concern first, the suggestion that we should move beyond doing Christology in the framework of history to doing Christology in the framework of nature. My question concerns how far nature provides an appropriate framework for Christological thought. The second issue concerns how useful the category of nature is in theological engagement with the ecological threats of our context. I am not so much making a criticism here as seeking to raise a topical issue for discussion. My final question concerns Professor Moltmann's understanding of time as it underlies the inspired eschatological *tours de force* toward the end of his paper.

1. 'Christology in the Framework of Nature'.

New Zealanders take some pride in the comparatively unspoilt, natural beauty of this land. This serves to intensify concerns vis-a-vis ecological threat. The increase in malignant melanoma due in part to the depletion of the ozone layer, possibly through the pumping of toxic wastes into the atmosphere; the ecological effects of growing pollution in the Antarctic region and in parts of the Pacific — in part as a result of nuclear testing, and other activities mean that we can identify, therefore, with Professor Moltmann's fear that we are fast reducing 'nature to a human rubbish heap'. In the church we would also warm to his suggestion that a rethink is needed in Christology and a rediscovery of the cosmic Christ as the one who 'can save men and women from their despair and preserve nature from annihilation.' Simply to allot Christ a place within a general programme of salvation-history or to privatise or spiritualise his significance through body-soul dualisms is clearly to reduce the Christ of cosmic significance to a domesticated Christ — a Christ deprived of the opportunity to address such present day crises. I would endorse Professor Moltmann's comments here unreservedly.

My question, however, concerns whether new problems may emerge if our interpretation of God's activity in Christ is conditioned by a prior, intuitive interpretation of nature and the threats to it. What do we mean by Christology within the framework of nature?

My nervousness is basically the same as that to which Karl Barth gave expression in his opening lecture at the first Assembly of the World Council of Churches. He was given the theme, 'The Disorder of the World and God's Plan of Salvation'. In that lecture he offered a vigorous critique of the theme that had been set, because it is only in the light of God's redemptive engagement with our world that we come to a proper theological perspective on the nature and character of that disorder. If we start with *our* interpretations of its disorder then our perception of God's redemptive activity risks being distorted by this procrustean bed. I suspect the resulting debate that took place between Barth and Reinhold Niebuhr will be echoed during this conference the title of which is 'Christ and Context' as opposed to 'Context and Christ'.

The underlying suggestion is that, although there is no such thing as pure, contextless theology and, granted that there will invariably be a hermeneutical circularity in the dialogue between our contexts and Christology, the theological order or pressure of interpretation and revision should be from *Christ* to our context rather than from our *Context* to Christ. Otherwise, our interpretation of Christ too easily becomes a projection of a prior, unconditioned analysis and agenda (be it ecological or otherwise). A related question to Professor Moltmann is: if, in the light of ecological threat, we are encouraged to move beyond 'Christology in the framework of history' to do 'Christology in the framework of nature' may we not find ourselves simply replacing one procrustean bed with another? And may we not also find that this bed has been tailor-made to accommodate a prior ecocentric agenda? How do we avoid the cosmic Christ being regarded as a means to an end. The thrust of the cosmic Christology of Colossians is precisely that he is not subject to anything. He is Lord and must be so in relation to our questioning, our frameworks and our categories as much as to our answers.

A relevant issue emerges here from an article entitled 'Christ and Creation' by another of our speakers, Professor Daniel Hardy, when he comments that 'the physicist speaks of the fact that all processes generate disorder or entropy: an irreversible destruction of macroscopic order is going on. The biologist, appealing to our intuitive perception of the world as unfolding in time, suggests that everywhere order or information is being generated whereby a simpler state is being transformed into a more complex one.'[1] (103-104) So if we are to explore cosmic Christology within a 'framework of nature' may we not find ourselves in this kind of dilemma? Our interpretation of the cosmic Christ and his redemptive role will be construed in radically different ways if our perspective is that of a physicist, that of a biologist or, indeed, that of an alarmed ecologist. It was, after all, the reinterpretation of the redemptive function of Christ in the light of a foundationalist, biological perspective (with its conception of negative entropy, of positive evolution) that led to the errors of Teilhard de Chardin which you expose so lucidly.

It might seem that such comments are more appropriate to ivory tower discussions of theological method than to a relevant engagement

---

1. D. W. Hardy, "Christ and Creation" in *The Incarnation: Ecumenical Studies in the Nicene-Constantinopolitan Creed*, ed. T.F. Torrance, (Edinburgh: Handsel Press, 1981), pp. 103-104.

with serious contextual issues. However, it is clearly important that if we are to operate as theologians from within a 'framework of nature' we avoid the highly relevant dangers of incipient forms of naturalism or pseudo-naturalism creeping in. 'Reactive' reinterpretations of theology and christology in engagement with threats from the world around us have their own risks attached. Feminist theology has continually had to confront theologies and Christologies within the church which operate from naturalistic interpretations of creation and God's purposes read out of it.

The South African situation is, of course, an *extreme* case but also reflects the risks of operating in this way. The reinterpretation by Afrikaaner theologians of God's creative purposes and of the redemptive and the preserving activity of Christ (which has been mentioned) from within a framework of nature and amidst perceived threats of potential social chaos in their society led to oppressive ways of theological thinking. Appeal to natural reason and and its interpretation of nature led to the conclusion that certain people were created to be 'by nature' inferior to others or to develop separately from others.

Another example in our own context here is the Social Darwinianism which the church has had to challenge within our society. This was advocated in extreme form in New Zealand history when a past premier, Robert Stout, who was Chief Justice of the Supreme Court 1899-1926, and Chancellor of the University of N.Z. 1902-1923, supported the publication of a book which advocated a 'final solution' to the problem of the 'unfit', using sterilization and poison gas technology, to solve New Zealand's problems vis-a-vis those regarded as socially and morally deficient![2] "Survival of the fittest" may be an acceptable category in biology, but is immoral and utterly repugnant to the Gospel when it is applied, as it was by the Nazis, to human beings as a principle of selection.

So my question is: can we find adequate safeguards against these kinds of potential problems of method and praxis if we are to do Christology within a framework of nature?

2. For a fuller discussion see John Stenhouse, "Science Versus Religion in Nineteenth Century New Zealand: Robert Stout and Social Darwinism", *Pacifica* 2 (1989), pp. 61-86.

2. What do we Mean by 'Nature'?

There is an issue here which is basic to our discussion so far which I should also like to raise, though not as a criticism of Professor Moltmann — he is far more aware of the challenges here than I am. It is simply the question: what do we mean by the term 'nature'? How useful is it in addressing ecological issues from a theological perspective? It seems to me there is a dilemma here with which the Green movement finds itself struggling. A beaver builds a dam and it is natural, human beings build a dam and it is vigorously protested as being unnatural — although human beings are being encouraged to eat vast amounts of natural fibre precisely because they are 'natural beings'. Is there not an inconsistency in suggesting that dams, factories or even nuclear bombs are 'unnatural' while affirming that human beings who build them are 'natural' beings? What of course is happening is that a whole set of additional evaluative categories are being ushered in via the backdoor under the umbrella of a concept of 'nature' and the 'natural'. The word is being used to mean different things in different contexts and it is easy to trade on the ambiguity. This ambiguity emerged, for me, in your paper when you mention that women and men are 'natural beings' but then go on to refer to the abandonment of nature 'to its disastrous exploitation by human beings'.

So the first question here is: what do we mean by the term 'nature' — especially as those who use the term frequently seem to shift their ground? A second question is: what theological function can it possibly have?

As you mention in your critique of Teilhard de Chardin, the very essence of the evolutionary process (within nature) of natural selection is a competitive struggle for resources with 'nature' dictating who is to survive. If the outworkings of human nature are a series of ecological events which lead to the ultimate demise of our own species, can we condemn this as 'unnatural' or as 'an abuse of nature', because it clearly isn't — it is quite natural and thoroughly evolutionary? Can 'nature' really dictate what is and what is not an ecological catastrophe? What is cosmically inappropriate about such an event on planet earth? It may be that it is contrary to the best interests of the human species but to say that this is part of the sin of creation or ecological catastrophy in need of redemption is surely to make recourse to another principle — an anthropic principle (that is the approach which assumes that the universe centres around humanity). In this case we are not doing christology in 'the framework of nature', rather we are doing christology in 'the framework of an interpretation of nature carried out with recourse to the anthropic principle'. This means that when we use the term 'nature' in theology we are using it to mean something very different from what it means in the secular world and this is surely something we must be 'up front' about. In other words, in order to offset a mass of sinister consequences, we are overlaying the concept with further principles — not least those inherent within the the concept of redemption, to which you appeal, quite rightly.

In the light of the various concerns I have raised above, is it not perhaps the case that the primary theological challenge here is not so much the production of a christology in the framework of nature (which will revise our praxis vis-a-vis nature), as a theological hermeneutic of nature (grounded in the Christ of the cosmos)? If we are to use the concept of 'nature', despite all its ambiguity, it must surely be redefined in the light of the creating Christ. This will be critical if our ecological Christology is not simply to be a means of assuming divine confirmation or ratification of our present ecological analyses and programmes. Is it not the case that affirming Christ as Lord of the cosmos may lead us to support some form of carefully *qualified* 'anthropic' principle — rather than a bare 'phusic' principle which treats 'nature' as a controlling category?

Focussing on these issues, serves to highlight not merely questions which may be addressed further but also some of the thoroughly constructive ways forward which emerge from Professor Moltmann's paper.

1) First his critique of the nature-grace dualism and his rejection of the parallel separation of creation from redemption I see as enormously relevant and is something which I should like to hear Professor Moltmann expand much further.

2) Secondly, I find Professor Moltmann pointing to a hermeneutical key in and through his interpretation of the messianic Wisdom — the 'through whom', 'in whom' and 'for whom' of creation. I suspect this may address very effectively indeed, some of the questions I am raising. On this particular issue, however, I wondered whether the other reformed doctrine of a Triplex Munus — the threefold office of Christ as Prophet (in his being Word), Priest and King — might serve to enhance the threefold office of the rule of Christ to which Professor Moltmann refers. As Word Christ becomes the key to the interpretation of creation and the agent of an appropriately qualified conception of the God-given, intrinsic reality of the created order. As its Priest and its Servant-King he holds together in a unity the teleological and

eschatological elements. The intrinsic reality of this creation and its fulfillment of God's purposes is therefore 'in a manner present' (Calvin) in the midst of its alienation and incompleteness. Moreover, the God-given function of creation and our recognition of this function become two aspects of the same reality as these are held together, through the Spirit, in an integrated unity.

3. Space-time Issues.

This brings me to a concluding issue which I should like to raise in relation to the conclusion of Professor Moltmann's paper. If we operate from our basic or intuitive conceptions of the cosmos and conceive of the cosmic agency of Christ in these terms, we run the risk of absolutising those axes (like time) which accompany our prior, 'intuitive' conceptions of the cosmos. Without accusing Professor Moltmann of doing this, I do suspect that this is inherent in the church's conception of continuous creation (*creatio continua*), as it is usually interpreted.

The basic problem is that we stand in danger of seeing time as an absolute, over-arching axis whereas, properly speaking, time is inseparable from the objects of creation and must be seen in terms of the open and relative relations between things. To be more specific we can find ourselves thinking in terms of what D.C. Williams, the Harvard philosopher, supported by the Australian philosopher, J. C. Smart, has termed the 'myth of passage' — the fallacious idea either that we and other entities (defined with reference to three-dimensional space) are, in some sense, 'moving through time' or that time itself moves or is 'ongoing' (as we say). In other words, there is a misunderstanding latent in everyday language and thought relating to our intuitive conceptions of the cosmos, which leads us to think that we can talk coherently about 'the passage of time'. Williams shows that any such talk would necessarily have to make reference to hyper-time for the simple reason that any talk of movement or ongoingness must, by its very nature, make recourse to time. If we talk of time as 'passing' or 'ongoing' then we find ourselves postulating two levels of time. If we then say that hypertime 'passes' or is 'ongoing', we find ourselves in an infinite regress. As Williams argues, 'Nothing can move in time alone any more than in space alone, and time itself can not 'move' any more than space itself. 'Does this road go anywhere?' asks the city tourist. 'No, it stays right along here.' replies the countryman.

All this means that I suspect there is a need at least to unpack the metaphors which Professor Moltmann uses when he suggests that 'Continuous creation is creation's ongoing history.' or that '[t]he process of creation takes place in time' or that 'becoming inevitably involves transience.' Two problems emerge here. First, if creation takes place within time or is a temporal 'ongoing' then we are differentiating incorrectly between created realities and the time in which they are created. Secondly, to say that creation is 'ongoing in time' is as problematic as saying it is 'everywhere in space'. Or to put it another way, we can no more talk about creation continuing in time than creation's being an object in space.

These problems emerge as soon as time is conceived as an extrinsic axis as opposed to being conceived as integral to the defining coordinates of things and therefore inseparable from the relations between things and that means the very being of things at the most fundamental level. Strictly speaking, the notion of the continuous creation of things in time becomes inappropriate, as also the notion of an original creation (*creatio originalis*) taking place at the beginning of time. Creation simply should not be thought of as a temporal event.

All this is particularly serious for Teilhard de Chardin's conception of 'Le Dieu en avant' (the God ahead). It is as difficult to make sense of this statement as it is of the assertion that God is above us or, for that matter, that God lives in the White House! (He doesn't, by the way!)

However, parallel questions emerge for me with your statement 'What is eschatological is that eternity of the new creation which all things in time will experience simultaneously when time ends.' Similarly, the notion of a counter-movement is problematic — there can be no backward movement in or through time for the simple reason that there is no movement in time at all. As Williams shows, time does not run forward any more than it runs backward. Now Professor Moltmann would be totally justified in replying that we simply cannot escape from spatio-temporal thinking and so there is some warrant here in appealing to provisional metaphors which are 'reality depicting', to use a phrase from Dr. Janet Martin Soskice, without being literal expressions. But this does not alter the fact that it is dubious to make a distinction between Christ's spatial or cosmic role and his temporal or eschatological role. If we interpret the cosmos out of Christ seeing space-time as relative, such dichotomies begin to break down.

The way forward emerges, if we take more seriously the *ephapax* emphasis in the New Testament, that is, the 'once and for all' nature of the event of Christ. If we wish to see the Christ of the cosmos, i.e. the cosmic Christ, we should neither engage in some form of cosmic extension of Christology nor should we look to the end of time to an eschatological future. Rather, I think we should focus on the 'once and for all' fulness of God's spatio-temporal indwelling as we find it concretely in the person of Christ the 'place' in space-time (the *topos*) and the focus in space-time (*skopos*) of God's engagement with humankind. Strictly speaking, the 'new creation' is not to be found by looking to our future, nor in our present nor our past any more than we should conceive of it as occupying some particular space. It concerns the fulfillment of God's purposes of communion in a New Creation which, as Professor Moltmann rightly points out, is not simply a restored creation but is so radically new that our space-time categories may only function analogically in their reference to it. Testimony to its reality is to be found solely in the conditioned experience of the communion which stems from the grace of God in the once and for all event of Christ.

To summarise the questions I have raised above in a single question: would the issues which Professor Moltmann explores, combined with the New Testament emphasis that the cosmos is subject to Christ, not, perhaps, imply that his paper 'Christ in Cosmic Context' suggests a further analysis 'Cosmos in Christic Context'?

This would ensure that the Cosmic Logos could not be interpreted as the 'Logos' in the sense of an absolutised human logos or set of ideas i.e. where Christ may function to provide divine affirmation for prior, intuitive perspectives on nature and creation. The Christ who is Lord of the Cosmos is the one who, from our perspective, requires to be seen as the Counter-Logos, to use Bonhoeffer's expression — the One who radically redefines and conditions our perspectives on nature in such a way that God's whole creative intention may be opened up to us, by the Spirit. In this way, our theorising (with all the categories, axes and demarcations with which we operate) may be qualified and corrected by, what Professor Hardy calls, the 'divine pressure on us' which necessitates a radical differentiation of God from the sum of the domains of this world. Let me end this response by saying that these rather long-winded comments are really little more than the yapping of a dachshund at the heals of the master! They are not so much criticisms as questions posed for clarification. Personally, I found Professor Moltmann's paper to be a kind of *logos spermatikos* — a word of seminal wisdom and prophetic that challenges much that is inherently weak in our thinking about Christology and creation, suggesting highly constructive ways forward. If any comments are unfair let me take refuge in a comment you made in that same letter to which I referred at the start of this response, 'Polemics always makes one a little one-sided.'

Response by Gustavo Gutiérrez

First, I would like to express my gratitude for the invitation to participate in this symposium and share with you in our common faith and hope. I would also like to express my gratitude to Professor Moltmann for his deep and stimulating presentation. I did have some remarks about trends today in Christology and also about Teilhard de Chardin, but, after listening to Professor Moltmann's conclusion I have changed my mind.

1. Garbage

By way of comments on Professor Moltmann's paper, first: in his conclusion he mentioned, a very important theological word: garbage. It is one way of describing what is referred to as the Third World (maybe it is now the Second World, now that there is no longer a second world — our only promotion in recent years!). Listening to Professor Moltmann I recall a biblical book: the Book of Job.

It is said that Job spoke from the dust heap, from the ashes, but more exactly Job spoke from the garbage heap, the dung hill. Many Christians are trying to do the same, to reflect on God from this side of history, that is, from the garbage heap. Maybe it is for this reason that it seems paradoxical that we try to be sensitive to the central point in Job: that it is not the human being who is the centre of creation, but God. Remember in God's speech to Job in chapter 38, God tells Job that it is God who makes rain in lands where no one lives. This is a poetic way of speaking about the gratuitous love of God. The gratuities love of God is possibly the central message of the book. Job is a very ironical book, because in the same speech God says, speaking about wild animals, donkeys, oxen, etc, that they are not submissive to the human person, but that they are free. The notion of the gratuitous love of God certainly seems to be a central point in the book of Job, and we know this is the central point of the Christian message. We have this in other writers who are leaders in the Church (though Job is not exactly a leader), like Saint Paul for example. But the book of Job is very clear regarding this point. The notion of the gratuitous love of God is present from the beginning, and creation is the expression of God's freedom, as well as God's delight. This is creation.

The author of the book of Job is trying to answer, if not to be in opposition to another book in the Bible: the book of Genesis. In Genesis the human person is lord and king of creation, but in the book of Job represents another theological trend portraying God as the only King and Lord of creation.

Job could possibly be the patron saint of ecology today. Unfortunately he was not exactly a historical figure, but I think that in the book we find a very different basis for the very important matter which was the starting point of Professor Moltmann's presentation: ecology.

As I have already said the book of Job is very important. Perhaps it seems paradoxical to speak about the gratuitous love of God as the basis of a biblical and Christian conception of ecology when speaking from the garbage heap, but it only appears to be so in the first analysis, because there are many people in the world at present who are living on the garbage heap.

2. Poverty

To pass on to my second point, once again starting from one of Professor Moltmann's last points, I want to talk about poverty and pollution. To me it is very interesting that he spoke about these two points. My interest here is in how we reach the notion of creation as the first salvific act, how we reach the notion of re-creation, the renewal of creation, if we do not start from the effort to clean up the pollution and the poverty which are both ever-present in the world. I agree with Professor Moltmann's point of Christology in the framework of history and nature. Alan Torrance has also mentioned this point. But it depends on our sense of history. If by history we understand the relationship between human beings living in society with nature, if history is understood as not only the social relations but also relations with nature, then, it seems to me, in trying to establish a just society, trying to clean up the pollution and the poverty present today, then we are able to understand creation as a salvific act, the first salvific act (an idea which of course comes from the German biblical scholar Gerhard von Rad).

We have the same process in the Bible, because the first and deepest experience for the Hebrew people was the Exodus. From the Exodus, from this liberation from slavery, they were able to speak about creation, and also about the Promised Land. Today it seems that the experience of poverty, or the sensitivity to the inhuman conditions of so many people in today's world, is perhaps a way, not the only one, of avoiding the separation between history and nature. To take up my point again about history, history refers to both human society and the transformation of nature. Maybe the ecological issue, and our sensitivity to it, can assist us to understand this a little better.

To conclude my second point, we need to start from our historical experience in order to understand yet again the biblical message, and it is important to stress that this process is never finished. The notion has been clearly and deeply presented by Professor Moltmann. The Cosmic Christ — it seems to me — is not so far from our experience. Let me give a small example. Perhaps for Western theologians (and I am myself partly a Western theologian), it is not so easy to overcome the separation between history and nature, but for the indigenous people, for example those in my own country, but I am sure here in New Zealand as well, it is not so difficult because they are so close to nature. They cannot think about their history without nature. It is impossible for them to separate the two.

I would like to employ here one Indian word from my country: *Pachamama* (Mother earth). The *Pachamama* is the land, and is the central notion both culturally and religiously speaking. If we present the biblical message without relation to the *Pachamama*, it is impossible for many in Peru to understand it, because it is life. The *Pachamama* is life, it is nature. I think that we have something very important theologically to learn from the experience of people living on the garbage heap of humanity today.

3. Spirituality and Creation

My third and final point comes from Professor Moltmann's conclusion regarding spirituality and creation. In the material I prepared before I came I had some observations about Teilhard de Chardin, but I will not raise them here now. I agree with Professor Moltmann's point that Teilhard was not really a theologian. Maybe he was more than a theologian: a poet, or a mystic, because poetry and mysticism are gifts coming from God. Theology is the result of our effort. I admit that I think in Teilhard we have deep intuition, but systematically it is very difficult to agree with him. Teilhard did stress the importance of the spirituality of creation, which is a very important point I think.

At one point in Professor Moltmann's presentation we have the affirmation of Christ's resurrection. The *resurrectio mortuorum.* Here, in Christ's resurrection we encounter a very important question, which adds to the points that I have been making.

To believe in the resurrection is to affirm life and not death. The resurrection is the last word of history. For people who are familiar with an early and unjust death, the announcement of the resurrection is very important. Sometimes I think that there are many theological reflections on Christ's resurrection which are very empty, because the authors ignore the issue of unjust death, which is the reality for many in this world. Historically speaking it is only possible from the sensitivity to unjust death today to speak strongly about Christ's resurrection, because in it we understand the meaning of the affirmation of life. As Christians we believe in life, and it is a synthetic notion upon which to build a Christology.

The points regarding Christology and the reference to scripture and Patristics are very important in Professor Moltmann's paper. I would like only to stress these points, to overcome, once again, the separation between history and nature, and to avoid any confusion, the notion of life is really, very, very important.

Conclusion

To conclude, I would like to recall my three points. The first is the gratuitous love of God. The human person is not the centre of creation, but God. The second is the relevance of the praxis of liberation, the struggle for justice, the closeness of the poor to nature, so as to understand the other two points of creation and salvation (as well as the renewal of creation). Finally, I have said that life is an appropriate word to express these ideas. For this reason I was very happy, reading, and listening to Professor Moltmann underline Christ's resurrection in order to take up another perspective in our reflecting about the Christ of faith.

Reply by Jürgen Moltmann to Alan J. Torrance and Gustavo Gutiérrez

I will respond briefly to the two papers. We have had this dichotomy or dualism between history and nature in our culture since the beginning of the nineteenth century. You have it all the time in the division between the departments of science and of humanities. In this framework history was understood as a dynamic reality and anthroprocentric, always understood human history, and nature was regarded as the static reality or merely the stage on which the human history takes place, just a framework which is not important. Human drama or the God-human drama is the main thing. And this meant they left nature to science and technology, without any theological reflection on the salvation of nature or on the redemption of nature. There was, interestingly enough, one science which nobody knew where to put, either in the science department or in the humanities department. It was medicine. In Germany, medicine up to 1850 was part of the Geisteswissenschaften, the humanities, and then it changed over to natural science, to the Naturwissenschaften, with the application of the methods of natural science. Why? Because the human being is not just an historical being, the human being is a natural being as well. Because we all *have* bodies and *are* some-body and the body is part of nature as well as part of the person and therefore this dichotomy could neither be applied to the human person nor to medicine. What I am trying to do is to integrate this paradigm of reality as 'human history' into the larger framework of 'nature', and by 'nature' I mean, very specifically, the living organism of the earth in which human beings live and have their history. So I am not talking about philosophical concepts of nature, I am just speaking about the framework of this life-giving earth in which we live and have human history. This framework gives certain limitations to human history which we must observe otherwise we destroy ourselves. There is a certain ambiguity in our everyday language and our feeling. When we speak about the Earth we think about the reality on which we walk and can trample etc. But is this the Earth? If you look at pictures made from spaceships etc, and you look at the globe, then all of a sudden you discover that human people do not live on Earth, they live in the Earth, because the atmosphere, the biosphere, they all belong together to one big life-giving system in which we live. It is difficult to realise it, but it's not too difficult I believe, and therefore I try to work with an integrated paradigm — human history in the nature of this earth. Of course the nature of the earth is affected by human history and human history is limited and affected by the nature of the Earth. But there are certain limits which must be respected otherwise human history is destructive to nature first and then to itself.

Now for Christology, I followed the old regulation of the Patristic Fathers. I think it was Gregory of Nysa who said that what is not accepted, cannot be healed. So God in Christ accepted the whole human being not only the soul, but also the body, in order to heal the whole human being. And I think this must now be extended to the whole of reality in which human beings live. Therefore we can say that in the incarnation, God accepted not only human nature but — by and with human nature — the nature of the Earth as well. What is not accepted cannot be healed. God does not forget even one of his own creatures, otherwise he would not be God. So this then would be a concept of nature in Christology and I'm not quite sure whether this opposition of; cosmos or nature in Christ vs. Christ in the context of the cosmos, is in fact a real alternative. This is a typical Karl Barth question, an either/or question. That is, do we live in God or does God live in us? I think it's a mutual indwelling because the one who remains in love remains in God and God in him. This is a scripture quotation, and therefore the Cosmos in Christ is the Cosmos, it's not a real alternative, it's a mutual indwelling. I spoke about a text and a context in a hermeneutical way on this point. I prefer the term 'nature' because by nature, *natura nasci* in Latin, we mean a life-giving reality not just an object, but something which is life-giving in itself — producing life, plants and trees etc, and therefore the source of life. This is the what we have meant for a long time by the term nature. Of course nature has two sides; one side is called Mother Nature and there you have the life-giving form, and the other part is called death-giving nature — nature which takes away human beings. This is the on-going process of life and death in the world which we call nature, it has two sides. I prefer this term over against 'environment' because if we called the reality in which we live environment, we would mean our human environment, and would ignore the fact that this is also the environment of the plants and the trees and the fish and the sea and the birds etc. We environmentalise the whole world and make it human centered. Thus the term environment could be the last aggressive term against nature. When we speak about nature it's more mutual. We speak about what is giving life to us and the other living beings. The term in theology which we use is 'creation' and if we use the term 'creation', we invoke a creator, a family of creatures. We then refer to creature and co-creature etc. So this is a whole different world recalling a reality outside — not nature but creation. We respect the rights of the creator over his creatures, so it cannot be conceived of anthropocentrically and environmentalised to human culture. We must respect God as the source of all being and God as the one who has the right over his own creatures. As a result we use the term creation in the ecological movement in Germany as a term of resistance against the destruction of nature. And strangely enough for the first time in a German legal text on the preservation of animals, we find the term creature and co-creature — Mitgeschöpf — used, and I think we can introduce these terms, 'creation' and 'creature', into our constitution if we formulate something along the lines that one of the goals of the society is to preserve nature as creation. If, on the other hand, we call creation nature, what we mean is the present state of the creation, and by this we mean that creation for the time-being is not paradise any more and therefore we don't believe in natural evolution and the idea that everything is a paradisic state. It's also not yet the kingdom of God. This is therefore the situation of creation between the 'creation in the beginning' where everything was very good and the 'new creation' where everything is glorious. The mystics in the mediaeval time, Hildegard of Bingen for example, spoke about the present situation of creation as a winter of creation, expecting the new creation to happen as a spring of creation where everything blooms again. I think this is a very good poetic symbol — the idea that we live in a kind of a winter of creation expecting the new creation as a spring of creation, when everything becomes alive again as in spring in Germany. Now I am aware that you live on the other side of the seasons.

I think I should not go into a debate about the concept of time because this will take too much of your time. As Old-European as I am, I still believe that there is a 'before' and an 'after', and I still believe that one is allowed to speak about future, present and past, and that there is a certain irreversibility because future can become present and then past, but past cannot become future again, so future is associated with possibilities while past is associated with reality out of possibility. Possibilities can be realised, but reality cannot again be possibility. For there is that irreversibility and I think every living creature knows about that. No more of this.

Now to the points Gustavo Gutiérrez made, I agree with all of them and I like them very much. I would like in addition to call your attention to Psalm 8. There a human being is indeed something like a lord and king in God's creation. Everything is done under his feet etc. And then there's Psalm 104 where the human being is just a fellow creature and everything is well ordered. At night the human being sleeps and the lions go out and have their meal and when the sun rises the lions go to sleep and the human being goes out. Everything is well ordered in the family of creatures according to Psalm 104. I think we look too much to Psalm 8 and to little to Psalm 104. At least there are these two sides, on the one hand the human being as lord and king in the creation and on the other hand as one of the family of creatures. This ambiguity is perhaps constitutional of human beings. We are part of nature and we have nature. We have a body and we are somebody. It's an ambiguity in ourselves — we are inside ourselves and we can transcend ourselves. Similarly, we are inside of nature and at the same time we can transcend nature. We need a balance in this ambiguity, because we experience reality in the category of being, and in the category of having. In our modern culture the categories of having are extended enormously and the categories of authentic human being are mostly underdeveloped.

To the second point I would like to add that the Exodus upon which liberation theology rests so much, leads, according to the biblical story, to the covenant, and the covenant, according to Genesis 9, is established "with you and your descendants after you and with every living creature that is with you", so the living creatures are partners in God's covenant together with human being according to the covenant of Noah. Out of this "covenant with you" I think human rights follow. From this "and your descendants after you", come the rights of future generations, and the rights of nature come from "and with every living creature". So at least this is a biblical proposal to understand all the other living creatures as partners in the covenant and to respect their covenant with God.

The other point I would like to make is that equivalent to the Exodus motif and paradigm, is the Sabbath theology in the Old Testament, and also in the New Testament, and the Sabbath theology is a theology for all creatures because they all have the right to rest on the Sabbath day and especially on the Sabbath year. The justice of God is restored in the people of God and in the land of God. There is one interpretation of the Babylonian exile in the Old Testament, which says that Israel was driven out of the land of God because Israel neglected the Sabbath of the land, and that Israel had to remain in the foreign country for seventy years so that the land of God could celebrate it's solemn rest and Sabbath which it has not had during the time that Israel dwelled in the land. So there is a special relationship between the Sabbath and the land, and perhaps we should reintroduce into our agriculture and into our life-system together with nature this Sabbath rest, because the Sabbath gives an opportunity to restore energy not only in our human life but also in the life of nature.

When I was a young boy in the northern part of Germany, there was a fallowing principle followed by the farmers so that every fifth or seventh year the land had to be left free from human exploitation so that it could restore its energy. After the war, with all the fertilisers etc, the earth was forced into on-going fertility and this destroyed much of the land in Germany so that we are now thinking about reintroducing the Sabbath principle to agriculture and the land.

The last point is very important I think. History and life come together, and nature belongs together with the concept of life, and with what we call the resurrection of the dead. This is a very strong (the strongest) affirmation of life not only for those who are living but also for those who die and therefore I am very grateful for this last point. The affirmation of life is also the experience in the Spirit of God which we participate in from day to day. Thank you.

8

The "One World": A Challenge to Western Christianity

Johann B. Metz

I.

In its essence Christianity is not a dualismin which the world and its history are untouched by salvation and this salvation is removed from the world and its history. The peace of God wills us to become peacemakers. The justice of God destines us to resist the injustice in this worl, and the heaven which is promised to us desires that there be no heaven without the earth.

In its essence Christianity is not a spirituality secluded from the world and its history. It does not teach, if I may say so, mysticism with eyes closed, but rather, a mysticism with eyes opened. The Gospel calls not only for hearing, but also seeing! In matters of faith Jesus puts the emphasis on being able to see — to our continual amazement — "Lord when did we see you ...when did we see you naked, see you hungry, see you imprisoned?" Jesus desires that religion, instead of closing its eyes to the world, gives new eyes to see, an increasing perception for the suffering of the stranger, for the affliction that is invisible or made invisible. In short, he teaches — for example, when one really reflects on the parable of the Good Samaritan — a mysticism with eyes opened.

This type of mysticism becomes more and more important in our modern world of the mass media. For television, which already almost transcendentally encompasses our lives, does not actually teach us to see and perceive, but merely to observe. Instead of turning us into "seers", we become voyeurs, ultimately, possibly, the voyeurs of our own decline.

It is true that Christianity appears in its essence as a great exaggeration. The standards that Jesus proposed for being attentive, for loving, for being responsible for others are intolerably high. There is an air of anarchy about his message. Who can possibly live it without compromise? And so for the last 2000 years we have sought to whittle down these standards, to shrink them down so that we can get along with them without risking too much conversion. Yet time and again the restlessness, the rebelliousness within Christianity breaks forth: that these standards will not be arbitrarily cut down, or proclaimed with a merely aesthetic radicalism. The tension between discipleship and world, between mysticism and politics remains rooted in the center of Christianity. This tension marks at the same time the greatness and the constitutional risk of Christianity, its apocalyptic restlessness, so to speak.

These (admittedly sporadic) descriptions of Christianity belong to the necessary premises of my subsequent (and now more academic) reflections on "The 'One World' as a Challenge to Western Christianity."

II.

Christianity does not encounter the experience of the "one world" only from the-outside. Actually, it is itself already on the way toward a real World Christianity. Christianity was for almost 2000 years bound to a relatively united cultural sphere, namely, the European and Western sphere. It is today expanding toward a World Christianity which is rooted in a variety of cultures. It stands today at perhaps the most fundamental historical turning point since its very beginning. It is on the way from a culturally more or less unified, thus a culturally monocentric European and North American Christianity toward a World Christianity rooted in many cultures, and in this sense culturally polycentric. For the Catholic Church the recent Vatican Council stands out as the institutionally tangible expression of this awakening.

At this point the theme of the "one world" becomes crucial for Christianity, both practically and in theological reflection. I begin with the problem that starts from the empirical situation of our present day world, and the processes toward uniformity emerging within it. The discussion of a World Christianity which is culturally polycentric presupposes that indeed such a living cultural variety in our modern world does exist. But this is in no way as obvious at it might seem at first glance. More and more the question imposes itself whether the macrocultural variety in our world is invisibly disappearing, whether this variety — slowly, but surely — is being broken down and leveled by that secular westernizing of the whole world that we call "science" and "technology", or even "technological civilization." This process with its information and culture industries rumbles like a bulldozer across the planet. It affects not simply the praxis, but clearly also the mentalities of peoples. A woman from Bali who drives a car is already a half-secularized Westerner. A South American Indian who watches television and no longer listens to the tribe's story-teller is just as much so. This modernizing of minds in the Western fashion is at work everywhere. For a long time non-western countries have been under siege from a "second colonization": Through the invasion of the Western culture industry and its mass media, especially that of television which holds people prisoner in an artificial world, a world of make believe. It alienates them more and more from their own cultural images, from their original language and their own history. This colonization of the spirit is so much harder to resist because it appears as a sugar-coated poison, and because the gentle terror of this Western culture industry operates not as an alienation, but as a narcotic drug. For a long time, the opium of the poor has no longer been religion, but much more the culture of the mass media, which breaks down the power of resistance in these poor and exploited peoples, before they have a chance to become subjects, bearers of their own freedom. This mass media culture robs them of their own memory, scarcely before they have become aware of their own history of suffering. It threatens their languages, even before they have finally managed to express themselves, before they learn the "alphabet" of their own culture. It seems at least as if the non-western peoples and cultures have fallen into a Western whirlpool. As the German writer Hans Magnus Enzensberger remarks: "What causes one's heart to sink is not the fact that the population of a poor country is compelled with a gentle but elementary force toward an improvement of their living conditions, but rather the path of the forced imitation that they thereby take... The 'idée fixe' of progress for Europeans and North Americans has fallen more and more into doubt; it now reigns unchallenged only in the 'developing' countries of Asia, Africa and Latin America. The really Western oriented people — these are precisely the "others." Even if one thinks that this formulation is exaggerated, it cannot be disputed that the non-western peoples and cultures in the meantime have fallen under a massive pressure to conform to the secular westernizing of the world.

Has not then the cultural polycentrismin our world already been undermined in its foundations? Is there still enough cultural identity and resistance to fight against such a mass-produced world civilization so empty of substance? What does it mean then: the "one world", in other words, the "Oikumene" in its literal sense of the "inhabited earth"? This question draws attention to a deep-seated conflict: the one world now being formed as a result of the secular westernizing wins its unity through the triumph of one dimensionality. It wins it through the shrinkage and leveling of cultural differences and othernesses, by turning their special historical and ethnic characteristics into folklore, as it were. Opposed to this, Western Christianity as it transcends itself toward a polycentric World Christianity in the course of enculturation seeks the one world precisely in its ethnic and cultural diversity and dignity.

2.

Yet exactly at this point when we assume that such a diversity in our one world of today still exists and that it must be preserved, there arises — as the second problem — the real theological question: how should Western Christianity form a bond with these non-western cultures when it clearly cannot regard the project of the technological world civilization, and thus the secular westernizing of the world, as an innocent and neutral catalyst for World Christianity? This question, as you know, is treated in present day theology under the catchword "enculturation". I am not able here to expound thoroughly the entire breadth of meaning of this concept in its use in theology and in the church. It is here simply a question of excluding from the start a misunderstanding that very often occurs when people discuss Christianity's taking root in non-western cultures. It seems to me essential to point out this misunderstanding if we do not want to misrepresent theoretically the challenge of the one world to Western Christianity, and if we want to understand the project of enculturation as a project for peace.

There are today many well-meaning attempts to protect Christianity from ethnocentrlc fallacies, and, by taking into account foreign peoples and cultures, to prevent a second late takeover of World Christianity by the West. These attempts are often accompanied by proposals like this: Christianity must finally discard its Western clothing, it must finally strip off its Western shell, and so forth. Evidently, underneath this approach there is hidden the idea of a non-historical Christianity, of an ethnically innocent Christianity which is free from cultural limitations, whose identity one can conceive like one of Plato's ideas. I could also say: Behind this is hidden the idea of a "pure" or "naked" Christianity whose substance at first only consists of itself, and then later dresses itself in the various cultural robes. But this idea is a fiction; it is nourished by the unproven, metaphorical talk of "bare facts" or of the "pure truth". Christianity that was pre-existent to culture and history, or a culturally divested, a culturally naked Christianity does not exist.

The culture which Christianity cannot simply take off as one takes off a piece of clothing is that European and Western culture that was formed from the Jewish and Hellenistic Greek traditions. With this arises the crucial question: if Christianity cannot simply strip off this historically contingent cloak in order to slip into this or that cultural mantle, how can there be a World Christianity that is rooted in truly diverse cultures ? With this starting point, how can a real enculturation of the Gospel take place which would be something more than simply an expansion of Western culture concealed for tactical reasons Thus, is what we call cultural polycentrism in World Christianity ultimately anything more than the continuation of a monocultural colonization of the souls of foreign peoples and cultures, only now carried out with less drastic means than used previously in the history of the Church?

III.

The attempt to respond to these questions outlines the challenges which are posed to Western Christianity in the face of the one world. A culturally polycentric World Christianity which cannot and must not strip off its Western historical origins is possible under the presupposition that this Christianity remembers two fundamental characteristics of its biblical heritage. It must more and more realize these traits, realize them above all as a dangerous memory within the Western world itself in order to break the one-dimensionality with which today it overshadows the whole world. Western Christianity must, as its first characteristic, remember its biblical heritage and actualize it as the ferment of a *political* culture that seeks freedom and justice for all. It must, as the second, remember the biblical heritage and actualize itself as the ferment of what might be called a *hermeneutical* culture, that is, a culture that recognizes the others in their otherness, as should be well-known to us from the early history of Christianity. Both characteristics of the biblical heritage belong inseparably together. Actually, the suggested distinction between the two is relative, for the hermeneutical culture is also of vital political relevance — and not least in view of the contribution of Christianity toward the peaceful living together of the peoples of the world. Enculturation, when properly understood, is really also work for peace.

1.

I would like to treat here very briefly the question in what way Western Christianity has to protect and to fulfil the biblical heritage as the ferment of a political culture of freedom and of universal justice. In the last few years there have been significant contributions made in the discussion about a new political theology and about liberation theology. I would thus like here to limit myself to treating the threats to this political culture within the Western world .

First of all, a word about the threats to the basic concept of *freedom*. Has not an economic sense been superimposed upon the understanding of freedom that was painfully won and gradually developed in the history of the West. Has not the goods and exchange principle of our civilization in the meantime extended beyond the economic sphere, reaching into the spiritual foundation of our society and in its own way "colonizing" the relationships among people. Does not in principle everything appear marketable, even relationships among human beings in which freedom concretely lives and actualizes itself? And has not technology also already superimposed itself upon our freedom? The precipitous acceleration in which we live, the abrupt changes in consumption and in styles, extending even to the cultural fashions, cannot be concretely comprehended. Our impressions become less and less concrete because we can at most quickly glimpse back at the people and things around us. In this way the individual is trained more and more toward accommodating himself to an abstract, ungraspable, to an opaque world. Even the return to the images of childhood seems blocked, because in our automated world, we have smothered these images before they could develop. Everything becomes capable of being technically reproduced, even the productive human being himself. It seems that the human person becomes less and less his own memory and his freedom rooted within that memory. Instead, he becomes only his own experiment. What will become of the human person? In your country the official search for a successor to the human person has already begun. Time magazine portrayed him as "Man of the Year" on their cover a few years ago: the robot,a gentle machine that works without complaint, resistant against all crises, a computerized intelligence that is not capable of remembering because it also cannot forget. In other words, an intelligence without history, without the ability to suffer, without morality. It is true that this may sound like science fiction (still?), but it forces us to question the substance of our freedom, and the consequences of a secular westernization of the world.

With a view toward a political culture which seeks justice for all, I would like to indicate a further potential danger. My concern is based on the impression that I have received in the last few years above all in my own country, but also throughout Europe, and which continues to grow within me. It refers to a change in our attitude toward the poorer countries of the world as they seek justice, and in this way toward commitment for universal justice. Isn't there in our countries of the West a new mood, new "habits of the heart" (Bellah), so to speak, which push the misery and need of the poor peoples of the so-called Third World further back into a greater existential distance? Doesn't there spread among us a new provincialism, a new form of privatization in our lives, a rather voyeuristic approach to the great situations of crisis and suffering in the world? Are there not in our enlightened Western world more and more signs of a regression back to a second immaturity, so to speak, which is fed from the conviction that, indeed, today we are better informed about everything than ever before, above all even about what threatens us. That we know about all the crises and all the fears in the world, yet the step from knowledge to action has never seemed so great and never so futile as today? Does not such an impression lead us toward resignation? Or also toward flight into myth and its dreams of innocence (removed from the world of action)? Is there not growing among us more and more an attitude of getting accustomed to crises and to the human misery in the world? We become numb before the crises of poverty which continually seem to reoccur. In response, we shrug our shoulders and delegate the problem to an impersonal social evolution: Does the Third World really exist? Is it not finally merely a projection? Does it exist, perhaps, only rhetorically?

For the Church, however, sorrow-filled reality of these poor countries has become a vital question and a test case for proving itself as a World Church. Finally, the Church no longer "has" a Third World Church, but in the meantime it "is" to a great degree a Third World Church, with an unrenounceable European and Western history as part of its roots. The Western Church must not therefore — almost in postmodern it not finally merely a projection? Does it exist, perhaps, only rhetorically?

For the Church, however, sorrow-filled reality of these poor countries has become a vital question and a test case for proving itself as a World Church. Finally, the Church no longer "has" a Third World Church, but in the meantime it "is" to a great degree a Third World Church, with an unrenounceable European and Western history as part of its roots. The Western Church must not therefore — almost in postmodern fashion — allow itself to be talked out of its standards or allow them to be discarded under the pressure of circumstances. It cannot withdraw from the tension between mysticism and politics into a mythical thinking removed from history. With its creed — "suffered under Pontius Pilate" — it is and remains bound to concrete history, to that history in which people have cried and loved, but also hated, tortured, crucified, and massacred. No myth can give back to the Church the innocence that it has lost in such history. Of course, the Church is not primarily a moral institution, but rather the bearer and transmitter of hope. Its theology is not primarily an ethics, but an eschatology. And it is here that its strength is grounded, that even in a situation where it is powerless, it does not surrender its standards of responsibility and solidarity and does not simply abandon the "preferential option for the poor" to the poorer Churches themselves. This is what I mean when I say that our Western Christianity should remember and realize its biblical heritage as the ferment of a political culture in which freedom and justice are sought for all. In this way it will mature into a culturally polycentric World Christianity which accepts the challenges of the one world in the spirit of the gospel.

2.

I would like now to treat the other challenge which the one world implies for Western Christianity. If Western Christianity is to mature into a culturally polycentric World Christianity, then it must remember and realize its biblical heritage as the ferment of what can be called a hermeneutical culture, that is, a culture of the acknowledgement of others in their otherness, a culture of togetherness, of the earthly "Oikumene" which in its heart is freed from "the will to power" (Nietzsche).

This question does not only involve the living together of the various cultures and the one world. It has to do first with what we today call the "ecological crisis" and what is described in Christian terms as the mission of the "stewardship of creation". From all sides we are called upon today to practice ecological wisdom. Here, nonetheless, we must guard against a theoretical naïvité. In order to exercise this ecological wisdom, we cannot simply in feigned innocence begin with nature itself. Nature itself cannot become the principle of a new way of acting without social and anthropological mediation. We must rather concentrate on the cultural history of nature, that is, the history of human beings interacting with nature. This history, however, is a history of domination, or of subjugation, a history of the will to power.

At the beginning of what we call the Modern Age, the limits of which we are now reaching with ever-increasing clarity, there unfolds — embryonically and overlaid with many religious and cultural symbols — this anthropology of domination. In it (and here I consciously employ the exclusive term) man understands himself as a dominating, subjugating individual over against nature; his knowledge becomes, above all, knowledge via domination, and his praxis is one of exerting power over nature. In this dominating subjugation, in this activity of exploitation and reification, in this seizing power over nature, man's identity is formed. Man is by subjugating. All non-dominating human virtues such as gratitude and friendliness, the capacity for suffering and sympathy, grief and tenderness, recede into the background. They are deprived of social and cultural power or, at best, in a treacherous "division of labor" they are entrusted to women, who are deprived of power anyway in this dominating male culture. These non-dominating attitudes become undervalued also as unique kinds of knowledge.? What dominates is knowledge as subjugation, knowing as "grasping", as "appropriating", as a kind of taking possession. Other forms of sensitive-intuitive access to reality, such as through the eyes and their gaze, are forced aside into the realm of the private and the irrational.

In the meantime this principle of subjugation has long since permeated the psychic foundations of our total sociocultural life. It has become the secret regulating principle of all interpersonal relationships; the psychosocial pathologies of our times provide a surfeit of illustrative material on this. In this sense, we could and should speak, not only — and not even primarily — of a poisoning through unrestricted technical exploitation of the outer nature surrounding man, but also of a poisoning of the inner nature of man himself. An identity thus formed through the principles of domination and subjugation makes the individual profoundly disconnected and, in the strict sense of the term egoistic. It makes the human being incapable of seeing himself and judging himself through the eyes of his victims.

These marks of a dominating anthropology may have long since elapsed us, since the drive to subjugation which belongs to this form of anthropological identity shifted its focus very early on outwards, against foreign minorities, foreign races, and foreign cultures. The European history of colonization has its roots therein, and the fact that the history of Christian missions accompanied this all too closely, arching, as it were, over this history of subjugation, may serve as an illustration of the pervasive way the mechanism of subjugation has also penetrated our church life and religious life.

For me the ecological questions, whether there will be a new cultural history of nature, are closely tied to the question whether there can exist at all in our Western world a new hermeneutical culture which is divested of the will to power. Its touchstone is not primarily our relationship with "nature" but rather our behaviour toward the multicultural diversity in a world which over our heads has long since grown into the one world. Here again I repeat the challenge to our Western Christianity that wants to become a culturally polycentric Christianity: it must develop itself into this hermeneutical culture based on the acknowledgement of the others in their otherness by taking up this early Christian impulse.

For from the beginning Christianity has wrestled with this culture of acknowledgement. The argument between Peter and Paul (cf. Gal 2:11ff) and the struggles at what is called the "council of Jerusalem" (Acts 15) whether the circumcision of the Gentiles should be observed may serve as examples. The refusal of the Jewish Christian Paul to submit the gentile Christian to circumcision is an expression of this acknowledgement of the others in their otherness. This calls to mind that the compassionate acceptance of the stranger is a genuine biblical quality which is also continuously commented upon in the accounts of Jesus' ministry. Moreover, many parables of Jesus point toward the character of promise that lies in the acknowledgement of the stranger, of the others in their otherness. Thus, the impulses toward a hermeneutical culture of acknowledgment lie at the roots of the Jewish-Christian tradition, even if in the course of European history it was later overshadowed and pushed into the background. This hermeneutical culture did not gain at all the significance in church history which would one have expected from these biblical sources. Exempla docent.

In his book *The Conquest of America. The Problem of the Other*? Tzvetan Todorov, a researcher living in Paris, shows that the conquest of America in the sixteenth century succeeded above all because the Europeans were hermeneutically superior to the natives. For example, the Aztecs could recognize and evaluate the small troop of Spanish soldiers led by Cortes only within their own "world view" (in this case, falsely). In contrast, the Europeans had the capability of perceiving these strange others in their otherness, of grasping them with the Aztecs' own "system", so to speak.

Yet, as we know, this grasping of the others in their otherness did not serve for their true acknowledgement: it was a perception of the others in the interest of sizing them up and outwitting them. It was the expression of a hermeneutic of domination, and not that of a hermeneutic of acknowledgement to which all acts of violence, any "will to power" in the acknowledgement of the others in their otherness is foreign. 1992 is the 500th anniversary of America's "discovery". With which eyes was this continent "discovered"? Did the early Christian hermeneutic of the acknowledgement of the others in their otherness play the predominant role? Or was the process of Christianizing America rather much more — and all too much — directed by a questionable hermeneutic of assimilation which could not see the trace of God in the otherness of the others and which therefore turned the uncomprehended others more and more into victims.

Allow me in this context to make very briefly two suggestions about how this almost epochal concealment of the culture of acknowledgement could occur, theologically and ecclesially. If I am not mistaken, the development of the hermeneutic of acknowledgement *in theology* has been obstinately prevented because of the acceptance early on within Christian theology of an epistemological principle which arose from the Greek philosophy of identity (since Parmenides). This principle became effective religiously in Mediterranean Gnosticism. It finally flowed through Plotinus into Christian theology and then left a substantial imprint on the form of Christian thought and Christian philosophy of religion from Neo-Platonism up through German idealism. I mean that principle of epistemology according to which "like can only be known from like". If, however, one does not follow the Greek ontological thinking, but rather the covenant thinking of the biblical traditions, if one follows Paul (e.g., in his conflict with Peter), then one should really formulate another theological principle of knowing: precisely the unlike recognize — in acknowledging — one another. Only with this hermeneutical axiom can, in my opinion, the problem of "Unity and Plurality" as it is today given to us in the face of the one world be approached hopefully.

What led *ecclesially* to the suspension of the biblical hermeneutic of acknowledgement? Now, clearly, the Church fell again and again into the temptation of confusing the universality of the mission entrusted to it with the universality of the Kingdom of God, and thereby neglected or ignored the eschatological difference between the Church and the Kingdom of God. That is why its mission was not guided by a hermeneutic of acknowledgement, but by a hermeneutic of assimilation, even of subjugation. The tragedy of the Jewish people in the history of Christianity has here one of its roots.

It is true that there are signs of a new consciousness and new orientation in present-day Christianity. Looking at the Catholic Church, I recall the recent Vatican Council where clearly the beginnings of a culture that acknowledges the others in their otherness, a culture sought by the Church itself, are to be found. Thus in the "Declaration on the Relation of the Church to Non-Christian Religions", there is recommended for the first time a positive evaluation of these religions and their cultures in contrast to the previously purely apologetic and defensive attitude. Clearly, one would have wanted to have heard more: whether and to what degree the Church itself needs to listen to the external prophecy from these non-Christian religions. And above all one would have wished — especially in the face of the catastrophe of Auschwitz — a more detailed appreciation of the unsurpassable relationship to Israel and to the Jewish religion itself as the root religion of Christianity and Islam. And yet in the "Decree on Religious Freedom", the Church of the Council expresses itself as an institution of a religion of freedom, which in the preaching and sharing of its convictions renounces explicitly any use of coercion which would counteract this freedom, because the Church does not want (any longer) to be guided by an abstract right of truth, but rather by the right of the (alien) person in her truth. We have good reasons to promote precisely these principles in an offensive faithfulness to the Council.

The biblically rooted culture of the acknowledgement of the others in their otherness does not aim at a romantic elevation of the alien others. But it makes possible that the tendency toward universality interiorized in the Western spirit itself be joined with the wisdom and the memories of suffering of other cultures in a promising way. In these cultures there is resistance against an abstract logic of evolution in which finally history is substituted by economical laws of nature, and memory is replaced by the computer. To me, this attitude seems to be capable of becoming allied with that Western spirit which today itself is genuinely searching — and indeed searching not for the dismantlement of our scientific technological world and its achievements, but rather toward new ways of working with it. This search takes place against the cultural background of our Western rationality and its increasingly self-running, increasingly subjectless processes of modernization in which the human person — as mentioned — is less and less his own memory and more and more only his own experiment. Here the death of that human person, as we historically know it, already seems to be taken into the planning. Probably such a creative exchange between the worlds of culture would be what today most deserves the name "progress". At any rate, the suggested hermeneutical culture seems to me to be the indispensable precondition for the continuously threatened peace in the world. Could a Western Christianity which matures into cultural polycentrism even become a productive model for the shaping of world peace? This question is directed to all of us, to us who are part of Western Christianity.

IV.

It is true that the isolated individual stands powerless and helpless before such a question. She can really hear it only as pure rhetoric, as an empty appeal. But Christianity is neither individualism nor existentialism. No one is a Christian for herself alone. Christianity lives, when it lives, in its communities of memory. It is committed to the one undivided discipleship of Jesus which does not permit a dualism between mysticism and politics, between spirituality and responsibility for the world. The liturgical celebration of the *memoria passionis mortis et resurrectionis Jesu Christi* thus becomes the expression of a dangerous memory that continually intervenes in our daily lives. These communities of memory resist a life that is dictated by the will to power. They resist a life that is more and more incapable of discovering a trace of God in the countenance of the alien and uncomprehended other. And they resist a life in which the substance of our freedom is threatened when this life becomes more and more apathetic and without bonds to other human beings, when the happiness of this life ultimately becomes nothing more than an unhappiness free of longing and suffering, nothing more than the apocalypse of banality. These communities finally allow themselves, continually failing, continually trying again, to be committed to a great solidarity, to the solidarity in memory with the dead whose past sufferings have not been erased, to the solidarity of presence with those who are today suffering unjustly, to a solidarity of anticipation toward the coming generations. And so they become a persistently and not without reverses, bearers and witnesses of a vision without which there will be no peace, no justice, and no saving of the earth.

Will this vision prevail? Will there be enough time? Time enough for a political culture of freedom and of universal justice and a hermeneutical culture of acknowledgement to arise among us? We Christians are not optimists of progress. Our hope is not based on a gentle, evolutionary-flavored eschatology. We are not ashamed of our apocalyptic traditions. Time is for us not an empty and surprise-free endless continuum in which we project our progressive advance, and which, nevertheless, continuously swallows us up. For us, time is and remains in the hands of God.

Response by Neil Darragh

1. The Challenge

My response to Professor Metz's presentation involves me first of all in a self-interrogation about my own theological geography. For in a discussion of "one world", a "polycentric world", the "western Christianity", etc., it is the map of our planet that supplies the model on which the discussion is based.

I accept the basic thrust of Professor Metz's paper which I understand to be a challenge to articulate a *polycentric* Christianity which remains yet a ferment of both a *political* culture, (seeking freedom and justice for all), as well as a *hermeneutical* culture (recognizing the others in their otherness).

In that case, however, my own first decision needs to be whether or not the challenge to *Western* Christianity constitutes also a challenge to *my* Christianity. I speak now as a Pakeha male New Zealander. And starting from that point, my "theological geography" becomes a matter of some interest and some complexity. Aotearoa-New Zealand is west of, say, Tahiti, and indeed of Peru. But that is hardly the point I think. I understand the term "Western Christianity" to refer to the practices and articulations of Christianity which took shape in the western Mediterranean and Europe. But these places are not, of course, "west" of us. They are north of us. Or more accurately, they are on the opposite side of the planet to us. And, as every school child knows, if we were to go there by the most direct route, namely by boring straight down through the earth, we would at some stage have to turn upside down in order to be the right way up when we got there. To these traditional centres of Christianity I think we have to add North America whose theologies have become all-pervading and unavoidable in this part of the world, unprotected as we are by any language barrier. And so, it is simpler for us here, when we hear of "Western Christianity" to translate that as "North Atlantic" Christianity. Then we know where we stand and can focus our own concerns on South Pacific Christianity.

There is then a challenge to the current forms of North Atlantic Christianity from a polycentric world and a polycentric Christianity. There is also a challenge, but a rather different one, to those of us who live on the peripheries rather than at the centres of traditional Christianity. And it is very important that these two challenges not be confused. Specifically, in our case, i.e. the case of those who stand on the periphery of historical Christianity, the challenge takes the form of a challenge to self-assertion as a part and only a part, though a distinct part, of a larger whole. More specifically again, it takes the form of the question: What is our specific contribution to the Christian understanding of God? For this contribution cannot be made from anywhere else.

2. My Task in Response

I therefore interpret my task here to be a simple one: it is to attempt a brief articulation of Christianity from the point of view of the male Pakeha New Zealander. A contemporary polycentric Christianity can only come about if Christianity is practised and formulated by those who live at what used to be the peripheries of our theological geography. At the periphery there are a variety of starting points. So far the most prominent of these theologies have begun either from a condition of oppression, or of integration with an indigenous spirituality.

Pakeha theology has had neither of these beginnings. Rather it begins as a superfluous plant uprooted and replanted in an unfamiliar soil seeking life for itself yet dangerous to that soil's familiar life-forms. And in so far as the theology of this place is Pakeha, it's inescapable feature is the *ambiguity between continuity and discontinuity* with its theological origins.

It is *continuous* with its past because this historical Christianity has been carried here in our flesh and our bones, in our DNA. For the Pakeha, the Christianity we have inherited has already been integrated with a "foreign" culture, but a foreign culture from which we ourselves have only recently become detached. Thus our spiritual capital, so to speak, is clearly "offshore" capital. Our Christianity carries at least the fingerprints, and possibly the entire travelling wardrobe of its immediately previous owner, i.e.. in most cases, the cultures of Europe.

Almost any attempt to create an indigenous, contextual, local, etc. articulation of Christianity will at some point be accused from within its own community of wanting to "take off western Christianity as a cloak"; and it will be pointed out that this (a) ought not to be done, and (b) cannot be done. But the experience of Pakeha theology is I think that when we take off the cloak of our "western" Christianity we find European labels on our underclothes.

Our Christianity exists *both* in continuity and in discontinuity with North Atlantic Christianity. If we conceal the *discontinuity* we become religious serfs abandoning responsibility for our own religious consciousness and content to borrow the religious solutions of our theological mistresses and masters. If we conceal the *continuity* we enter not simply into wilderness but into delusion. It is the continuity that still currently holds power. But it is the discontinuity that provides us with the clues to our specific contribution to a polycentric Christianity, i.e. a Christianity in which we are contributors and not just receivers.

Pakeha theology is *discontinuous* from its past; it is discontinuous because feminist theology has challenged the value of its past; it is discontinuous because Maori theology has challenged the value of its past; and most of all, it is challenged by the overpowering symbolic reality of the Pacific ocean, the radical historical, social and psychological reality of migration.

Thus we live consequent upon the non-negotiable fact of migration and this has produced three levels of discontinuity from our past:

1.The generational discontinuity which arises between first and second generation migrants because the childhood experience of "being at home" and of "where I came from" is quite different for these two generations;

2.The discontinuity from the more remote past which occurs through *identity with* those same parents or grandparents who themselves made a radical break with *their* own past by the fact of migration;

3.The inescapable "foreignness" of the place of ancestral origin revisited: that ancestral place which second and consequent generations have come to know only secondhand, i.e. not as immediate experience but as parental interpretation, and to which they relate as family visitors or tourists or amateur genealogists but rarely as those who belong there.[1]

3. The experience of being Pakeha

What shape then might a Pakeha theology take? What is our specific experience which contributes to an understanding of God and of Christianity and which does not simply ape in pale form the practice and articulation of North Atlantic theology?

i) Belonging with shallow roots: paradigm of Faith.

The experience of migration remains strong within the family stories of the Pakeha. It is the experience of tracing one's roots to places close at hand only to find them suddenly turning sideways and shooting across the sea. The indigenous people of this land find their roots in this land itself. The matriarch in Witi Ihimaera's novel tells her grandson: "You are descended of many tribes . . . *But this is where you were born. . . . But this is where you belong..* And because this is your land, you must know it like it knows itself, and you must love it even more than it loves itself. You must get to know its very boundaries, e mokopuna, and every part of it because without this knowledge you are lost.. . . You become a person without a homeland. You become a man who will never know aroha ki to iwi, love for your people and for the land. If you do not know this love then you cannot fight. Someday, you may need to know so as to challenge any person who might wish to take this land from you."[2]

By contrast, those who are the children or grandchildren of migrants find deep roots neither in this land nor in the land of their ancestors. It is specifically this "belonging with shallow roots" that is a primary characteristic of their identity. This is the "radical" experience of "hanging on with one hand, and the other hand full of seas".[3] And those who can consciously capture this kind of real experience can

---

1. I have discussed this threefold discontinuity before under the heading of the "The Catholic church in Aotearoa-New Zealand", *The Australasian Catholic Record* 65 (1988) 315-329.
2. Witi Ihimaera, *The Matriach* , (Acukland: Heinemann, 1986) , p. 95.
3. This phrase was used by Robin Hyde in the 1930's to describe the ambiguity of being a third generation pakeha New Zealander (but with one's poem from England) in her novle *The Godwits Fly*, (Auckland University Press, 1970, originally published in 1938), p. 101.

reread the stories of Abraham and Sarah and their journey of faith, or indeed the death-resurrection journey of Jesus, in a way which re-enlightens their own journeys and grounds their own faith. And the Pauline Law-faith contrast looks less like a contrast between order and freedom, and more like a second generation migrant's reinterpretation of the ancestral values — a journey both physical and spiritual whose basis is faith in a benevolent God or a risen messiah.

Thus the experience of migrancy may become a primary paradigm of the search for God: — a leaving behind and a taking with, a pilgrimage with no return, an experience of crossing, of being home and not yet quite at home. But we need to note too, that such an experience may produce its opposites: — a need for security founded on unchanging certainties, and belief in the superiority of ancestral "civilization", a need for a parental refuge (a "mother England", or a "holy Ireland").

ii) The moral limits to growth: paradigm of sin as excess.

The Pakeha is not simply a migrant but a migrant *majority*. Most European migrants to Aotearoa-New Zealand sought a better standard of living for themselves and their children. Only a few have been purely political refugees, or have been wealthy when they arrived here, or have migrated for explicitly religious motives. But the desire for more and more land and the hope for more work turned the landless into exploiters. As the numbers of European settlers increased they showed they were prepared to trample over both Maori rights as well as those of immigrants of other races.[4]

Perhaps only those who have realized too late that their own legitimate aspirations have been accomplished at the cost of oppression and discrimination can understand the insidiousness of evil which corrupts aspiration and hope. Only lately have we realized that progress has its own limits, i.e. eventually reaches a point where progress itself becomes destructive. Like the willows, the rabbits and the opossums, our own hopes have become a destructive excess.

And so a central image of "sin" is not the contrary of "good", not a choice between two paths, but a threshold, a limit to the very

---

4. Claudia Orange's *The Treaty of Waitangi* (Wellington: Allen & Unwin, 1987) provides extensive historical evidence for this in respect to Maori land; and Jye Kang's novel *Guests of the New Gold Hill* , (Auckland: Hodder and Stoughton, 1985), illustrates this in the case of the early Chinese migrants.

development of good itself. Sin is not so much a privation of good, or something which overpowers good from the outside, but rather the point at which good itself in its own growth becomes destructive. Hence the moral need to set limits to growth. And so today we begin to set limits to our diets, to our possessions, to our use of resources, to our desire to work, to our production of waste, to our conversion of wilderness. But the paradigm for this morality is already within our own history of regret.

iii) Individuals and networks: paradigm of a church.

The New Zealand experience of individualism is complex and variable over time. The Pakeha are children of the European "enlightenment" in their resistance to authority and belief in the individual. Our individualism is probably not that of the enlightenment entrepreneur nor of the American frontier myths, but may be more that of individuals seeking security from the state.[5] But our experience of individualism contributes, I think, to our valuing of the human person against a coercive collectivism and the ideologies of power. And this itself joins with our experience of smallness, so that individuals can count in a way which cannot be in those cultures where the sheer mass of human beings trivializes the individual.

But when we compare ourselves with Polynesian groups, the Pakeha sense of the individual is evidently much stronger than its sense of community. We have difficulty in accepting the leadership of another, in conceding personal opinion to the wisdom of the group, of acting in solidarity with others. If the redeemable element of our individualism consists in our valuing of the individual human person, its weaknesses leave us isolated or reliant on the state. And so our sense of being a church is more voluntary, more fluid, more occasional, less kin-based than our theology would hope for. Our religion turns out to be "my own religion" more than cooperative involvement with other Christians. As our churches lose their ethnic allegiances and our state becomes more authoritarian, the churches begin to reorganize themselves to cater for the community dimension of our lives. But this reorganization has less to do with the traditional church structures of ethnic allegiance than with care paid to individual integrity, with

5. This interpretation is proposed by Colin James in *The Quiet Revolution: Turbulence in Contemporary New Zealand*, (Wellington: Allen & Unwin/Port Nicholson Press, 1986) esp. pp. 14-17.

reliance on networks and neighbourhoods, and with solidarity on issues of social justice.

iv) A dream of equality: paradigm of a divine commonwealth.

Our experience of how society can be organized, and our beliefs about how it should be organized, are perhaps similar to those of the new settlers of Australia except for the harshness of their penal settlements. Certainly, our experiences and beliefs were originally very different from the indigenous inhabitants of Aotearoa, and they proposed to be different from the class and industrial systems of the European countries from which our early settlers originated. For the most part, their migration was motivated by, or they acquired soon after arriving here, the hope for a more humane, more equal society than the one they had left. This was a hope for a society where there was a chance of justice and freedom for all. But this once powerful dream of "equality" is now under heavy attack within our political system and is rapidly being replaced with an ideal of "efficiency" where masters and slaves are again justifiable in the interests of productivity.

4. The Other as Partner

As a speaker here I am not just an individual but also one in a condition
of belonging *with* some people,
of being different but *in alliance with* some people, and
as strictly "*other*" to some people.

The condition I want to investigate in particular here is that of "alliance". An "alliance" is always to some extent "uneasy". This is why it is an alliance and not simply a "belonging". But it is a good deal closer and more inter-related than simply "otherness". At the same time, it cannot work at all unless a degree of "otherness" is respected in the other party.

The particular form of "alliance" that is important for us at the present time is that of "partnership". These partnerships are uneasy alliances, often inequitable, often unjust, but containing the seeds of complementarity. These are primarily the ethnic partnerships (and the one that occupies me particularly here in this context and at this time, is the ratial partnership), and the gender partnership — male and female. But the most difficult partnership of all I think, is the ambiguous and uneasy partnership between Pakeha Christianity and North Atlantic (and more specifically in this case, "European-British") Christianity — an ambiguous partnership in which the primary concern of Pakeha Christianity is not so much to acknowledge the other as "other", but to recognize itself as "other" to North Atlantic Christianity.

Thus for the Pakeha, the primary experience of "other" is the realization that

(**a**) we ourselves have become "other" to the people of our ancestral culture, and that

(**b**) this experience of being "other" to our own past has been brought about primarily through the encounter with those who are ethnically and culturally "other" to us — primarily Maori, then also Chinese and Indian "others" and more recently migrant Polynesian "others".

One of the (to me at least) most interesting articulations of Maori theology is the articulation of what we may translate as "virtues".I want to outline briefly here Henare Tate's articulation[6] of Maori theology in terms of the "virtues". I have neither the experience nor the expertise to deal with Maori theology. But what an encounter with this kind of articulation of Maori theology does to the Pakeha (or to me at least) is to provoke a similar, though different, articulation of Pakeha "virtues" which in turn are recognized as different, though not completely independent of, older European articulations of the virtues. Thus the recognition of the "otherness" of Maori theology, provokes a Pakeha theology, which in turn recognizes its "otherness" from the theology of its ancestral past.

In my understanding, then, a Maori Christian definition of how to act rightly may be summarized in the three "virtues" of *Tika*: justice, acting rightly according to one's responsibilities to kin, expressed in marae protocol, and especially in addressing the "tapu" of people. *Pono* : faithfulness to justice, integrity, being true in spite of difficulties or criticisms or fads. *Aroha*: love, affection, compassion.

These ways of acting are lived out within the framework of "tapu", "mana", and "te wa".

---

6. Unpublished, but part of the Maori Pastoral Plan for the Catholic Church in Aotearoa-New Zealand.

What I need to seek next is a Pakeha response which redefines its own Christian spirituality in a similar, but different, summary of virtues. I propose the following: —

i) *Respect*: the recognition of another's right to their own feelings and hopes, the acknowledgement of a boundary protecting another's self-esteem and value, an unmanipulatable centre independent of my own beliefs or designs. This is the redeemable component of the "live and let live" of Pakeha spirituality (or at least of Pakeha male spirituality). It is the ingredient by which actions and programmes of, for example, governments and churches, may be judged to be fundamentally valuable or mischievous. It is a virtue whose importance I personally learnt not from formal theology but from prison inmates. To treat others with respect appears as the greatest of the virtues to those living the experience of being utterly unrespectable. The object of respect is not just towards other individuals, but also to groups and organizations of people, as well as towards other species, towards waterways, towards springheads, towards forests, etc.

The vices which contradict this virtue are the uses of power to belittle, to patronize. And its excesses are indifference, not getting involved.

ii) *Integrity*: this is the redeemable component of our individualism and individual freedom, our anti-authoritarianism, and our demands upon the state. It is the value we place on an individual's stance against society, its authorities, and its structures. Primarily, though, it is a way of living where an individual or organization lives consistently by its principles and convictions even when the costs of its principles are high.

The vices which contradict this virtue are dishonesty, conformity, the desire for success or acclaim. Its excesses are the inability to concede or to apologize.

iii) *Participation*: this is the virtue of being involved. It is closely related to the "dream of equality" in that it hopes for a society where classes do not exist and where the assumption that some people exist for the benefit of others no longer stands. But at the same time it does not assume that all people are simply the same. It seeks the balance between cooperative and competitive relationships with others. It values sharing. As a corporate virtue it has both an active and a passive form. Actively it means "pulling your weight"; passively it requires the opportunity for corporate decision-making.

The vices which contradict this virtue are the policies of line-management, competitiveness. Its excesses are wimpishness, lack of assertiveness, over-involvement, inability to say "no".

iv) *Fairness*: this is the virtue which seeks universal justice. It seeks to open for others a chance at economic equality, at opportunity to match talent, and a sharing of power. It seeks a relativity between one person or group's gain and another's loss. It is not about removing disappointment from life, but it is about eliminating crippling effects from our relationships and our organizations.

The vices which contradict this virtue are market thinking which ignores "externalities", efficiency as an end rather than a means, the various forms of discrimination. Its excesses are "the great New Zealand clobbering machine", the discouragement of brilliance.

I am not proposing here that the above four "virtues" are how Pakeha in fact behave. I am proposing a set of ways of acting which Pakeha Christians in their better moments can recognize as a good way of acting even if they do not yet in fact behave in this way. I am proposing also that these ways of acting are indeed implementations of the Christian commandment of love.

Again I am not proposing that these ways of acting are peculiarly Pakeha in the sense that they distinguish us from all other groups of human beings. This is clearly not the case. What is important is that they be recognizable as importantly *ours*. For then we are in a position to make our own contribution to a polycentric Christianity.

Finally, a quick glance across the Tasman. I would like to have been able here to explore the white Australian spirituality of "no-thing", the experience of wilderness at the heart of the Australian, the strategy of "knocking" or debunking of all things and especially those which pretend to be most sacred — a theology of negation.[7] For I suspect that the foundation for a New Zealand Pakeha spirituality is very different. Our experience of wilderness tends more, I think, to be a wilderness not of "no-thing" but a wilderness teaming with "wild" untamed life; a wilderness of uncontrolled flora, of beautiful and suddenly dangerous rivers, of sandflies, of multiple shades of green. Or even more common is our experience of the beach, the sea, the sand, not so much as the holiday beaches of sun and sea, but the sand-shifting margin between solidity of land and fluidity of water, a standing-upon, walking-upon, lying-upon margin of sound and touch and taste and smell and sight. And so our images of God are not iconoclastic or "knocking" images, but images too many and too

---

7. See especially Tony Kelly, *A New Imaging: Towards an Australian Spirituality*, North Blackburn: Collins Dove, 1990.

different to hold together all at once. But it is important to notice, I think, that in both cases we seem to want to turn back again to nature to renew our spirits.

My response, then, to Dr. Metz's paper has been to begin to articulate a theology which contributes to a polycentric Christianity from within the limits and hopes of that group of Christians whom I know best. And in attempting this in a public way, I dare to suggest not only that others should do the same, but that this is how theology ought to be done anyway.

Response by Elisabeth Moltmann-Wendel

J. B. Metz's position is that of the white Western male. He criticizes this world view and dominance but he often gets stuck in his critique midway.

1. The language which he uses is not the "inclusive language" prevailing in ecumenism, that is, a language which includes women rather than excluding women (for example: instead of man-humankind or humans). A sensibility for the connection between language and patriarchal culture which stems from man is indeed present in his work when in the description of the subjugation of nature, man is clearly spoken of as the actor of this (man is by subjugating). Women are mentioned as those to whom one assigns tasks which keep them distant from the power, as well as the patterns of behavior like "gratitude, friendliness, the ability to suffer, and to develop pity, sorrow and tenderness."

However, instead of only complaining about the dominance of the man, woman wishes that the reduction of the domination would already be practiced in the language.

2. Metz deals with the Roman Catholic problem: How is diversity in unity possible? He starts with the Roman, European, Western unity of Church and Culture and asks for cultural polycentrism. The *ecumenical problem* (of the non-Roman Catholic churches) is exactly the opposite: How is unity in diversity possible? Here we start with ecclesiastical and cultural diversity and ask for community.

3. Metz starts with "Western Christianity", which in fact is *Constantinian Christianity*, Christianity as imperial religion of the Roman, the European, the Western empire. He overlooks the *non-Constantinian* churches in Africa (Egypt, Ethiopia), Asia Minor (Syria), India, now minorities in all countries and nowhere dominant. To diversify "Western Christianity" is not yet ecumenical and not yet an acknowledgment of the other.

4. Why does Metz speak so strongly about *cultural polycentrism,* but nowhere about ecclesiastical polycentrism and an acknowledgment of "the other" Christian Churches (orthodox, protestant, episcopalian, pentecostal) in their "otherness" by Rome ?

5. The *acknowledgment of the other* is good, but not enough: Who has declared others to "the others"? Is there not a barrier of prejudices against humans?

And there is no honest acknowledgment of the other without a *new self-experience.* The pure acknowledgment of the others is as actively dominating as the prejudices, by which they are made "the others".

If I am acknowledged, I do not want to remain "the other".

6. The problem of indigenization in Western Christianity next of all would have to be shown in respect of the women and the uncovering of their own culture. As long as women as seen as the "others" in Western Christianity and in their Churches, Christianity and the Church are not credible if in their own house they do not try out tolerance towards those who are different. Over the last 20 years, women of Christianity have uncovered their own culture which was dominated and colonialized by the male culture so that here we are dealing with parallels to other oppressed cultures. The difference however, is that women have also participated in the patriarchal culture as "accomplices" (Thurmer-Rohr). Nevertheless, the women's culture, in its different patterns of thinking and living as compared to the male culture, is no longer to be overlooked. "In a Different Voice" (Carol Gilligan), "Women's Reality" (Anne Wilson Schaef) show that from different social experiences comes different thinking and acting. Historical examinations confirm this for the various eras of human history.

An example: not the individual but rather the connectedness stand in the center of female thinking. "Wholeness" is one of the most important notions of feminism and of feminist theology. Interestingly enough, both notions have an important place in African and Asian thinking and are emphasized in relation to Western thinking! Also for the necessary theological indigenization women could make an important contribution: their images of God, of the Spirit, of Christ often have more reference to ethnic religious images than to Western-Christian tradition. But exactly here the being-different is seen as dangerous heresy. As long as Western Christianity ignores the being different of the women, it can not accept the being-different of other cultures. The judgement must begin in God's house!

7. Metz undertakes a very important approach for changing Western male culture when he gives up the dominance of the ear and with that, the dominance of hearing and obedience, and introduces seeing as an important form of knowing. With this, a first step is taken to re-think the dominance of the senses in our Christian tradition. The rationality of our thinking is a taking possession with a claim of domination which has led to the submission of intuition, empathy, and phantasy and has placed them in a private and female space, standing in contrast to rationality. The result is a contamination of the human (that is, man!). A split of the humans who are intended for wholeness.

Metz encounters here women's research which teaches to see the human anew in its totalness and in its bodiliness. The re-discovery of the eye and of vision is, then however, only a part of a much more comprehensive revolution: the knowledge that humans understand with the body (B.W. Aarrison, Christa Wolf). If we were to learn to understand with all senses and organs (for example, through the skin, through touching!) then we could experience the world, nature, the others anew.

8. This leads to the last point: the question: Who is Jesus here? The one who teaches us to hear and see as Metz sees it? Is not the Jesus-figure very reduced and predefined? And in the end, rationalized and while its wholeness (life, bodiliness, relationship, mutuality) is still not discovered?

9

The Spirit of God in Creation and Reconciliation

Daniel W. Hardy

Introduction: Contextuality and the Trinitarian God

It may seem surprising for a paper on 'the Spirit of God in Creation and Reconciliation' to be offered to a Symposium on Christ and Context. The title is a rather coded one, indicating that I propose to discuss the relation of the Trinitarian God with the dynamics of humanity and nature. The paper will attempt to deepen the discussion of 'Christ and Context' by relating it to the Trinitarian God, to the nature of contextuality and to the dynamic relation between them. It may be best to start by suggesting why these issues are important.

Contrary to our usual suppositions, 'context' does not indicate that which surrounds us, as if that were distinct from us, as if it were an envelope in which we are contained. Nor, much as we might suppose otherwise, are 'contexts' clearly distinct or disjoined from each other. This is true both conceptually and in actuality. Conceptually, the notion of context derives its original meaning from the Latin word contexere, which designates the interweaving or braiding together of what might otherwise be considered distinct. So contextuality designates the interweaving of human subjects with their cultures and the natural world, and of cultures with each other and the natural world. In actuality also, it needs to be recognized that 'context' is a mental, if not also a cultural, construct, one which serves to tidy up the often confusing mixture of situations in which we find ourselves. There is some danger in this tidying up that we lose the vibrancy of the very mixture which we seek to clarify — that we 'murder in order to dissect'.

It also needs to be understood that the Trinitarian God does not designate one alien to this world, the world in which human beings and cultures and the natural world are interwoven. It often seems to be thought nowadays that, as a matter of principle, Christian speaking about God must somehow be alien to the wide multicultural, multireligious world which we inhabit. That is not necessarily the case; whether it is has still to be decided. It is that issue to which this paper is addressed. We shall attempt to find how the Trinitarian God is present in the interweaving of human subjects with each other, their culture and the natural world.

On Poesis, Theory and Truth-Telling

If contextuality is itself a dynamic, and if the Trinitarian God is to be sought in the braiding together of human beings, their cultures and the natural world, we will need to approach these issues by means of a dynamic of thought which transcends the limitations of our usual habits.[1] To put this very succinctly, we will need to develop a creative perception by which to sing our world as a hymn of praise to God; fashioning such a song is actually the task of theology.[2]

---

1. 'I believe that learning to admit transcendence may be one of the major undertakings of a man's life, perhaps the major undertaking, so that if it is ignored his personality may be stunted or destroyed.' Monica Furlong, *Contemplating Now,* (Cambridge: Cowley Publications, 1983), p. 50.
2. Poetry, in its creative perception, provides a concentrated opportunity by which to 'sing reality'. Bruce Chatwin, in *The Songlines* (London: Pan Books, 1987), says of the Aboriginal Creation myths,

> [They] tell of the legendary totemic beings who had wandered over the continent in the Dreamtime, singing out the name of everything that crossed their path — birds, animals, plants, rocks, waterholes — and so singing the world into existence... By singing the world into existence, the ancestors had been poets in the original sense of poesis, meaning 'creation'.

So the multistranded reality in which we live needs to be 'sung into existence'. For a Christian, this means that it needs to be sung as a hymn of praise to God the Creator. It is the task of theology to fashion the creative

Attractive and valuable though it might be, such a creative perception cannot simply be 'poetic' in the normal sense, providing an explicitly poetic concentration of the nature of God's presence in our interwovenness. To be sure, such a thing has the advantage of freeing itself from the norms which often operate in analytical-empirical 'science'.[3] But if we are to remain in touch with the factors which are formative of modern life and understanding, we cannot so easily distance ourselves from the the empirical and theoretical considerations of other disciplines and of theology; we must probe and test them. But the theoretical character of what follows should not obscure its place in the task of building a creative poesis or heuristic. And, as a poesis, it starts within — and remains within — the field which it explores; it does not stand outside, in a position of supposed neutrality.

Hence, as we speak of our contextuality and the presence there of the Trinitarian God, we shall be doing so from the position of those in whom they intersect, as those for whom God is present in our interweaving. To use more poetic images, we shall be engaging in a concentrated 'song of reality' even as we attempt to find better ways of following the line of the melody; and the song will draw its inspiration — and I use that word advisedly — from the very reality which is sung. Such a thing is far more important than it may seem. For what we seek are the intellectual conditions for a true poesis, by which we may fully participate in the work of the Trinitarian God in our interweaving. They are the intellectual conditions for truth-telling about God's presence in our interweaving, the intellectual conditions for what John de Gruchy called the 'promised land', for what Jurgen Moltmann called the 'mutual indwelling of humanity and nature'.

---

poesis by which it is sung as a hymn of praise to God. In more technical terms, poetry — or theology — provides a wisdom, heuristic or direction for exploration, which serves to orientate a search, much as the Aborigin-als' songlines provide a 'map and direction-finder' for travel.

3. To the consternation of many in the literary community, George Steiner has suggested that 'there is some fundamental encounter with transcendence in the creation of art and in its experi- encing', and that works of art manifest 'a root impulse of the human spirit to explore possibilities of meaning and of truth that lie outside empirical seizure or proof...'; they constitute a 'wager on survivance, [and] are refusals of analytic-empirical criteria of constraint.' *Real Presences,* (London: Faber and Faber, 1989), pp.228, 225f. While this view is helpful, it is an overstatement to claim that 'it is... poetry, art and music which relate us most directly to that in being which is not ours.' [p.226, emphasis mine]

A true poesis — in which we participate more fully in the presence of the Trinitarian God in our interweaving — is not a field which (more or less) approximates to a truth somehow independent of God. Its truth is God's; and our seeking for it is an activity in which the Trinitarian God participates. The truth of this poesis is God's performance of the truth. This makes truth somewhat different from what we usually expect. It is not something fixed, like a fixed star which is near or far away which serves as a simple point by which we can check the position of everything else. Rather it is an active truth, active everywhere, working to bring all things, including our understanding and actions, into its movement. The inner pattern of this Truth is Trinitarian, active and lifting and livening. But that is a discussion for some other time.

At the same time, we are in the position of those who think and live in a contextuality of falsehoods, one in which — in thought and deed — we suffer from the illegitimate divisions into which our contextuality is now divided, and in turn enhance them. Finding the intellectual conditions for truth-telling about God's presence in our interweaving will give us a means of combating the illegitimate division of human thought, of human beings and cultures, as well as the illegitimate separation of human beings from nature, by discovering the way in which God is present through the interweaving of human beings, cultures and nature. But, as I have already implied, the search will take us into Trinitarian, as well as other, ontology. In good English fashion, I was going to say, 'Sorry about that!'; but I'm really not, because the difficulties start as far back as that.

The results of such an inquiry have a peculiar position. I am sure that if theological work is to have maximum impact upon today's world, it cannot simply be evocative and exhortative; it must be explanatory, and as such interact with the means by which people in other disciplines explain the world. That is the modern, as well as the ancient, form of prophecy. That is not to say that theological explanations should be *identical* to the explanations by other disciplines, only that they should *interact* with them. For theological explanations are concerned with what ought to be, and its contrast with what is. This explanation of 'what ought to be' can be placed either historically — as protology or eschatology, or naturally — as transcendental; but in either case, it is interactive/interwoven with what is, as a form contrasting to what is. However, affirming this 'what ought to be' and bringing it about in historical-natural life, are the only ways by which it may be understood and effected. This is always costly, both to the understanding and to the actual living of life in history and nature. In other words, reconciling the two is always affirmative but costly.

Let me put the same point differently. The rather theoretical form of what follows may lead you to suppose that it is impractical. I assure you that it is not. No, it is not 'reflecting from the garbage-heap or dunghill', in the fashion mentioned by Professor Gutierrez, though I would be far from denying the value of that. But — like reflecting from the dung- hill — it does suppose that visions are influential and capable of changing practice. This is not only true of evocative language, but also of the much more empirical and theoretical language of the disciplines which form modern understanding and life. An explanatory description of what is the state of affairs has a normative effect, influencing performance. What is believed about God's presence in the world and human life forms what is done by human beings; and good practice rests on good belief (and vice-versa). What, therefore, I am attempting here is a critical realignment of the explanations we use for God and the world, supposing that the very act of doing so will bring about a change in our practice.

Two last preliminary comments. The first is that my allusions to the 'song of reality' in which we are engaged are both epistemological comments and more. They free us from the supposition that our apprehension of reality is based in certain axioms, and that reality is fact-like, consisting of fixed states of being for God, us and the natural world, fixed orders of being. As we will see, many of our habits of thought are still based on such assumptions.

It is a strange irony that theology has been only half-purged of the notion of fixed orders of being which arise from God's creation. At least by those whose 'order of being' was relativized by the person and work of Christ, these 'orders' were seen to result in the assignment of superior and inferior status in Nazi Germany, hence they were expunged from the doctrine of creation. But the notion of orders has been retained through the persistence of the supposition that there are fixities which pertain to God's being, ours and that of the natural world. The allusions to the song of reality suggest a purging of these orders of being from theology itself, and their replacement by *dynamics* of different kinds within a harmony of being. They open us to the possibility that God, human beings and nature interact *dynamically* in ways to which our habits of thought blind us.

This is not to say that the 'fixities' which we habitually prefer are not important. But they are to be seen more like the capturing of the rhythms of movement in static forms than as the primary characteristic of the 'nature' and interrelation of God, human beings and nature. A suitable analogy is the position of individuals in the interwovenness of human beings: the fact that human beings are interwoven does not preclude individuality — only individualism; there is still 'space' for individuals to be, and to move to other relationships, while carrying the benefits (or the harm) of the previous relationships there. Likewise, the locating of the patterns in which the rhythms of movement consist is a means by which they can be found and seen elsewhere.

The second of these last preliminary comments is this. By encouraging you to think in dynamic terms, I do not wish simply to set up 'dynamic movement' as a mediating category, and to collapse theology, and indeed the understanding of humanity and nature, into a philosophical or quasi-theological middle-ground which does justice to none of them. That may be very attractive, particularly where it seems to provide a thematic place in which different religious traditions may meet. This seems to me to be the fallacy into which the now famous address by Chung Hyun-Kyung at the Canberra Assembly of the World Council of Churches fell. It is also the kind of strategy which is the most common fault of current discussions of theology and science.

The dynamics on which I wish to focus are no such middle- ground, but a category which will need to be developed in various ways according to the ontological domain being discussed, whether God, humanity or the world. At this point, I am simply signalling a change needed for present-day understanding of theology, humanity and the natural world, one which may move us beyond the static ontology which predominates, at least in theology; and it is the development of a dynamic ontology which is suitable to theology, humanity and the natural world which concerns us here.

The Modes and Operation of Contextuality

It will be well now to specify the range of issues which we are to discuss. I can do that by resuming the discussion of the nature of contextuality. As I have already mentioned, contexts are not so clearly distinct — either from us or from each other — as we normally assume. Neither conceptually nor actually are contexts so distinct; they indicate an interwovenness or braiding. A conference on Christ and Context is therefore concerned with the question of how God is present in our interweaving.

But there is a vast variety of modes of contextuality, of those elements which are interwoven in us and for us; and we cannot proceed without identifying them, at least in a rudimentary fashion. Our contextuality is the presence in/for us of those factors by which we are constituted. There seem to be two sets of such constituting factors. For human beings, one set is social: symbolic signification (linguistic and cultural procedures), political order (the distribution of responsibilities), economic order (the distribution of benefits) and customary/legal structures (the regulation of practices). These, whether formal or informal, are the social elements which constitute our contextuality. The other set of factors is *natural:* cosmic order (comprised of elements both spatial and temporal), and the order and distribution of animate beings and of human beings. Again, these factors constitute our contextuality. Taken together, social and natural factors meet in us, and provide the fields in which we interact with others.

'What about me as an individual?' you may ask. I will only repeat what I have already said, though in slightly different terms. The fact that human beings are interwoven in a full contextuality through the meeting of social and natural factors does not preclude individuality, together with a sense of meaning (symbolically expressed), individual responsibility (manifested politically), benefits (arranged economically) and rights (either customary or legal). Furthermore, such individuality is based on the possibility of occupying a place, being an undamaged human being and having access to suitable resources. To have all these, however, is a *privilege,* and can only be attained if social and natural circumstances permit. And they often do not, whether by accident of circumstance or design of other people.

It is well to recognize how fragile is this interweaving of factors in our contextuality. Natural and social circumstances, separately or together, can savagely undermine the contextuality — the interweaving of factors — which is necessary for the well being of individuals or social units. We see this increasingly in the world today.

But there is a further issue which needs much more recognition than it receives, the creativity with which human beings use their contextuality. For the interweaving of these factors in contextuality is not fixed, and human beings creatively develop their own contextuality. As one scientist said recently,

> Human thought and action are the most prolific sources of order in the world as we know it. Speech, writing, music, painting and sculpture, dance, and the ordinary activities of

everyday life are at once the most familiar and the most mysterious of all order-generating processes.[4]

The items listed, to which one should add the humanities, science and technology, and all institutions, are the means by which human beings and their societies not only understand their contextuality more deeply, but also readjust it. And the effects of this readjusting ripple through the contextuality. The major question lies not in whether the rebalancing does or does not affect others, but how far it does so, and how far it harms the contextuality — impoverishing others or nature. For this reason, the human creative reordering of contextuality provides one of the most basic moral and theological questions. For it can be a prime means of securing and enhancing privilege — precisely by manipulating social and natural contextuality (so far as it is possible to do so) to the benefit of some. As one sees in Church of England debates about women's ordination, or in the politics of South Africa, the room for protecting privilege through creatively readjusting contextuality is very great.[5]

By now, you may see that talking of the modes and operation of our contextuality is a way by which to identify the issues with which we must be concerned in discussing creation and reconciliation. The factors which meet us in our contextuality are interwoven in our very being. They are intrinsic to us, and it is a strange act by which we externalize them, as if they could be treated as extrinsic, even incidental, to us.

Let me make three comments about these externalizings. Firstly, the idea that we are actually autonomous, and everything else — God, others, world — external, is based on privileging ourselves within a contextuality, supposing that everything else will 'hold still and behave itself' while we see and use it. The notion of human autonomy is based on a very limited notion of contextuality, an essentially separatist and instrumental view of others and the social and natural worlds.[6]

---

4. David Layzer, *Cosmogenesis,* (New York: Oxford University Press, 1990), p.16.
5. See my response to the paper by John de Gruchy elsewhere in this volume. The debate about women's ordination in the Church of England also provides an instructive example, where convictions about the necessity of a male priesthood are perpetuated by appeals to the symbolic necessity of such a priesthood, and by political, economic and legal means.
6. See D.W. Hardy, 'God and the Form of Society' in *The Weight of Glory,* ed. D.W. Hardy and P.H. Sedgwick, (Edinburgh: T. & T. Clark, 1991).

Secondly, the same holds true for other factors in the contextuality. It is a mistake to suppose that any of the issues which we listed before — social and natural — can be isolated from each other. Yes, of course, they can be separated temporarily for purposes of study. And much of the success of modern academic understanding rests on such separations. But such separation is a privileging of a particular subject-matter which rests on its interconnection with all the others.

Thirdly, the supposition that God is fundamentally isolated from the contextuality is also highly questionable. Powerful as this supposition is in the Christian tradition, and richly suggestive as it is for the richness of the Divine Being, we only know God through his relation to the contextuality which is ours. Karl Rahner's famous dictum, 'the immanent Trinity is the economic Trinity', expresses this, albeit in very formulaic terms. The economy through which the Trinitarian God is himself is our contextuality, that rich interweaving of all the social and natural factors which we have seen. The question is how he is himself in this economy, or — as we have posed the question previously — how he is present in our contextuality.

That is the heart of the issue before us, and to it we must now turn.

The Dynamics of Contextuality

The first question to which we must address ourselves is, 'what are the dynamics of contextuality?' It is at least possible to answer the question in general terms, by looking more closely at the evidence of life in the world. That will at least provide us with an 'arena' in which we might identify the economy through which the Trinitarian God is himself.

If we confine ourselves to animate creatures, the evidence of life in the world suggests a diversity in a complex contextuality (interwovenness). Central to this is the fact that life manifests itself

> through a closed organization of production processes such that (a) the same organization of processes is generated through the interaction of their own products (components), and (b) a topological boundary emerges as a result of the same constitutive processes.[7]

---

7. M. Zeleny, ed., *Autopoesis: A Theory of Living Organization*, (New York: North Holland, 1981), p.6.

In other words, the organization of production processes for life is a closed one, yet generates self-same processes in the interaction of the components of particular life-forms; thereby emerge boundaries by which they are distinct from, and yet related to, what is not themselves. If we take human beings, the overall organization of life-processes is such that each human being manifests the same organization of interactive processes, and from these develops its distinction and relation to others.

An interesting human example appears in Shakespeare's 'Merchant of Venice'. There, Shylock seeks acceptance by pointing to the self-same interactive processes by which human beings are constituted, following the closed organization of the production processes of life. He cries: 'When I am cut, do I not bleed?' But later he does something different. He turns such interactive processes into a device for structuring his relations to another man; he asks for a 'pound of your flesh' as security for a loan. When the loan cannot be repaid and he claims his bond, however, the claim is disallowed because he had made no mention of the blood to be shed in taking the pound of flesh. Ironically, for one who had appealed to a common humanity on the basis of inter- active processes ('when I am cut, do I not bleed?'), he had over-looked the same interactive process, that cutting out flesh means the loss of blood.

Following the same closed organization of production processes for life, any life-form is itself through its interactions in its place, two aspects of its contextuality:

> This structure conditions the course of its interactions and restricts the structural changes that the interactions may trigger in it. At the same time, it is born in a particular place, in a medium that constitutes the ambience in which it emerges and in which it interacts. This ambience appears to have a structural dynamics of its own, operationally distinct from the living being.[8]

Between the living being and its ambience (what is often — in the more common sense of the term — called its 'context'), there is a structured relation, a structural congruence. And within this, there are undetermined interactions — perturbations — which 'trigger' changes for both. The interactions produce changes which serve to preserve or

8. H.R. Maturana & F.J. Varela, *The Tree of Knowledge*, (Boston, 1988), p. 95.

destroy the organization (and hence the identity) of either living being or environment. These may be summarized as four domains:

> a.Domain of changes of state: viz., all those structural changes that a unity can undergo without a change in its organization, i.e., with conservation of class identity
> b.Domain of destructive changes: all those structural changes that a unity can undergo with loss of organization and therefore with loss of class identity
> c.Domain of perturbations: all those interactions that trigger changes of state
> d.Domain of destructive interactions: all those perturbations that result in destructive change.[9]

At first, this appears to be a very bare catalogue, including only those interactions (c) which trigger the structural changes which would be considered normal to a living being (a), and all those destructive interactions (d) which would trigger structural loss incompatible with its identity as a living being (b).

But the list may be more inclusive than it first appears, especially if the various domains are understood with sufficient sophistication. For example, the domains of destructive changes and interactions go a long way toward providing the possibility for understanding contextual imbalance and damage. It ought also to be recognized that domains may have a recursive dynamic, through which the effect of a damaging perturbation may be 'doubled' by repetitions or by being internalized in the structure of a living being. A contextuality may become so asymmetrical that contextual interweaving becomes the domination of a living unit by external forces. In this case, the external forces 'becomes *domination,* [and] the internalization of shame *legitimates* the system of domination. The more shame is internalized, the less is brutal force needed in order to integrate a social structure.'[10] Hence, through domination the structure of a living being can be changed to undermine itself. That, by the way, accounts for the power with which poverty undermines the structure of a living being.

---

9. *ibid.*, p. 97f.
10. Agnes Heller, *The Power of Shame,* (London: Routledge & Kegan Paul, 1985), p. 40.

This is a very basic picture which requires supplementation in two ways. One is the recognition of interaction with the natural factors which also figure in the contextuality of a living being.

> The most dangerous tendency in modern society, now rapidly emerging as a scientific-industrial ambition, is the tendency toward encapsulation of human order — the severance, once and for all, of the umbilical cord fastening us to the wilderness or the Creation. The threat is not only in the totalitarian desire for absolute control. It lies in the willingness to ignore an essential paradox: the natural forces that so threaten us are the same forces that preserve and renew us.[11]

For if living beings structure themselves through interaction with each other in constructive and destructive ways, they also do so in interaction with nature in constructive and destructive ways. And the logic of the self-structuring of human beings is to get bigger and more elaborate, which requires that they develop an increasing asymmetry in their interaction with the environment: nature becomes simply a resource for the self-structuring of human beings or a receptacle for their waste.

The other is to recognize that the basic picture presented is more appropriate to primitive situations than to well-developed ones. As Habermas observes of cultural anthropology, 'primitive societies have the advantage of being units that are relatively easy to delimit and relatively static.'[12] Where more developed situations are involved, societies and their norms must be taken into account as maintaining themselves through self-structuring in interaction with wider social environments, and individuals seen as interacting with such societies and the codes through which societies structure themselves can become indistinguishable from the societies themselves. A notable example is the patriarchal code by which most societies are structured, which identifies the position of women in society as the position in which they *are put* by men.

Such an explanation provides a general account of the dynamics of contextual interweaving. It shows the possibility of innovative change

---

11. Wendell Berry, *The Unsettling of America: Culture and Agriculure,* (San Francisco: Sierra Club Books, 1977), p. 130.
12. Jurgen Habermas, *On the Logic of the Social Sciences,* (Cambridge: MIT Press, 1988), p. 78.

or destruction, whether in living being or nature or their interaction, albeit constrained by the previous structuring of the living being and its congruence with its environment. Furthermore, it maintains a complex view of self-maintenance through turbulent interactions. Boundaries, which are relative not absolute, are a natural counterpart of the self-structuring by which this self-maintenance occurs. The result is a picture of ongoing generativity (or diminishment) in all the elements of the picture (structured living being, interaction and nature) which may be doubled through the restructuring of them.

In sum, the advantage of this form of explanation is the explanatory diversity which it incorporates. It opens a vision of ontological diversity, which is very important for survival in a changing world.

> Social diversity works to preserve the system's personal, psychological, and economic flexibility, and thus helps to maintain the single most important condition for long-range survival in relation to the environment, which is of course all the more significant if the environment is changing or being changed (by society): what Gregory Bateson called our 'uncommitted potential forfuture change'.[13]

In this form of explanation, both self-structuring and the boundaries which it brings are both relatively open and contingent, in the sense that they require constructive response to interaction. The perturbations in these interactions are then possibilities for constructive change. The implications of this form of explanation for behavior are also advantageous. For the world is seen as a place of diversity which invites freedom in self-structuring through interactions, yet a freedom constrained by the conditions of previous structures. These constraints guide what may happen, but their open texture allows far greater freedom for diversity. Neither these constraints upon behaviour, nor the explanation in which they figure, are overdeterminative. Instead, there is what could be called 'affirmative underdetermination'. There is a rich and fascinating poem by the Irish poet Micheal O'Siadhail which gives some indication of such affirmative underdetermination.

---

13. Anthony Wilden, *The Rules Are No Game: The Strategy of Communication,* (London: Routledge & Kegan Paul, 1987), p. 105.

> O my white-burdened Europe, across so many maps greed zigzags. One voice and the nightmare of a dominant chord: defences, self-mirroring, echoings, myriad overtones of shame. Never again one voice. Out of malaise, out of need our vision cries.
>
> Turmoil of change, our slow renaissance. *All things share one breath.* We listen: clash and resolve, webs and layers of voices. And which voice dominates or is it chaos? My doubting earthling, tiny among the planets does a lover of one voice hear more or less?
>
> Infinities of space and time. Melody fragments; a music of compassion, noise of enchantment. Among the inner parts something open, something wild, a long rumour of wisdom keeps winding into each tune: *cantus firmus,* fierce vigil of contingency, love's congruence.[14]

Despite the 'dominant nightmare' of defensive, reflexive, shameful, changeful, perhaps even chaotic, contexts interwoven in us, what we have called an 'affirmatively underdetermined' world has two outstanding features which suggest the possibility of the presence of God. One is the vitality present in the 'turmoil of change' itself, the 'slow renaissance' of the realization that 'All things share one breath.' The other is the presence of an open structure: 'among the inner parts something open, something wild, a long rumour of wisdom [which] keeps winding into each tune' as a 'fierce vigil of contingency'.

These features of the interweaving which occurs in our contextuality enable us, at least in some degree, to identify the economy of the Trinitarian God. As we do so, however, we will need to locate substitutes with which these — both our contextuality and the economy of the Trinitarian God — have been confused. We shall hope to rediscover the proper form of contextuality by reference to specifically Christian (Trinitarian) understanding, while disengaging them from sub-contextual and sub-Christian forms of understanding. In more familiar categories, this will be an attempt to find the impact of the presence of God (Revelation or Grace) on the forms of our contextuality (Nature).

---

14. Micheal O'Siadhail, 'Motet' in *The Chosen Garden,* (Dublin: The Dedalus Press, 1990), p.82.

'A long rumour of wisdom... fierce vigil of contingency, love's congruence...'

We have been attempting to provide an account of the dynamics of contextuality. Furthermore, we have been able to identify two primary aspects of these dynamics, 'all things share one breath' and the open structure of contingency. If the possibilities latent in such accounts of the dynamics of contextuality are carried into theology, the activity of God is also seen quite differently. As you will quickly see, while we can make a notional distinction between the immanent and the economic Trinity, this should not be turned into a division between the two.

First, as regards the economic Trinity, and employing the kind of explanation which we have been using for worldly contextuality, we find a Trinitarian God who is himself by the economy of his presence in the world. He is himself in maintaining the consistency of his life in an ordered but energetic congruence with his world; he is capable of self-restructuring in a controlled response to the perturbations (constructive or destructive) which occur in that interaction and in those with whom he interacts.

As regards the immanent Trinity, his own unity is that of a dynamic consistency, not inert but energetic in the consistency of his self-structuring in self-sameness. Such an explanation of the immanent Trinity provides for an energetic (Spirit-driven) unity in the Godhead which is yet true to its own initial conditions (what we designate by the word 'Father') and ordered in its interactions (that which we call 'the Son' or the 'Logos'). But this is not so much an explanation of a 'state of affairs' in God as it is an explanation of the energetically consistent congruence with the world by which he remains himself. 'Energetic' refers to the operation of the Holy Spirit, 'consistency in following initial conditions' refers to the Father and 'congruence with the world' refers to the Son. This is the 'fierce and excited contingency' of which Micheal O'Siadhail speaks, the Spirit 'exciting' the fulfillment of initial conditions through an ongoing self-structuring in which there arises a true congruence with the world in love. To use more formal words, God is a dynamic structured relationality in whom there is an infinite possibility of life.

But more needs to be said about the life of this Trinitarian God and its presence in the contextuality of the world, and what form it takes. I propose to discuss this a little because of the paucity in the Symposium so far of reference both to the Father and to the Holy Spirit, but I do not wish thereby to abandon the discussion of Christ. The activity of God in the contextuality of the world is not to be confined to the presence of Christ, but it is not simply to be identified with the Holy Spirit either. The activity of God in the contextuality of the world requires recognition that the operation of the Holy Spirit achieves its consistency by following the initial conditions which we conventionally identify as the 'Father' and the congruence with the world which we identify as the 'Son'.

What occurs in the life of the Trinitarian God is an outpouring of energy through which the initial conditions of God are fulfilled, and this fulfillment is in God, but occurs also through the congruence of God with the world by which God is himself. What occurs in God, therefore, is a self-enhancement, but this occurs also in both his constitution and active sustenance of the contextuality of the world. Words for this are difficult, but the language of 'blessing' and 'glorifying' may be best, for they signify the intensification of *ordered life* (the combination of words is significant) which occurs in God and from God in the contextuality of the world. So far as God himself is concerned, it brings a concentration of energy in the initial conditions by which God is himself and which are manifest in the fullness of ordered relationality in God, and also with the world in the Logos. Thus, from the implicit relationality of 'the Father', the Spirit can be seen to generate the fullness of the Father through the Son and through the Son's work in the world.

What are the *marks* of the activity of the Trinitarian God in the contextuality of the world? It is the active source of contextual interweaving, constituting and sustaining this contextuality. I agree with Professor Moltmann's remarks elsewhere in this paper that there is a transcendent unity which arises through God's creation, but I disagree that it 'precedes' the diversity of all things. There is, as he says, an immanent unity, but it is an active unity which arises in their diversity, rather than preceding it; it is therefore more correctly called an active contextuality/interweaving, and should be attributed to the Trinitarian activity of God by which God is one. By the way, this changes the character of universality, and avoids the monistic tendencies — whether logocentrist or phallogocentrist — against which the post-modernists rightly protest.

At the same time, with this contextuality, the Trinitarian activity of God sustains a complexity of particularities, establishing 'relativities' with their own integrity in fully contextual interweaving. This is to be sharply distinguished from the post-modernists' notion of particularism, which opposes a false universalism by a false particularism. Their notion of particulars rests on privileging, and the supposition of the inaccessibility of others with whom we are interwoven/contextually related. The active sustenance by the Trinitarian God of a complexity of particularities is also to be distinguished, if I may say so, from those who suppose that becoming indigenous requires severance from others, especially those considered outsiders. These are over-statements, understandable for those who need to recover their particularity from submersion in a monolithic world, but fundamentally a denial of the wider interweaving which contextuality involves.

And the 'relativities' or 'particularities' are linked into active and contingent ways, in the fashion appropriate to an actively self-ordering God. Perhaps two stanzas of another poem by Micheal O'Siadhail may lighten this 'heavy' discussion while also showing the character of the network of particularities which is sustained through the activity of the Trinitarian God. The first recalls the task given to children by their knitting mothers.

> Like pegs, our forearms held the skein's coil. Arcs of the knitter's hand unloop and ball by turn. Sweep and detail. A feeling of beginning in childhood's wind-up I keep on recalling. Somehow I'm between a yarn uncoiling to a tight ball of destiny, a ball unravelling back the promise of a skein. Plain stitch and design; point and infinity. Who changes the world? Oh, this and that, strands as they happen to fall, tiny ligatures, particular here and nows, vast loopings of pattern, the ties and let-gos of a knot, small X-shapes of history; our spoor and signature a gauze of junctures, a nettedness of things.
>
> Whose music? A quiver enters like a spirit, a murmur of tension from and back into space. A tune of trembles in catgut. The pride of an instrument as at its beck and call the heart vibrates: pulse-sway, dominion of rhythm, power before the slack and silence. 'Pride before a fall' we say, sic transit ... Should we've been puritans, taut, untouchable, our unshakeable self-mastery a vacuum of muteness? O noise of existence shake in me a tone you need; sweet friction of rosin, play me limp or tense. Possessor of

> everything, owner of nothing. Whose bow shivers its music in my string?[15]

The poem makes clear the active bestowal, by its source, of the highly contingent complexity of the contextuality of our being and activity, in which are interwoven nature, sociality and God. It is that very contingency which 'opens' our freedom, while also providing the scope and parameters within which it may operate. At the same time, this freedom in our contextuality is activated and energized by the free ordering of God, by which it is blessed/enriched.

But the proper use of our freedom-in-contextuality follows the pathway followed by God's Spirit, the pathway constituted by the initial conditions of 'the Father' and fulfilled in the ordering of the Logos. This means that the right use of our freedom is ex-centric, outward turning, conferring the benefits of our particularity upon those with whom we are interwoven. Our freedom confers freedom through our love.

It seems, therefore, the relatedness of God to the contextuality of our life and activity is far more complex than it is generally thought. God's ongoingly active/energetic self-structuring in the bestowal and sustenance of the highly contingent complexity in which our contextual being-in-freedom consists, provides a far more complex and contingent relation between him and our contextual being. That is not to say that the marks of God's presence in our contextuality cannot be found, preeminently in the ordered energy which activates our freedom to love and therein to confer freedom upon others. This is no 'heroic' freedom which magically transforms all in sight. Much as we might wish for the capacity to work an overnight transformation, without having to attend to all the factors by which we and others are shaped as we are, our freedom to confer love and freedom is itself contextual, mediated through all the factors — natural, biological, social — which locate us and render us finite there. The sign of the blessing which God confers is in our conferral of such blessing on others, with all the natural and social modifications that may require, and even the creativity by which to fashion new and more humane contextual interweavings.

15. Micheal O'Siadhail, 'Perspectives', *The Chosen Garden,* (Dublin: The Dedalus Press, 1989), p.86.

The Contextual Loss of God

The active achievement of such fullness within the contextuality of life rests on the ongoing participation in the blessing which God confers, the God who reaches 'his' fullness through the energizing of his loving congruence with natural and human contextuality. In that sense, the natural-human contextuality is a radically contingent one. Insofar as it structures itself in accordance with God's actively benevolent presence, it is blessed, energized for its proper order. That is, it moves towards an interweaving which is just towards all, where benefits and responsibilities are fully shared. So it can be said that the conditions for the full contextual interweaving of human beings and other animate creatures, as well as nature itself, are already actively present in the contextuality of human life, and that we here are simply uncovering what already is by God's grace, so that it may be seen and performed more fully. But in another sense, it is also accurate to say that it is not actively present there. This is because there are those in a contextuality who fail to orientate their interweaving with others to the active presence of God and the energetic order which that provides. The consequences are seen in the impoverishment of contextual relationships. These are the contextual counterpart of sin, 'missing the mark', with the loss of energy and order which that involves. The evidences are readily seen. Let me take some examples from the social sphere.

One is what can be called 'social narcissism', where society develops its interrelations while at the same time supposing that it is itself encapsulated from the natural world. This is a certain kind of self-structuring by society of its dynamic relations with the natural world. As the dynamic self-structuring of human beings and societies has led them to greater and greater complexity, they have structured their relation with nature as one of use or domination; the 'guest who came to dinner' gradually centred the household on himself. This structuring has led human beings to see the natural world as 'only a resource' upon which human society may endlessly draw, or a 'receptacle' into which the waste-products of society are discharged. The same structuring, though in a different form, is present where it is said that nature has its 'limits' beyond which it cannot be imposed upon.

In other forms of 'social narcissism', society structures its interrelations in 'totalities', thereby encapsulating them from smaller social groupings; the result is — in the name of ideals of 'purity' — to eliminate the very social diversity by which society preserves its flexibility and long-term survival. The reverse form of the problem arises where society structures its interrelations in 'localities' or 'individualities', thereby encapsulating them from wider social contexts. Still another form of the problem is seen where society structures its interrelations as encapsulated within a 'present' which bears no relation to its past or future, thereby losing sight of the sources and effects of its own structured dynamics.

From a theological viewpoint, all these are 'missing the mark' in that they show society as structuring its dynamic relations in self-encapsulation from God. The social universe is 'simplified' by reducing its dynamics to those of human autonomy, whether social or individual. And God is seen to have been the false projection (self-alienation) of ideal human attributes, whether those of individuals or societies. It is then thought to be an act of human responsibility to end this alienation:

> The madman jumped into their midst and pierced them with his glances. 'Whither is God?' he cried.'I shall tell you. We have killed him — you and I. All of us are his murderers.'[16]

The self-structuring of the dynamics of society by such means are the products of social power seeking to consolidate or expand its position by disadvantaging others, not to mention nature itself.

Reconciliation in Contextuality

Much of this is the result of human anxiety, and the desire to compensate for what is not — by blindness — found in a God understood as barren. The growing complexity of contextuality is not in itself a problem, so long as it is accompanied by the realization that there are resources with which to develop an active and ordering love, both amongst cultures and societies and between them and the natural world. But it may easily be seen as a deficiency (an emptiness where there should be a fullness), and therefore a cause for anxiety.

The response is typically to meet the sense of emptiness occasioned by the growth in this complexity by consuming energy for self-structuring from elements beyond and within ourselves. We take action

---

16. Friedrich Nietzsche, *The Gay Science,* trans. Walter Kaufmann, quoted in Anthony Flew, *An Introduction to Western Philosophy,* (London: Thames and Hudson, 1971), p. 468.

to remedy the deficiency (fill the emptiness), and do so by fundamental strategies of isolation, self-love and domination; by these means, the 'originative' or 'fundamental' sin becomes actual, whether for individuals as societies. The effect is to exteriorize (alienate), reconceive and instrumentalize (dominate) those sources upon which I/we draw our energy. These we may do to ourselves, our fellow human beings and our environment ('the context'). This is a deception which 'builds our being' (fills our emptiness) by diminishing others to 'non-being' (no value) or a 'supply' (limited value).

Underlying the conception of human being as emptiness, and also the stratagems by which we attempt to overcome it, is a key question about the nature and supply of energy for the development of new forms of unity and reconciliation in contextuality. What is available, and how? It is commonly assumed that dynamic order is derivable only from what is available through human life in the world, that is in the bounded situation of an ecosystem; only such energy as can arise within this context will count as 'kinetic energy' usable for work. Since the supply is limited by this limited context, human life will become a competitive struggle for the available supply of energy.

But this is a reductionist account of the energy available for the development of relationality, and will serve as grounds for human beings to distort the dynamic order of their social and ecological environment, and to refuse to develop the necessary kind of contextuality. There is, of course, a sense in which the ecosystem must be taken as limiting the energy available, and therefore requiring an appropriate balance within it; the material resources of the ecosystem are, for practical purposes, limited, and the balance of these resources (their diversity-in-unity) cannot be damaged without dire consequences. But in a still more fundamental sense even this ecosystem operates within and from a fuller dynamic order, and without reference to this dynamic order, treating the ecosystem as a limited source of energy is reductionistic.

The fuller dynamic order from which the ecosystem operates, by which it is energized for its unity and reconciliation, is the dynamic order of God himself which he confers on human beings in and through their world. This confers not only a richer source of energy on the world than that which is available simply by reference to the ecosystem itself, but a higher quality of relationality than is available therein; taken together, these provide a higher order of dynamic order than that available by reference to the world alone.

The act of God's reconciliation is the renewal of his presence in the contextualities of existence, whereby he provides the ordered energy of his own being as the means by which is restored the full contextuality of human beings with each other, with the animate and with the natural order. This is not simply an illuminist view of the act of reconciliation, for the principal means by which God reconciles is to be interwoven in the lives of those most 'decontextualized', those most diminished in their contextuality, providing new life for them in their abandonment — and for those who meet them in the gift of love by which they and their contextuality are restored.

Conclusion

In this discussion, we have followed a difficult path But nothing less is necessary if we are to answer the question of how God is present in our contextuality. What I have sought to show is the kind of interweaving which occurs in our contextuality, and therein to show the economy of the life which derives from the immanent Trinity of God and from the reconciliation which is brought by this same God in our loss of contextuality.

Biographical Notes on Contributors

1. **Veronica Brady.**
   Lecturer, Department of English, University of Western Australia, Perth, Australia.

2. **Douglas Campbell.**
   Lecturer, Department of Religious Studies, University of Otago, Dunedin, New Zealand.

3. **Neil Darragh.**
   Lecturer in Systematic Theology, Catholic Institute of Theology, Auckland, New Zealand.

4. **John W. De Gruchy.**
   Professor of Christian Studies and Head of Department, Department of Religious Studies, University of Cape Town, South Africa.

5. **Gustavo Gutiérrez.**
   Director of the Instituto Bartolomé de Las Casas, Lima, Peru.

6. **Daniel W. Hardy.**
   Director, Center of Theological Inquiry, Princeton, New Jersey, United States of America.

7. **Stephen May.**
   Lecturer in Systematic Theology, St John's College, Auckland, New Zealand.

8. **Johann B. Metz.**
Professor of Catholic Theology and Director of the Institute for Fundamental Theology, University of Münster, Germany.

9. **Jürgen Moltmann.**
Professor of Systematic Theology, University of Tübingen, Germany

10. **Sue Patterson.**
Knox Theological Hall, Dunedin, New Zealand

11. **Janet Martin Soskice.**
Department of Theology and Religious Studies, and Fellow Jesus College, University of Cambridge, United Kingdom.

12. **Alan Torrance**.
Professor of Systematic Theology, Knox Theological Hall, Dunedin, New Zealand.

13. **Elisabeth Moltmann-Wendel.**
Journalist, writer on religious topics, Tübingen, Germany.

Index — Author

Index — Subject

Sponsors

The support of the following individuals, groups and instittutions for the Symposium is most gratefully acknowledged:

Otago Southland Synod, Presbyterian Church of New Zeland
Dominican Friars, New Zealand
University of Otago, Dunedin
Sister Emmanuel Wallis O.P. (Bequest)
Selwyn College, Dunedin
Todd Foundation, New Zealand
Anglican General Synod, New Zealand
Christian Brothers, New Zealand
Sisters of Our Lady of the Missions, New Zealand
Marist Sisters, New Zealand
The Sisters of the Good Sheperd, New Zealand
Congregation of the Dominican Sisters, New Zealand
Cenacle Sisters, New Zealand
Rosminian Instittute of Charity, New Zealand
Holy Faith Sisters, New Zealand
Presentation Sisters, New Zealand
Little Company of Mary, New Zealand
Sisters of Mercy, Dunedin,
St Columban Mission Society, New Zealand
Anonymous donor
The Society of Missionaries of the Sacred Heart, Australia
Sisters of Mercy, Adelaide, South Australia
Sisters of Mercy, North Parramatta, New South Wales
Pacifica, Australian Theological Studies, Melbourne, Victoria
St John of God Brothers, Australia
Little Company of Mary, Australia
Scotttish Journal of Theology, Edinburgh, Scotland
Sisters of St Joseph, Australia
Benedictine Monastery of the Holy Spirit, Croydon, Victoria
Missionary Sisters of Mary, New Zealand
Mrs MM Regan, Adelaide, South Australia
New Blackfriars, Oxford, United Kingdom
Roman Catholic Archdiocese of Auckland, New Zealand
TrustBank, Otago, New Zealand

College House, Christchurch, New Zealand
Bank of New Zealand, University of Otago Branch, Dunedin, New Zealand
Anglican Diocese of Wellington, New Zealand
Anglican Diocese of Dunedin, New Zealand
Rev Maurice Andrew, Dunedin, New Zealand
Anglican Diocese of Auckland, New Zealand
Roman Catholic Diocese of Auckland, New Zealand
St John's College, Auckland, New Zealand
Women Authoring Theology Conference, Sydney, New South Wales
Cadbury Confectionary, Dunedin, New Zealand
Associate Professor A C Moore, University of Otago, Dunedin, New Zealand